REWORKING GENDER

REWORKING GENDER

A Feminist Communicology of Organization

Karen Lee Ashcraft
University of Utah

Dennis K. Mumby
University of North Carolina at Chapel Hill

SAGE Publications
International Educational and Professional Publisher
Thousand Oaks ▪ London ▪ New Delhi

For information:

Sage Publications, Inc.
2455 Teller Road
Thousand Oaks, California 91320
E-mail: order@sagepub.com

Sage Publications Ltd.
6 Bonhill Street
London EC2A 4PU
United Kingdom

Sage Publications India Pvt. Ltd.
B-42, Panchsheel Enclave
Post Box 4109
New Delhi 110 017 India

Printed in the United States of America

Library of Congress Cataloging-in-Publication Data

Ashcraft, Karen Lee.
Reworking gender : a feminist communicology of organization / by Karen Lee Ashcraft and Dennis K. Mumby.
    p. cm.
Includes bibliographical references and index.
ISBN 0-7619-5354-X-ISBN 0-7619-5355-8 (pbk.)
    1. Organizational sociology. 2. Communication in organizations. 3. Sex role in the work environment. 4. Feminist theory. I. Mumby, Dennis K. II. Title.
HM786.A84 2004
302.3´5—dc22

                                                              2003016116

Printed on acid-free paper

03   04   05   06   07   08   09   10   9   8   7   6   5   4   3   2   1

Acquiring Editor:	Todd R. Armstrong
Editorial Assistant:	Veronica Novak
Production Editor:	Claudia A. Hoffman
Copy Editor:	Jamie Robinson
Typesetter:	C&M Digitals (P) Ltd.
Indexer:	Molly Hall
Cover Designer:	Janet Foulger

Contents

Preface

L ike most scholarly projects, this book evolved through a number of unforeseen turns. Although it is the result of our collaboration (and our names appear on the book in alphabetical order in recognition of our coauthorship), we did not begin this book together. Originally, Dennis conceived of the book as a way to productively explore the burgeoning scholarship on postmodern feminism and to assess its potential contribution to radical organization studies in light of the "discursive turn." In this sense, the book began as a largely metatheoretical project—an effort to position feminist scholarship within a larger set of disciplinary discourses that had arisen in organization studies around questions of epistemology, ontology, methodology, and axiology. It asked what feminism—and, in particular, postmodern feminism—could contribute to these discussions. As the project took shape, however, it became clear that such a metatheoretical focus inadequately captured the myriad ways in which feminist scholarship was beginning to influence the project of radical organization studies. Dennis's concerns about the inadequacy of this frame led to his inviting Karen to collaborate with him in "reworking" the project. Her research on feminist alternatives to conventional organizational forms explores the relationship between theory and practice and, in addition, suggests directions for an explicitly communication-based conception of feminist organizing.

Once Karen signed on, a joint vision for the book began to develop. Several shifts in emphasis emerged from the meeting of our respective orientations to, and frustrations with, the scholarship we read and practice. We decided to integrate the original agenda for the book with these concerns, expanding the book's focus to include matters of disciplinary identity (that of organizational communication and feminist organization studies), as well as empirical and pragmatic considerations, particularly those related to feminist politics and praxis. After much conversation, the following themes came to focus our thinking.

A first point of interest involved tensions in the relationship between feminism and critical organization studies. For the most part, feminism has existed as an "outsider within" radical organization theory and research. Even today, it is still often framed as derivative from, or as a corrective to, critical scholarship and its neglect of gender. Our own field of organizational communication was particularly slow to engage feminist approaches to organizing, with published research appearing only in the early 1990s. Despite that sluggish start, we have seen the virtual explosion of gender and organizational communication research over the past decade. We hoped to build on this momentum by positioning feminism as more central to the critical project than it is typically assumed to be, both in terms of what it has already contributed and as a guide for the future. We also wanted to articulate a distinctively *communicative* feminist approach to the study of organization, which led us to a second theme—the place of communication in organization studies.

It is our sense that, in the face of the discursive turn that has defined much critical organization scholarship in the last 20 years or so, our own field of organizational communication continues to hover at the margins of this body of work, despite our focus on the communicative constitution of organizing. To be clear, we are referring here to the (in)visibility of our disciplinary community, not that of individual scholars. This book thus represents an effort to not only develop a *communicative* feminist perspective on organizing but also to articulate organizational communication as a recognizable and relevant voice in the scholarly conversation about organization, discourse, and power.

Of course, calling for such a shift requires reasons for doing so, and it was in spirited discussions of such reasons that we began to truly redefine the project. We started by spinning the matter less defensively and, we thought, more productively. Rather than presume that communication studies ought to be central because so many organization scholars now care about discourse, we asked ourselves a different question: What *are* communication's distinctive contributions, given that so many organization scholars already address discourse? Exploring this question took us down several paths. For one, it pushed us to be more precise about the term *discourse*. In particular, we wanted to elucidate varied meanings and applications of discourse across the gender and organization literature—thus Chapter 1 is an adaptation of Karen's chapter in the *Handbook of Organizational Discourse* (in press, Sage). The question also led us to specify and delimit our conception of communication and to clarify the relationships we envision among discourse, communication practice(s), materiality, temporality, and so forth—groundwork that shaped the way we present and refine our communicative feminist "model" in Chapters 5 and 7. Finally, discussing our field's distinctiveness led us to characterize our model as one template for *communicology*. With this term, we mean to parallel other disciplinary approaches (for example, the *sociology* of gendered organization). While the term may strike some as an unnecessary neologism, we see it as a useful way to capture the contributions of a communication approach in a language at once familiar and curious to broader audiences.

Third, we wanted to explore gender as one important discourse of difference that necessarily intersects with others. Given recent turns in both of our research agendas, we initially expected to focus the book on masculinity and organizing. And yet, as Karen began to sift through some data from her airline pilot project in preparation for the analysis in Chapter 6, it became apparent that masculinity alone provided an insufficient explanatory frame—that, in fact, masculinity became a much more visible and sensible force when she simultaneously considered the role of femininity. Put simply, certain forms of masculinity played against certain forms of femininity to engender particular outcomes. And the "certain forms" clause here is crucial, for all constructions of gender summoned other discourses of difference—in particular, race, sexuality, and class—and relied on these discursive affiliations to accomplish multiple forms of privilege and exclusion at once. Consequently, we tried to do more than merely issue another call for further attention to gender relations and intersectionality—we aimed to illuminate how gender becomes central *and* how it never works alone.

Finally, we wanted to stay mindful of the relationship between metatheoretical issues and mundane practice—to show that philosophical debates carry significant implications for organizational life. This point seemed imperative, in part, because of an abiding feminist commitment to praxis and ambivalence about "high theory." Relatedly, one of our goals gradually became to disabuse readers of an idea often aligned with a social constructionist bent—namely, the notion that to focus on how discourse constitutes organization is to abandon "the real world." In this book, we are at pains to theorize and demonstrate the connections between discursive processes and their material consequences for human beings.

The development of what we call a feminist communicology of organization represents our efforts to address these themes. In doing so, we hope to "rework gender" in several ways—among them, (a) to situate organizational communication as central to the discursive turn and, specifically, to understanding gendered organization; (b) to show how feminism can model scholarly practices (such as balancing multiple discourses of difference or embracing ambiguity and mediating irony instead of claiming incommensurability) that are vital to the critical project in organization studies; and (c) to connect theoretical conversations to empirical and practical projects.

As with any scholarly endeavor, we have been helped along the way by numerous people, and we wish to recognize a few of them here. Many thanks to Patrice Buzzanell, George Cheney, Charley Conrad, and Cynthia Stohl for their invaluable feedback and support at various stages of the project. We would also like to thank the Department of Communication Studies at the University of North Carolina at Chapel Hill and a few agencies at the University of Utah—the Department of Communication, the University Research Committee, and the Tanner Humanities Center—for providing us with research leaves that enabled the completion of this project. We are additionally grateful to the 99s Museum of Women Pilots in Oklahoma City for granting Karen access to the archival materials that ground the analysis in Chapter 6; we owe particular gratitude to Saundra Lapsley, the museum manager who gave generously of her insight, time, and energy as Karen gathered this material. We also want to thank the airline pilots whose reflections are featured in Chapter 6. Karen is most grateful to Ken Davis not only for his unqualified support of the book project, but also for his priceless stints as "research assistant" on the ongoing airline pilot study. We both wish to thank Todd Armstrong at Sage for his enthusiasm, editorial expertise, and willingness to take on this project at a relatively late stage in its development. As we honed the final draft, Jamie Robinson's copyediting skills were invaluable. We are indebted to Lisa Flores, Marouf Hasian, Helga Shugart, Stephanie Wahab, and Greg Holles for their inventive book title suggestions, all of which we clearly and stubbornly ignored. Finally, we owe a considerable debt to Thoney (a.k.a. Catherine Ashcraft), who kept us sane throughout the project.

Introduction

Situating Gender in Critical Organization Studies

The history of gender studies in organization scholarship is, at best, patchy and discontinuous. Twenty years ago, Jeff Hearn and Wendy Parkin provided "a selective review and critique of a neglected area" (Hearn & Parkin, 1983). Five years later, Albert Mills (1988) confirmed that "gender is a crucial, yet neglected, aspect of organizational analysis" and characterized that neglect as "inexcusable in the face of a growing concern with the experiential aspects of organizations" (p. 351). In 1990, Joan Acker observed (in a special issue of *Gender & Society* devoted to organizations), "Writers on organizations and organization theory now include some consideration of women and gender, but their treatment is usually cursory, and male domination is, on the whole, not analyzed and not explained" (p. 140). Six years later—and a full thirteen years after Hearn and Parkin's landmark article—Fiona Wilson (1996) inveighed against a state of affairs in which "organizational theory is tenaciously blind and deaf to gender" (p. 825). Most recently, Patricia Martin and David Collinson (2002) bemoaned the fragmentation of gender and organization research across the United States and Europe, inviting gender scholars to "strike out" on their own to establish a field of "gendered organization" studies.

Has the neglect of gender as a cohesive domain of organization studies really been as sweeping and systematic as these authors claim? Sylvia Gherardi (1995) wonders if they protest too much: "It is extremely difficult to take seriously the contention that 'gender and organization' is truly a neglected area, given that so many articles have been written to make precisely this point" (p. 25). So where does the truth lie? Not surprisingly, both positions can stake claims to validity.

❖ THE STATUS OF GENDERED ORGANIZATION STUDIES

Over the past 30 years of organization scholarship, gender has been visible and invisible, subject to intense focus yet ignored. On the one hand, scholars have vigorously investigated gender as an important independent variable affecting such factors as leadership or conflict style (e.g., Eagly & Johannesen-Schmidt, 2001; Eagly & Johnson, 1990; Monroe, DiSalvo, Lewis, & Borzi, 1990; Todd-Mancillas & Rossi, 1985). Yet in most of these studies, gender remains marginalized—a binary factor pertinent to specific interpersonal practices, not a basic pillar of organizing. Other researchers have examined gender as a key aspect of work and family matters; predictably, much of this scholarship is addressed to the concerns or consequences of working mothers (Belsky & Eggebeen, 1991; Greenhaus & Parasuraman, 1999; Milkie & Pelotal, 1999; Scarr, Phillips, & McCartney, 1989; Vogel, 1993). To date, the most prolific work on gender and organization has stressed the plight of women in management, exploring barriers that range from sexual harassment to discriminatory policy to exclusionary interaction patterns (Burke & McKeen, 1992; Fagenson, 1993; Reardon, 1997; Staley, 1988). Notably, the work-and-family and women-in-management literatures expand the variable-analytic view by calling attention to gender as a political and systemic matter. Across these studies, however, gender becomes relevant to organizations only when (white) women enter them. Put simply, women appear as visibly gendered "others," while men are erased as the genderless norm.

Challenging the view that gender is a special concern limited to women, scholars have begun to consider gender as a deep-seated organizing principle:

> To say that an organization . . . is gendered means that advantage and disadvantage, exploitation and coercion, action and emotion, meaning and identity, are patterned through and in terms of a distinction between male and female, masculine and feminine. Gender is not an addition to ongoing processes, conceived as gender neutral. Rather, it is an integral part of those processes, which cannot be properly understood without an analysis of gender. (Acker, 1990, p. 146)

The claim that organization is fundamentally gendered suggests several radical premises, which together form a foundation for this book. First, gender is constitutive of organizing; it is an omnipresent, defining feature of collective human activity, regardless of whether such activity appears to be about gender. Second, the gendering of organization involves a struggle over meaning, identity, and difference; this ongoing, discursive struggle occurs amid, and acts upon, gendered institutional structures. Third, such struggle (re)produces social realities that privilege certain interests. It follows that gender is inextricably linked with power; it is medium and outcome of the vested interests of organizational life. This implies, finally, that the struggle for gendered meaning is a deeply material matter, for it produces not only preferred truths, selves, and courses of action but also tangible systems of "advantage and disadvantage, exploitation and coercion."

The notion of "gendered organization" has been taken up by numerous scholars in organization studies. In particular, feminist authors have investigated the politics of organizing to illuminate "the ways in which gendered subjectivity is constituted within relations of dominance" (Hegde, 1998, p. 277). Over the past decade or so, sustained programs of feminist research have examined the intersection of gender, organizing, identity, and power. In our own field of organizational communication, for example, a "critical mass" of feminist scholarship has emerged (e.g., B. J. Allen, 1996; Ashcraft, 2000; Buzzanell, 1994; Clair, 1998; Gregg, 1993; Holmer Nadesan, 1996; Jorgenson, 2002; Mumby, 1996; A. G. Murphy, 1998; Trethewey, 1997). This trend is particularly striking, for it was not so long ago that Judi Marshall (1993) strained to hear any feminist voices in the field. The management and organization studies literatures have seen a similar, and slightly earlier, emergence of feminist perspectives. Scholars have deconstructed the gendered foundations of organization theory (Calás & Smircich, 1992a; Holvino, 1997; Mumby & Putnam, 1992), developed alternative forms of theorizing (Acker, 1992; K. Ferguson, 1994; Gherardi, 1995; Jacques, 1992), and commenced empirical study of gendered organizing processes (J. K. Fletcher, 1998; Gherardi, 1995; Gottfried & Hayashi-Kato, 1998; Kondo, 1990; J. Martin, Knopoff, & Beckman, 1998; Pringle, 1989). A growing strand of work on masculinity and organizing further challenges the view that gender is a matter made for women. Recently, an interdisciplinary cluster of scholars has converged in an attempt to "make the one the other" (Hearn, 1996) and interrogate the social construction of masculinities at work (e.g., Cheng, 1996; Collinson, 1992; Collinson & Hearn, 1996a, 1996b; Hearn, 1994; Knights & McCabe, 2001). Their efforts expand the terrain of gendered organization studies well beyond "the woman question." In this book, we seek to do the same, giving life to our theoretical model with an empirical emphasis on the organization of masculinity.

Masculinity theory and research has generated pivotal insights that inform our project. For one, masculinity is not a stable or unified phenomenon; its meanings shift over time and in relation to culture, context, person, age, and so forth (Spitzack, 1998a). Multiple narratives of manhood circulate concurrently, offering versions of self and social relations that, when practiced, yield differential, consequential access to power and resistance (Corey, 2000; Mechling & Mechling, 1994; Nakayama, 2000). In particular, feminist theories of intersectionality push us to recognize that masculinities, like all gender identities, are inevitably raced and classed (C. Crenshaw, 1997; K. Crenshaw, 1991; Dace, 1998; Orbe, 1998). In other words, talk of "men" and "the masculine"—however generalized—always refers to a specific form of masculinity (Dines, 1998; Eng, 2001; Wiegman, 1993). Scholars emphasizing gender are increasingly accountable to these insights, for to study gender in isolation is to risk furthering the normalization of partial (e.g., white, middle-class, heterosexual) identities, relations, and interests. Accordingly, our theoretical model of gendered organization and empirical analysis of professional masculinity share a guiding interest in the historically, culturally, and politically specific nature of gender discourse.

In addition, most masculinity scholars coalesce around a concern shared with feminists: the need to mark masculinity and men as gendered subjects. Scholars especially challenge the invisibility of dominant masculinities, since all forms of manhood do not enjoy similar privilege. Perhaps ironically, however, studies of dominant masculinity run the risk of recentering the white, heterosexual, middle-class, male subjects they seek to deconstruct (e.g., Penley & Willis, 1993; Robinson, 2000).[1] Not oblivious to such danger, many masculinity scholars assume the risk to shatter illusions of homogenous, indelibly privileged male selves (e.g., Eng, 2001; Spitzack, 1998b) and to unearth the institutionalization of particular masculine forms (e.g., Mumby, 1998). This book shoulders a similar risk, for to illustrate the theoretical model we build, we examine the social construction of "airline pilot" as an elite, romanticized professional identity. Potentially, our focus could be read as reinscribing this figure in the popular imagination. To minimize this risk and to develop the lens of masculinity studies, we attend to the coevolution, or dialectical interplay, of specific masculinities and femininities. In other words, our analysis demonstrates how the formation of airline pilot identity entailed weaving an intricate and precarious web of gender, race, and class symbolism—with immense contemporary consequences.

In sum, our efforts in this book are informed by a vast and growing literature that explores the meeting of gender and organization. Particularly, three recent themes in that literature begin to focus our interests: (a) organization as fundamentally gendered, (b) the social construction of masculinity and work, and (c) the inevitably partial character of any gender identity. We argue that, while gender and feminist research can hardly be described as part of "mainstream" organization studies, there has been a noticeable shift in scholarly sensibilities about the gendered character of organizing. Attesting to this trend are recently developed journals like *Gender, Work and Organization* and several anthologies of feminist viewpoints on organizing (e.g., Buzzanell, 2000; Cheng, 1996; Mills & Tancred, 1992; Savage & Witz, 1992). Given this shift, we think it time to move beyond general debates of legitimacy and toward examining the implications of specific feminist perspectives for enhancing understanding. For us, the central question then becomes, "Out of the many possibilities that feminism offers, which approaches best enable us to map the complexities of gendered organization?"

Nonetheless, authors continue to ponder, "Can one legitimately study gender in organizational life?" or "Why isn't feminist scholarship published more frequently in organization studies?" We see these persistent anxieties over credibility as an outgrowth of current relations between feminist and critical organization studies; namely, that feminist perspectives are typically viewed as a recent offshoot of a larger, more sophisticated body of radical organization scholarship.

❖ FEMINISM AND CRITICAL ORGANIZATION STUDIES: REREADING THE RELATIONSHIP

By *radical* or *critical organization studies*, we refer broadly to a tradition of theory and research that analyzes the social construction of organizations and, specifically, the ways in which institutional(ized) meanings mold power relations and identity (Alvesson, 1985; Clegg, 1989; Deetz, 1992a; Huspek & Kendall, 1991). Critical approaches to organization emerged in the wake of the so-called linguistic turn in philosophy and social theory (Rorty, 1967), which situated language as the basic ontological condition of being and experience. Applied to the study of organization, this paradigmatic shift took human communication not simply as one element of organizational life, but as *the* essential process—that which calls organization into being, crafting actuality from possibility. Communication produces, not merely expresses, the realities of organization (Grant, Keenoy, & Oswick, 1998; Pacanowsky & O'Donnell-Trujillo, 1982; Putnam & Pacanowsky, 1983). In this sense, the linguistic (or discursive) turn transformed the way we can see organizations as objects of study.

The discursive turn generated a wave of research concerned with organizational language and symbolism, and the critical approach represents a particular intervention in such studies. Drawing on 19th and 20th century developments in hermeneutics (Gadamer, 1989; R. Palmer, 1969), phenomenology (Heidegger, 1977; Merleau-Ponty, 1960), and humanist Marxism (Gramsci, 1971; Horkheimer & Adorno, 1988; Lukács, 1971), critical scholars articulate a "discourse of suspicion" (Mumby, 1997a; Ricoeur, 1970). Thus, where interpretive or cultural scholars look to understand the ways in which organizational actors create shared, collective meaning through interaction (M. H. Brown, 1990; Pacanowsky & O'Donnell-Trujillo, 1982; Putnam, 1983), critical scholars explore the "underbelly" of organizational life, arguing that apparent harmony and consensus hides underlying structures of domination, resistance, and interest-driven discourse strategies (Deetz, 1992a; Hardy & Phillips, 1999; Mumby, 1987). In other words, organizational reality is not constructed spontaneously or consensually; negotiating meaning is a political process that is both constrained by and constitutive of power structures. From a critical perspective, then, organizations are sites where various organizational actors and groups strive to fix meaning in ways that will serve particular interests (Deetz, 1982; Mumby & Clair, 1997).

Central to understanding the politics of organizing through a critical lens are the concepts of ideology and hegemony, which we briefly introduce here. In radical organization scholarship, the term *discourse* is invoked liberally yet with various meanings, which range from mundane communication to language or text to abstract societal narrative. One common premise that cuts across this variation is that discourse—in all its forms—does ideological work that shapes our relationships to the world in ways that are not always apparent to us. Here, ideology is more than ideational; it entails systems of representation that construct identity, securing and obscuring structural inequalities and contradictions. Furthermore, these systems of representation do not float above social practice; they are materially grounded in the practices of everyday life. As Althusser (1971) states, "Disappeared: the term *ideas*. Survive: the terms *subject, consciousness, beliefs, actions*. Appear: the terms *practices, rituals, ideological apparatus*" (p. 169). While ideology predisposes people toward certain ways of making sense, it by no means exhausts the interpretive possibilities at their disposal. Consequently, attempts to ideologically fix meaning are always contested processes. As Hall (1985) states, ideology "sets limits to the degree to which a society-in-dominance can easily, smoothly, and functionally reproduce itself" (p. 113). Criticisms notwithstanding, this formulation of ideology has significantly influenced the agenda of critical organization scholars—namely, their guiding interest in explicating discursive processes of ideological struggle (Collinson, 1992; Graham, 1993; Huspek & Kendall, 1991; Markham, 1996).

Gramsci's notion of hegemony has also become integral to critical accounts of ideological struggle. Although hegemony has been widely read to capture ideological domination of one class by another, it is more appropriately interpreted to theorize power as a noncoercive, dialectical struggle between competing groups in the realm of civil society (Mumby, 1997b). In short, hegemony explains "the ability of one class to articulate the interests of other social groups to its own" (Mouffe, 1979, p. 183). Gramsci's work is particularly vital insofar as it marks a shift from viewing power as simply coercive, or as the imposition of some fixed ideology on subordinate groups, to a dynamic conception of lived social relations, wherein various tensions constantly unfold among groups. For Gramsci, political struggle is less a "war of maneuver" (i.e., the direct confrontation of state power) and more a "war of position" (i.e., the struggle of classes to diffuse their worldview via the institutions of civil society). Hence, hegemony involves the cultivation of a "collective will" through "intellectual and moral reform" (Gramsci, 1971, pp. 60–61). Guided by such claims, critical scholars conceive of organization as a primary domain for the enactment of hegemonic struggle in contemporary civil society (e.g., Deetz, 1992a; Mumby, 1988).

Traditionally, critical organization scholarship rests on at least some modernist principles. Most pertinent to our project are (a) the emancipatory interest that guides critique of power relations, (b) an associated view of power as a dialectic of control and resistance, and (c) confidence (however qualified) in the rational subject from whose consciousness emancipatory possibilities can spring. Postmodern organization theory, based initially on the work of Cooper and Burrell (Burrell, 1988; R. Cooper, 1989; Cooper & Burrell, 1988), has begun to pose serious questions about these premises. A first challenge concerns the moral imperative of emancipation (Deetz, 1992a). Although critical scholars reject narrow, technical visions of enlightenment and progress through scientific knowledge (such as those embedded in positivism and empiricism), social transformation remains the primary impetus for analyzing organizational forms and articulating alternatives (M. Parker, 1995). Simply put, critical theorists tend to criticize the dominant path to, not the very notion of, emancipation. Postmodernists are much less sanguine about the emancipatory potential that critical scholars argue is latent in contemporary institutions. Indeed, some argue that "emancipation" is one more modernist, totalizing discourse that disciplines people, reproducing institutional mechanisms that create docile subjects (e.g., Foucault, 1979, 1980a). Speaking generally, postmodern authors refuse any kind of normative base from which to critique social processes, maintaining that such bases lead to imposed consensus and, thus, to more forms of terror (Lyotard, 1984). Hence, they urge multiple, local ways of explaining dominance and representing resistance, with particular attention to the possibilities of play, parody, and pastiche for deconstructing relations of power.

Second, the dispute over the desirability and possibility of emancipation reflects contrastive accounts of power. Critical modernists often define power as domination and harbor utopian possibilities of coercion-free contexts for social interaction and knowledge production. For example, even Gramsci's conception of hegemony, while it illuminates the dialectical processes of consent and domination, ultimately holds that a ruling bloc retains power by controlling such repressive apparatuses as law enforcement and the military. Postmodernists, however, tend to view power and truth as inevitable partners, with power as an inescapable, defining element of human identity (Foucault, 1979, 1980a). The distinction is perhaps best exemplified in the debate between Jürgen Habermas and Michel Foucault. Habermas (1971, 1979) articulates a theory of truth that excludes the exercise of power. Indeed, his ideal speech situation is predicated on the possibility of a communication context, free from domination and its inevitable distortions, in which validity claims can be tested. In contrast, Foucault depicts power as endemic to everyday life and argues for an intrinsic and dialectical (although *not* isomorphic) relationship between knowledge and power (1979, pp. 27–28). From this view, power does not forbid; it enables. The question becomes how it enables, and what and whom it makes possible. In several projects, Foucault (1979, 1980a, 1986) traces the ways in which specific power-knowledge formations facilitate and normalize certain ways of being. Such works reflect the premise that power-knowledge relations articulate systems of possibility—resources from which social actors fashion coherent senses of identity. Characterizing the matter broadly, then, critical modernists tend to promote a "sovereign," top-down, negative account of power, whereas postmodernists put forth a disciplinary, productive, positive conception.

A third challenge posed by postmodernism concerns the reasoning subject to which modernity clings as a fount of knowledge and emancipatory potential. Postmodernists (in particular, Derrida) are perhaps most (in)famous for "decentering" a humanist conception of identity, which they fault for reifying metaphysical notions of "the mind." Certainly, many critical theorists also attempt to undermine metaphysical accounts of reason. Habermas, for example, replaces a transcendental notion of consciousness with a linguistic one. Yet there remains a tendency among critical scholars to hypostatize critical self-reflection as the primary means through which relations of domination are interrogated and overcome. Despite their unyielding rejection of subject-centered models of knowledge, postmodernists by no means reject the construct of subjectivity entirely. Instead, they treat the subject as an *effect* (rather than as the origin or author) of numerous discourses and disciplinary practices. In short, the subject is decentered, not discarded. As hinted above, postmodern scholars often "recenter" the subject, asking "who" is called into being by various discourses of truth and power.

It is worth noting that, while both critical modernists and postmodernists conceive of discourse as constitutive of social reality, critical modernists are much more prepared to recognize the material world as impinging on that reality. For postmodernists, Derrida's (1976) claim that "there is nothing outside of the text" (p. 157) is a rallying point for articulating an isomorphic relationship between discourse/text and reality. Indeed, many of the deconstructive analyses in management studies make little or no reference to "the world" in which particular discourses are situated (Calás, 1992; Calás & Smircich, 1991; Kilduff, 1993). A critical perspective, on the other hand, explores discourse as a communicative accomplishment that exists dialectically with the political economy of the workplace (Burawoy, 1979). It might make sense, therefore, to consider what we have called "critical modernist" and "postmodernist" positions as part of an emerging and potentially useful dialogue about tensions in critical organization studies.

For roughly 30 years, then, radical organization scholarship has centered attention on the complex relationships among power, ideology, identity, and discourse. The linguistic turn facilitated the study of organizations as pivotal sites of political struggle to secure meaning and identity. More recently, and within the context provided by the linguistic turn, postmodern insights have begun to challenge—we think, productively—conventional critical models of organized discourse, power, and subjectivity.

Against this conceptual backdrop, feminist scholars of organization appear like latecomers, borrowing critical insights to assess one specialized dimension of organizational discourse, power, and identity: gender. The following rationale for the absence of feminism from an anthology on critical management studies encapsulates the prevalent view: "Most if not all phenomena involve a gender aspect, but it would be reductionist to capture most aspects of management, production and consumption basically in feminist terms, although we recognize that critical feminism provides an invaluable complement to, as well as critique of, Critical Theory" (Alvesson & Willmott, 1992b, p. 9). Such justifications may appear tortured, if not patronizing, particularly in light of the above feminist claim that organizations are fundamentally gendered. Simultaneously, the notion that feminist research is a specialized area of critical organization inquiry is not without merit. As we explain in subsequent chapters, much feminist organization scholarship overtly appropriates critical concepts—such as hegemony, ideology, and so on—to explain the gender relations of organizational life (e.g., Clair, 1993b).

Yet, although there is a sense in which feminist studies is a subsidiary arm of radical organization scholarship, other possible readings spin the relation differently and, we argue, constructively. One such reading acknowledges that feminist scholars of organization draw on more than critical perspectives. In fact, they bring to the table their own long-standing, independent tradition of conceptualizing societal relations of power: feminist theory. Given this foundation, one might muse with Fine (1993) that

> researchers who espouse the utility of a feminist perspective in communication are frequently asked how their ideas differ from

those of critical theorists. (Both feminists and critical theorists should be interested in exploring why the reverse question is never asked). (p. 143)

Moreover, although fairly new to the scene, feminist *organization* theories have already demonstrated the centrality of gender to radical accounts of organizing. Specifically, feminists have compellingly argued that critical and mainstream organization studies can prove unwitting allies in the tacit assumption of men as universal working subjects. From this vantage point, critical scholars who wish to deny the relevance of gender to analyses of organizing power and identity ignore a primary way in which difference and subjectivity are configured and thus obscure the gendered subtext of such analyses. Long before rendering such critique, however, feminists pursued an organizational agenda distinct from, and more pragmatically radical than, that of many critical theorists. This contribution comes into view only if we cast our eyes beyond the exclusive domain of academic activity.

The interpretation of feminist approaches as derivative of critical perspectives remains viable—albeit tenuously—only when we spotlight the scholarly exercise and overlook other arenas of social practice. For example, if we include political activism as part of our discussion, we are compelled to recognize that feminists were busy experimenting with alternative organizational forms just as critical scholars were beginning to envision them. Guided by the assertion that bureaucracy serves as a structural arm of male domination, many feminist movement groups (variously focused on consciousness raising, domestic violence, rape crisis, reproductive health, and so forth) developed functional communities that strove to minimize hierarchy and maximize egalitarian relations, to enact group authority via consensual decision making, and to value emotions and other "private" matters as relevant political and organizational concerns (Ahrens, 1980; Iannello, 1992; Maguire & Mohtar, 1994; Morgen, 1994; Reinelt, 1994; Ristock, 1990; Rodriguez, 1988; V. Taylor, 1995). Certainly, many other activist groups also implemented democratic, collectivist, and other participatory alternatives to bureaucracy (Kanter & Zurcher, 1973; Mansbridge, 1973; Newman, 1980; Rothschild-Whitt, 1976, 1979). Arguably, at least in the United States, feminist organizations have negotiated considerable institutional staying power, and they remain one of the longest-standing social movement forms designed around counter-bureaucratic empowerment ideals (Ferree & Martin, 1995; Maguire & Mohtar, 1994;

P. Y. Martin, 1990; Reinelt, 1994). With this claim, we do not mean to paint idyllic images of triumphant social transformation. Rather, the struggles, failures, ironies, and innovations of feminist communities have produced (and continue to generate) a wealth of empirical insight about the pitfalls and potential of alternative organizational practices; we consider such matters in more detail as we survey relevant literature in Chapter 1.

For now, the point we are making is that these "grassroots" endeavors reflect an entrenched feminist commitment to do more than talk within the walls of an ivory tower; they embody the desire to create tangible forms of social change that enhance equality and justice in the lives of real people. Whereas critical organization scholars prioritized emancipation through ideology critique, feminists literally grounded their emancipatory interest in the trenches of practice. This observation prompts two claims. First, the contrast suggests that feminist approaches to organization exemplify a different sort of maturity—one that Fine (1993) calls "revolutionary pragmatism"—which critical organization scholarship has yet to develop and from which it could learn a great deal. Second, that feminist experiments with practice largely preceded feminist theories of organization (while the reverse typifies critical organization studies) signifies an abiding ambivalence among many feminists about philosophical debate and, specifically, about the simultaneous importance and impotence of such reflection. Indeed, the larger history of feminist studies is rich with ambivalence—struggles between epistemological and political imperatives, between symbolic and material realities, between deconstructive and reconstructive impulses, between conceptions of power as imposed and self-policed, between stable and fragmented accounts of "woman," and so forth. Importantly—and, of course, not coincidentally—this second claim implies that feminist approaches to organization have long embodied tensions akin to those between critical modernism and postmodernism. With its experience in juggling such tensions, feminism can serve as a model for or means of productively mediating them.

To clarify, we acknowledge the partial validity of both readings offered here: "feminism as offshoot" of and "feminism as central" to radical organization scholarship. Undeniably, however, the "feminism as central" position gets much less play in the reigning narrative of (critical) organization studies. By assuming that position throughout this book, we hope to underscore the pivotal place of feminist approaches in organizational theory and praxis.

❖ COMMUNICATION AS THE ORGANIZING PROCESS

In this book, we seek to develop a feminist communicology of organization, which centers human communication as the basic, constitutive activity of organizing. In other words, it is as people engage in communicative action that identity, action, and structure—individual and collective—become possible and meaningful. Given our roots in organizational communication theory and research, our interest in a communication-centered account of power, identity, and organization is not surprising. Yet we take this stance for more than disciplinary reasons; we believe it has much to contribute at this moment in feminist and radical organization studies.

To begin with, the above sketch of the discursive and postmodern turns in organization scholarship suggests the need to foreground communication while revising dominant conceptions of it. Specifically, many radical organization theorists take seriously the notion that communication lies at the nexus of what counts as truth—that communication is the fundamental ontology of human existence. This notion requires a radical shift from the traditional view of communication as self-expression, or as an intentional act in which the speaker verbalizes an already formed subjectivity. This "commonsense" lens sees communication as a medium or conduit for the transmission of ideas fully realized in the speaker's mind (Axley, 1984). Shepherd (1993) captures well the consequences of this Cartesian model for the study of interaction:

> Disciplines forward unique ontological views; they tell us what matters about Being and they represent essentialist ideas. From modernity's point of view, then, how can there be a discipline of communication? Nullius in Verba [Words are nothing]. How can one be a disciple of nothing? As a mere vehicle, communication has no existential status in modernity. In a sense, communication may carry Being, but in and of itself, communication is Being-less. What unique view of Being can a Being-less idea forward? Modernity said of communication what Gertrude Stein said of Oakland: There is no there there. (p. 87)

As this excerpt suggests, the conventional model of communication tends to reify the subject as a fixed entity who engages in cognition, then encodes these cognitions through the interaction process. This stance precludes precisely that which interests scholars shaped by the linguistic turn and the subsequent insights of critical modernist and postmodernist perspectives—namely, the ways in which realities and selves are *produced,* not merely expressed, through communication.

Deetz (1992a) argues against the commonsense view when he declares that "communication is not for self-expression but for self-destruction" (p. 341). This counterintuitive claim articulates a nonessentialist relationship between the self and communication. From a postmodern perspective, as noted above, we are the effect of various and often-competing discourses. In Hall's (1985) terms, "There is no essential, unitary 'I'—only the fragmentary, contradictory subject I become" (p. 109). In opposition to the traditional, representational view, communication as self-de(con)structive stresses the *productive* character of interaction. Deetz (1992a) continues, "The point of communication as a social act is to overcome one's fixed subjectivity, one's conceptions, one's strategies, to be opened to the indeterminacy of people and the external environment" (p. 341). This claim recognizes that our sense of identity is "subject" to the pull of other discursive possibilities that challenge who we are.

Crucially, a revised perspective on communication does not mean that we are always constituted anew in every interaction. We are all, to a greater or lesser degree, products of sedimented, institutionalized meaning systems that provide a frame for our ongoing, everyday experience. However, it is this very sedimentation of experience that predisposes us to adopt an unreflective stance toward self, world, and other. It is because we are at least partially sutured to certain dominant, institutionalized senses of ourselves and others that it becomes possible— even easy—to conceive of communication as simply the expression of what is in our heads. It therefore takes a fundamental shift in perspective to see communication as a self-de(con)structive phenomenon that, in its ideal form, challenges comfortable, preconceived conceptions of self as the Archimedian point of origin of meaning and experience. Such a shift allows and directs us to examine the communicative processes through which identities and organizations are (re)produced. In sum, centering communication means that reason and rationality, community and identity, must be placed within an intersubjective context, where organization entails the linguistic construction of shared assumptive grounds about what is real and meaningful. The matter of how such interactively constructed worlds measure up to the court of reality then becomes moot, for reality itself is destabilized, residing in the ongoing process of communication.

This is *not* to say that there is nothing real outside of discourse. A significant aim of this book is to step beyond such text positivism and to capture the ways in which communication is at once constrained by and generative of material conditions. We mean that in at least three senses. First, communication arises in response to (perceived) political and material exigencies. Second, communication takes the material world as its material. Thus discursive formations are inscribed on the body and performed in concrete practices; as such, discourse and communication generate ways of being, seeing, feeling, and acting in the world. Third, communication can produce material circumstances beyond lived subjectivities. By this, we mean to say more than that communication lends meaning to an existing material world. Taking a step further, we suggest that discourse and communication can literally create lasting institutional and economic arrangements.

On its face, the claim to communication's centrality may seem like a truism, but the extent to which it is neglected in organization studies (and in many other fields that profess to study human behavior) is astounding. Scholars study power, leadership, network structures, information processing, routines, and so forth, while paying little attention to the "real time" practices that give life to these phenomena. Often, even some who identify as interpretivists (or critical-interpretivists) do not draw the link between meaning and actual communication processes. We seek to illuminate that link and, specifically, to elaborate the connection between "micro" communication practices and "macro" systems of symbolic and material power. Our preceding claims about the materiality of communication begin to speak to the micro-macro connection. More broadly, we intend to engage the hotly contested "agency-structure" relationship, guided by an interest in unpacking the mechanisms by which mundane moments of interaction affiliate with enduring structures and institutions.

In these ways, we hope to expand extant notions (within and beyond our home discipline) of what counts as organizational communication, as well as why organizational communication counts. The feminist approach we develop investigates how communication across often-severed domains of symbolic activity—public and private, mediated and interpersonal, and so forth—organizes gender and genders organization toward tangible effects. Beyond the aims of our own project, we believe that such a perspective can enrich radical organization studies by strengthening the connection between criticism and the "real" world, where the privilege of certain interests means the experience of palpable consequences.

❖   TOWARD A FEMINIST
     COMMUNICOLOGY OF ORGANIZATION

Principally, then, we seek to articulate a communicological approach that can enrich conceptual, empirical, and practical understanding of the processes that organize gendered selves and institutions. Chapter 1 commences this effort by providing a fresh review of feminist organization studies. The aim of this chapter is, first, to ground our later theoretical discussion by establishing key themes that characterize empirical studies of gender and organization and, second, to situate that research in terms of the discursive turn. We argue that the literature reflects four tacit ways of framing the relationship among organization, discourse, power, and gender; and we link these perspectives to the critical modernist and postmodernist debates outlined above, demonstrating how empirical projects reflect metatheoretical tensions that generate partial insights and constraints.

The next three chapters explore these metatheoretical tensions in greater depth. Chapter 2 considers feminism in relation to modernist logics, Chapter 3 explores the emergence of postmodern thought in organization studies, and Chapter 4 delves into the relationship between feminist and postmodern analytics and its possibilities for radical organization studies. Reviewing the varied ways in which feminist theorists have engaged and struggled with modernism and postmodernism, we characterize feminist perspectives as critical of and sympathetic to both. Ultimately, our purpose is to demonstrate how this ambivalent posture positions feminism to mediate or navigate crucial dilemmas in contemporary critical organization scholarship. It is in these chapters that we develop more extensively the argument that feminism is not an offshoot or afterthought—and gender not a peripheral or specialized concern—of radical organization studies. Rather, feminism represents a useful place from which to negotiate conceptual fissures and to simultaneously pursue deconstructive and activist agendas.

Emerging from this theoretical context, Chapter 5 articulates a feminist communicology of organization. Among other implications, centering communication means that gender is neither merely an individual trait, nor a structural feature of organizational life; rather, it is an ongoing interactive accomplishment that creates possibilities for and limitations to the process of organizing. Feminism at the intersection of modernism and postmodernism facilitates a communicative perspective by destabilizing self and organization and directing attention to the mundane interactions wherein we consume, echo, and (re)invent institutional discourse. All the while, such a perspective retains a guiding interest in both deconstructing and reconstructing organization toward productive social change. Thus, a feminist communicology hinges on several premises, such as the communicative constitution of subjectivity; dialectical relationships between power and resistance, discourse and the material world, and masculinities and femininities; the historical specificity of gendered organizational formations; and normative, ethical commitment to the exploration of lived consequences and possibilities for praxis.

Chapter 6 demonstrates the empirical potential of this feminist approach. We apply the communicology model to data drawn from Karen's ongoing study of gender, race, and class relations among U.S. commercial airline pilots. The data include historical and contemporary discourse, which spans occupational, organizational, and popular culture, as well as individual experience. We chronicle how commercial aviator identity became symbolically and materially attached to the male body, yielding unprecedented professional standing in the process. Our analysis tracks the strategic institutional formation of two discourses—that of the "lady-flier" and the "pilot-as-professional"— and contends that their interplay engendered the requisite masculinity of airline pilots, which anchored the class status of the occupation. As explained above, gender identities are never generic or universal, though they may masquerade as such. Likewise, communication of and about airline pilots invoked a particular form of white, heterosexual masculinity, laced with class contradictions. We consider how contemporary pilots navigate such tensions and, specifically, how many cling to the emotional and material pleasures of white masculinity, even as they embrace efforts to increase diversity in the race and gender profile of their occupation. In these ways, Chapter 6 foregrounds the diachronic, dialectical, and material character of the communication processes that organize gendered labor. In Chapter 7, we conclude our efforts by stepping back from the empirical study to consider its implications for our project, as well as for the larger projects of feminist and critical organization studies.

1

Feminist Organization Studies in the Wake of the Discursive Turn

❖ ❖ ❖

It is one thing to assert that feminist organization studies does not ride the coattails of a larger critical venture and to therefore render it both independent of and integral to radical organization studies. It is another matter, and the explicit interest of this book, to substantiate the claim. This chapter commences that effort by introducing gender and organization studies as an interdisciplinary endeavor that encompasses a complicated array of theoretical and empirical projects. Our primary aim in this chapter is to provide a textured portrait of extant research, depicting the range of foci, findings, and perspectives that have characterized gender and organization scholarship in the past few decades of its development.

This chapter is distinct from previous reviews (e.g., Calás & Smircich, 1996; Hearn & Parkin, 1983; Mumby, 1996) in that it examines

AUTHORS' NOTE: This chapter is adapted from an initial version of Karen's chapter to appear in the *Sage Handbook of Organizational Discourse* edited by David Grant, Cynthia Hardy, Cliff Oswick, Nelson Phillips, and Linda Putnam. Reprinted with permission of Sage Publications, Inc.

feminist organization scholarship in light of the linguistic turn. As such, it is particularly concerned with works that place language and communication at the core of reality and knowledge construction. Over the past 30 years, scholars have developed complex accounts of connections among discourse, organization, gender, power, and identity. Increasingly, discourse is thought to constitute rather than simply reflect the seemingly inevitable intersection of gender and organization. This shift has disrupted the conventional notion of organizations as static entities and of gender as fixed identities that meet in measurable ways. It highlights how communication continuously creates, solidifies, disrupts, and alters gendered selves and organizational forms. As such, the discursive turn in this line of inquiry points to possibilities for revising relations of power.

Although many gender and organization scholars have come to embrace the centrality of discourse, they often diverge, at least implicitly, in how they cast relationships among discourse, organization, gender, power, and identity. Consequently, the terms assume variable meanings and alternately appear as figure and ground, producer and product, subject and context, leading and supporting character, and so forth. Our position here is *not* that diverse perspectives impede knowledge, but that the slippage of terms and relationships, when left unexamined, obscures key points of tension and alliance across the literature. We maintain that these conceptual conflicts and coalitions are more than cerebral matters; they are of profound practical and political significance. Consistent with the aims of our overall project, this chapter surveys relevant literature for the ways in which scholars depict the meanings of and relations among discourse, organization, gender, power, and identity. We identify four prevalent ways of seeing, or framing. With the term *frame*, we mean not to suggest durable mental maps but to evoke tacit, provisional viewpoints shared by certain approaches to research, which illuminate particular features yet remain open to alternative perspectives. As with any effort to characterize, this approach assumes the probable risks of reducing complexity and diminishing certain commonalties as it accentuates others. Certainly, we acknowledge overlap and convergence across perspectives, as well as the viability of other categorizations. Our hope is that this effort to organize and simplify scholarship can expose overlooked patterns and thus establish a vantage point from which to see differently.

Our discussion of each frame begins by broadly characterizing basic assumptions; we then offer illustrative literature and consider the frame's key contributions and difficulties. We order our discussion of frames in terms of their relative emphasis on "micro" to "macro" dimensions of discourse. Frame 1 highlights how gender identity shapes communication habits, while frame 2 underscores how daily interaction manufactures gender identities. Shifting to a broader, institutional level, frame 3 depicts organizational forms as gendered discourse communities, and frame 4 steps beyond discrete organizations to inspect societal discourses that arrange gender and labor. We conclude by exposing underlying tensions and alliances that cut across the frames; our purpose is to illuminate how empirical projects reflect metatheoretical struggles that translate into partial insights and practical constraints.

❖ COMMON WAYS OF FRAMING THE RELATIONSHIP AMONG DISCOURSE, GENDER, AND ORGANIZATION

Frame 1: Gender Organizes Discourse

The first frame treats gender as a defining element of human identity and highlights how it shapes interactional tendencies. From this view, discourse refers to communication style—predispositions toward ways of talking, using language, and orienting to human relationships. By defining discourse primarily as an outcome, manifestation, or reflection of an individual's gender identity, frame 1 downplays the constitutive function of discourse. In this sense, it leans toward what we previously called a representational view of communication, wherein communication amounts to a vehicle for self-expression. Through the lens of frame 1, gender is a socialized (but fairly fixed) individual identity and/or cultural membership, which is organized around biological sex and which fosters predictable communication habits. Here, identity connotes a relatively stable self, distinguished by core, group-based similarities and differences that largely transcend time and context. For frame 1, organization carries a dual meaning. First, it captures the guiding assumption that discourse is gendered in relatively ordered and consistent ways. In its more overt use, organization (read: the white-collar workplace) is a key context in which gendered discourse patterns play out. It is here that power enters on the edge of frame 1's scope. That is, power becomes relevant not to the actual configuration of gender differences but, rather, to how those differences are perceived and (de)valued within organizational settings.

The vast literature on gender differences best illustrates this frame. Much of the early research in this area took sex/gender as a fixed variable associated with communication differences; this work offered little account of sources or mechanisms that engender difference (for an extensive review, see Canary & Hause, 1993). The picture became more complex as scholars distinguished between biological sex classifications and gender identity, developing psychodynamic, social psychological, and cultural theories of gender-role socialization that variously portrayed behavioral differences as learned outcomes or social products, not static or intrinsic traits (Bate, 1988; Egendorf, 2000; Ivy & Backlund, 2000; Pearson, Turner, & Todd-Mancillas, 1991; Wood, 1997). Although many authors in this tradition acknowledge the distinction between symbolic (i.e., abstract social constructions of gender) and empirical (i.e., what actual women and men do), they nonetheless tend to presume a strong correlation between them.

Of particular prominence in the gender difference literature is the focus on "women's ways" or "feminine styles" of being and doing (e.g., Belenky, Clinchy, Goldberger, & Tarule, 1986; Gilligan, 1982). Specific to discourse, countless scholars depict men and women as inhabiting distinct communication cultures (Bate & Taylor, 1988; Johnson, 1989; Kramarae, 1981; Maltz & Borker, 1982; Tannen, 1990, 1994). Despite disagreement as to how language and difference implicate power, most of this work converges around a basic image of gendered discourse. In this image, women tend to approach communication as a process of building and maintaining relationships. They emphasize equality, responsiveness and support, emotion and personal disclosure, and a tentative or provisional tone. In contrast, men typically view interaction as an instrumental activity. Hence, they stress communication outcomes—like dominance, persuasion, or display of knowledge—and tend toward more abstract, rational, strategic, and assertive tones. Such broad variations in approach are thought to translate into particular discursive practices. For example, abundant research on conflict, criticism, and compliance-gaining points to women's preference for indirect, cooperative, egalitarian (or even deferential), and emotional tactics, in contrast to men's penchant for confrontational, competitive, assertive, and rational strategies (e.g., Monroe et al., 1990; Todd-Mancillas & Rossi, 1985). Several scholars have advised caution regarding such claims, citing inconclusive evidence (e.g., Conrad, 1991; Sternberg & Soriano, 1984). Nonetheless, the gender difference literature is organized around a binary view of gender, which, by and large, supports popular visions of men and women communicating.

Organization appears more explicitly in this literature as a key site where differences become manifest and consequential. Preoccupation with a particular kind of worker and workplace—female professionals in white-collar settings—is evident in the most prolific literature on gender and organization to date: studies of women in management (e.g., Billing & Alvesson, 1998; Calás & Smircich, 1996). A substantial share of this work examines how interaction patterns and perceptions thereof erect barriers (e.g., the "glass ceiling") to women's professional, hierarchical advancement (Buzzanell, 1995; Fitzpatrick, 1983; Horgan, 1990; Powell, 1999; Reardon, 1997; Reuther & Fairhurst, 2000; Staley, 1988; Stewart & Clarke-Kudless, 1993; Wilkins & Anderson, 1991). In her popular account of workplace communication, for example, Tannen (1994) explained that many women avoid self-promotion, share credit, and use hesitant and self-deprecating language—discursive habits that appear weak and, thus, ill-fit for upper management.

Given the overwhelming focus on managerial women, it is no surprise that leadership has engrossed more gender and organization scholars than any other discursive activity. Since the mid-1970s, the work of such scholars has shifted attention from women's alleged dubious capacity to lead to gender variance in leadership style (Natalle, 1996). More recently, a host of authors have positively spun such difference, celebrating "women's ways" or "feminine styles" of leading. Typically, they claim that women tend to prefer or exhibit distinctive, effective, and some even say superior leadership habits stemming from lifelong lessons in relationship formation and maintenance (Bass & Avolio, 1994; Helgesen, 1990; Loden, 1985; Lynch, 1973; Nelson, 1988; Rosener, 1990). Helgesen (1990), for instance, wove women's leadership as a web of associations, inclusive, emergent, and flexible. With metaphors like teacher, magician, gardener, and liaison, she conveyed women leaders' unique concerns for mentoring, nurturance, and equality. Similarly, Rosener (1990) portrayed women as "transformational" or "interactive" leaders who invoke informal, personal bases of authority to stimulate participation, share power and information, and enhance others' self-worth and energy. She contrasted this approach to the "transactional" tendency of men to view leadership as a series of exchanges that hinge on formal, structural authority and hierarchical control.

And yet, empirical studies yield limited support for such tidy, dualistic depictions. Nearly 30 years of investigation have yielded inconclusive evidence (Butterfield & Grinnell, 1999). In an extensive meta-analysis, Eagly & Johnson (1990) found that gender patterns confirmed in laboratory and assessment studies did not hold true in natural settings, particularly when men and women occupied similar organizational positions. Likewise, scores of studies report little or no difference in the styles of men and women in organizations, and several reviews note inconclusive findings (e.g., Butterfield & Grinnell, 1999; Walker, Ilardi, McMahon, & Fennell, 1996; Wilkins & Anderson, 1991). Strongest among the findings is the association of women with democratic or participatory leadership discourse and of men with autocratic leadership discourse (Eagly & Johannesen-Schmidt, 2001; Eagly & Johnson, 1990). Yet even this link must be qualified. Numerous studies suggest that it is complicated by perception and expectation (e.g., Carless, 1998; Staley, 1988), organizational context (Butterfield & Grinnell, 1999; Epstein, 1981; Hanson, 1996) or position (Mulac, Tiyaamornwong, & Seibold, 1999), a cultural preference for democratic leadership (Eagly, Makhijani, & Klonsky, 1992; Luthar, 1996), and ambivalence toward women as leaders (Eagly, Makhijani, & Otto, 1991).

Much gender and leadership research relies on self-report data and takes a psychological spin on communication, wherein interaction styles reflect cognitive orientations. In a leadership study rare for its explicit attention to discourse, Fairhurst (1993) examined the routine talk of women managers to understand the interactive accomplishment of leader-member relationships. Through conversation analysis and case comparison, she identified 12 communication patterns—such as provisional framing, polite disagreement, insider joking, and coaching—through which the women negotiated work relationships. Her detailed analysis revealed commonality (e.g., the primacy of relational concerns) and variation (e.g., ways of engaging in power games) among study participants, suggesting how close readings of discourse in practice can usefully nuance the tidy, dualistic depictions often rendered by communication difference studies.

Certainly, frame 1 serves vital functions. Most vividly, it demonstrates how even perceptions of gender variance in organizational communication can translate into tangible political consequences. As our review reveals, studies of gender differences in organizational communication reflect a preoccupation with documenting women's or "feminine" styles. While this work can be read to perpetuate the limited association of gender with women, it also serves to mark men as gendered communicators and professionalism as a biased construct.

For example, starting with the premise of masculine and feminine discursive cultures, several scholars have argued that dominant professional norms privilege men's culture (e.g., Haslett, Geis, & Carter, 1992; Marshall, 1993; Murphy & Zorn, 1996). Specifically, a legacy of research reports that management is usually defined in masculine terms (e.g., Brenner, Tomkiewicz, & Schein, 1989; Heilman, Block, Martell, & Simon, 1989; Sachs, Chrisler, & Devlin, 1992; V.E. Schein, 1973, 1975; Schein & Mueller, 1992). Thus, many women will likely experience "double binds," or clashing expectations for femininity and professional leadership (e.g., Jamieson, 1995; Marshall, 1993; Murphy & Zorn, 1996; Wiley & Eskilson, 1985). Even those who emulate masculine culture well risk negative evaluation, since similar behaviors look suspect in the light of gender prescriptions (Powell, 1993). In addition to exposing the tacit masculinity of professional interaction and the attendant dilemmas that daunt women at work, gender difference scholars have sought to raise esteem for feminine modes of discourse and to integrate them into organization theory (e.g., Fine, 2000; J. Fletcher, 1994).

Such important strides notwithstanding, frame 1 rests on a tired and problematic logic of difference. In response to shaky empirical foundations, many theorists acknowledge that masculine and feminine styles do not fit all males and females; simultaneously, they continue to mark those styles as "women's ways" or "the male approach" (e.g., Nelson, 1988; Rosener, 1990). This conflicted move reifies a binary view of gender despite a dearth of support, neglecting within-group variations that could problematize dualistic accounts (Kahn & Yoder, 1989; Pollitt, 1992). Specifically, frame 1 tends to treat gender as an isolated feature of identity, all but ignoring its inevitable intersections with race, class, sexuality, organizational context, and so forth, as well as how those intersections complicate the content of gender difference. Narrow attention to gender, coupled with the conventional research focus on white women professionals, has fed a tacit and misguided assumption that white, middle-class gender norms represent universal perceptions and practices (Calás & Smircich, 1996).

To put the problem another way, frame 1 suffers from a general lack of context—cultural, political, institutional, historical, and structural. Relatedly, frame 1 tends to underplay the production of difference, as well as the relation of difference and power. Typically, authors discuss gender difference in uniform, static, ahistorical, and uncritical terms. Questions like these—How did we reach our present configuration of differences? How do we preserve and alter it? What alternative forms compete alongside it?—remain largely unvoiced and unexplored. Moreover, if masculine communication entails "doing dominance" and feminine communication entails "doing deference" (West & Zimmerman, 1987), it makes little sense to simply appreciate gender difference as is, much less to embrace the devalued other, since the variation itself reflects relations of dominance and subordination (Ashcraft & Pacanowsky, 1996; Buzzanell, 1995). In other words, different-but-equal logic struggles to explain how opposites can ever be equal when they are born of hierarchy (Beauvoir, 1973; Irigaray, 1985; Kristeva, 1981). Perhaps worse, different-but-superior logic (e.g., "the feminine leadership advantage," see Fletcher, 1994) aims to reverse the hierarchy, overlooking potentially destructive elements of "women's ways," as well as the case of women who internalize the lesser worth of feminine styles (Ashcraft, 1999; Ashcraft & Pacanowsky, 1996; V. W. Cooper, 1997; Madden, 1987). Far from redefining women, both logics appropriate familiar visions of white, middle-class motherhood in the service of corporate interests (Calás & Smircich, 1993). Furthermore, both logics are easily directed toward exclusion (Buzzanell, 1995). For example, Rosener's (1990) popular claim that context determines which leadership style is best easily becomes justification for a gendered division of labor.

In sum, frame 1 holds that gender identity, while initially produced through interaction, is a primary producer of discursive patterns. Organizations appear as impartial housing in which variations assume significance, or in which masculine culture denigrates feminine speech. As frame 1 obscures more complex ways in which institutional discourse organizes gender, it carries several risks: It divides and essentializes women and men, emphasizing individual rather than systemic tendencies; it crystallizes and normalizes the current discursive norms of dominant groups; and it supplies difference as a rationale for organizational control. In contrast, frame 2 examines how difference is evoked and toward what ends.

Frame 2: Discourse (Dis)Organizes Gender

Like frame 1, frame 2 highlights the organization of gender identities around difference. But while the first frame treats communication differences as the product and evidence of orderly gender identity, the second frame examines how that apparent order is reproduced and/or undermined by discourse. Discourse assumes a more intricate and dynamic face, entailing micro and macro dimensions. First, it refers to the unfolding process of mundane interaction, *not* to the entrenched dispositions people bring to that process. On a larger scale, "a discourse" is a temporarily fixed (but never determined), relatively coherent (though also conflicted), context-specific narrative or symbolic abstraction of gender. Frame 2 posits a dialectical relation between these levels of discourse. On the stage of daily life, social actors are always "positioning" self and other in terms of available gender narratives or situated scripts, which, in turn, facilitate and delimit possibilities for action (Burr, 1995; Goffman, 1959, 1976, 1977; Weedon, 1987). Thus, identity is a partial, unstable discursive effect. Discourse becomes constitutive or productive, and gender identity a product always in progress.

In this way, frame 2 interrogates the link between the symbolic and empirical dimensions of gender, whereas frame 1 presumes its relative stability. Put another way, frame 2 is driven by two questions: How are societal and organizational narratives of gender invoked by people in particular situations, and how do these performances preserve and/or alter the veneer of a binary gender order? As in frame 1, organization carries a dual meaning here. First, it is a feature of gender (i.e., gender as organized). But rather than presume order (i.e., organiz*ation*), frame 2 stresses the ongoing social activity of (dis)ordering gender (i.e. organiz*ing*). Second, organization is a key social context in which gender becomes relevant (i.e., gender "in" organizations). However, whereas frame 1 examines the *expression* of gender identity at work, frame 2 investigates its organizational *formation*. Importantly, most adherents to frame 2 maintain that relations of power inhere in the construction of identity via the ongoing (re)production of difference.

The influential work of West and colleagues (Fenstermaker & West, 2002; West & Fenstermaker, 1995; West & Zimmerman, 1987) illustrates the conceptual shift. They theorize gender not as something we have or are as individuals but as something we "do" together. It is a situated and provisional accomplishment—the continuous activity of managing conduct in light of dominant expectations for appropriate gender behavior. Generally, prevailing norms call for the performance of gender difference, which affirms social faith in the masculine/feminine dualism. However, particular contexts afford a range of acceptable behavior and resources to assist the performance, and so, at least some room to maneuver. Applying this approach directly to organizational life, Gherardi (1994, 1995) argue that we do gender through "ceremonial work," which marks and celebrates men and women as members of separate symbolic orders. This work is largely conversational, performed "through the verbal appreciation of the 'gifts' of the other gender" (Gherardi, 1995, p. 132). Because most forms of work beget ambiguities that breach symbolic divisions, we also perform "remedial work" to repair such violations. For example, Gherardi (1994) reframes "women's lack of assertive style" as a remedial ritual that repairs the offense of infringing on "male domains: the public, production, conversation, and so on" (p. 605).

It is worth noting the radical shift from frame 1: No longer an expression of stable identity, "doing difference" becomes part of an ongoing and interactive effort to secure elusive gender identities through discourse. And the apparent veracity of gender difference attests to the tenacity of social scripts, *not*—as frame 1 implies—to the presence of some steady internal core. In Gherardi's (1995) words, "Doing gender has a prescriptive side to it, and expectations of coherent behaviour among the characteristics attributed to a sex are empirical evidence of it" (p. 144). Invoking other theoretical traditions, several scholars have advanced similar accounts of the relationship between discourse and gender identity (Alvesson & Billing, 1992; Bordo, 1990, 1992; Butler, 1990; Fraser, 1989; Kondo, 1990; Weedon, 1987).

This turn in perspective has stimulated research that explores how women and men "do gender" (West & Zimmerman, 1987) in various settings, "crafting selves" (Kondo, 1990) that (re)produce and/or resist gender difference and relations of power through organizational discourse (e.g., Alvesson, 1998; Ashcraft & Pacanowsky, 1996; Bell & Forbes, 1994; Edley, 2000; Hossfeld, 1993; Pierce, 1995). A common claim across this literature is that the performance of professional identity entails the symbolic and material manipulation of sexed bodies. Scholars have especially emphasized discursive practices—such as formal and informal storytelling about maternity leave (Ashcraft, 1999; J. Martin, 1990) or conversational tactics facilitating effective "passing" (Spradlin, 1998)—that discipline working women with respect to age, attractiveness, emotionality, desire, pregnancy and reproductive capacity, and sexual orientation (Brewis, Hampton, & Linstead, 1997; Dellinger & Williams, 1997; Hochschild, 1983; Pringle, 1989; Sheppard, 1989; Trethewey, 1999a, 2000, 2001; Wendt, 1995). Likewise, organizational communication scholars have usefully reframed sexual harassment as a discursive activity. For, even when it involves physical contact, the reality of harassment—its subjects, meaning, experience, consequences, and responses—gets negotiated among members within the constraints of specific organizational cultures and larger social narratives of gender, sex, and power (Bingham, 1994; Clair, 1993b; Kramarae, 1992; Strine, 1992; Taylor & Conrad, 1992; Wertin, Medlecker, & Pearson, 1995). More recently, authors have considered organizational sexuality as a unique form of sexual play and/or violence—discursive in nature, as it tends to hinge on symbol and talk, not private physical acts (Gherardi, 1995). Some have suggested the transgressive potential of certain "erotic"[2] discourse at work, which can disrupt engrained organizational rationalities and upset gendered order (Brewis & Grey, 1994; Brewis et al., 1997; Burrell, 1992; Pringle, 1989). Notably, much of the "doing gender at work" literature redresses a common criticism of scholarship on organizational discourse: that it discards or downplays things material (Cloud, 2001). Quite the reverse, these works demonstrate how discursive struggles translate into corporeal practices and effects, as well as how the body becomes a potent symbolic resource for identity formation.

Not surprisingly, most studies of this sort spotlight women. And yet, as we observed in the introduction, a growing body of research steps beyond "the woman question," probing the discursive construction of men's bodies and sexualities (Bordo, 1999; Collinson & Collinson, 1989; Faludi, 1998; Gherardi, 1995; Ray, 1999; Roper, 1996; Tasker, 1993a, 1993b). Indeed, recent times have brought a virtual explosion in masculinity scholarship (Brittan, 1989; Brod & Kaufman, 1994; Hearn & Morgan, 1990; Kimmel, 1996; Segal, 1990; Seidler, 1989, 1994; Stecopoulos & Uebel, 1997) and, specifically, in studies of masculinity and organization (Alvesson, 1998; Cheng, 1996; Collinson, 1992; Collinson & Hearn, 1996a, 1996b). One general finding of this growing literature is that "doing work" tends to facilitate "doing masculinity," albeit in dramatically different ways. It is precisely in its sensitivity to contextual variation that this work refines frame 1's sweeping claim of the male-bias of professionalism. Acker captures the point succinctly: "Individual men and particular groups of men do not always win . . . but masculinity always seems to symbolize self-respect for men at the bottom and power for men at the top, while confirming for both their gender's superiority" (p. 145). Scholars have documented variations in the enactment of masculine identity across technical, managerial, and working-class communication cultures (Collinson, 1988, 1992; Fine, Weis, Addelston, & Marusza, 1997; Gibson & Papa, 2000; Huspek & Kendall, 1991; Mumby, 1998; Willis, 1977; Wright, 1996).

Several authors have problematized frame 1's notion of "men's style" of leading, exploring the particular breed of masculinity embedded in dominant managerial discourse, as well as its connection to violence, sexuality, and the experience of actual men (Aaltio-Marjosola & Lehtinen, 1998; Hamada, 1996; Hearn, 1994; Kerfoot & Knights, 1993; Linstead, 1997; Roper, 1996). In recognition that manhood is not homogenous, and that all masculinities are not equally privileged, the term *hegemonic masculinity* has come to capture the socially constructed, institutionalized yet shifting form of masculine identity that systematically dominates femininities and alternative masculinities (Cockburn, 1984; Connell, 1987, 1993, 1995; M. Donaldson, 1993).

As an aside, it is worth noting the relative alacrity with which gender and organization scholars acknowledged that men's identities are not monolithic, even as scholars continue to debate essentialist images of the feminine (e.g., Fletcher, 1994). Arguably, the feminist propensity to paint masculinity in monolithic shades (Mumby, 1998), however regrettable, is no match for the cultural narrative in which men are depicted as varied individuals while women remain marked (and marred) by gender.

In sum, frame 2 illuminates how discourse constitutes gender. Rejecting essentialist accounts of identity, this frame recasts gender difference as situated social scripts to which we hold one another accountable. At a macro level, discourse refers to the scripts themselves; at a micro level, it is the infinite process of negotiating them, often adhering to but occasionally improvising and rewriting them. As the micro emphasis makes clear, frame 2 discards frame 1's representational, self-expressive view of communication. And, unlike frame 1, frame 2 encourages analyses that couch gender identities in political contexts. Most authors stress contemporary context, for example, by addressing how institutional norms (e.g., occupational cultures) present particular identity dilemmas and resources for resolving them. Emphasis on the multiplicity of masculinities and femininities also reflects attention to another sort of context: the interplay of gender with race, class, sexuality, age, and so forth (e.g., Ferdman, 1999; Higginbotham & Romero, 1997; Trethewey, 2001). In these ways, frame 2 offers a fuller account of interaction between the micro and macro facets of gender discourse. Some masculinity scholars have rendered vivid historical accounts of the discursive construction of manhood (e.g., Rotundo, 1993). Such work challenges those who study "doing gender" in organizational life to develop a richer historical consciousness.

A pervasive, though sometimes implicit, assumption of frame 2 is that (re)producing difference inevitably amounts to (re)producing inequality. Some critics contend that, by indicting difference itself, this premise obscures how dominant groups appropriate and deploy difference as a hegemonic tool (Collins et al., 1995). Put differently, frame 2 may grant too much constitutive power to discourse, especially its micro dimension, thereby diminishing the role of strategic, institutional, structural, and material factors. What's more, this conceptual move may be easier made from (and perhaps, comforting to) white, middle-class perspectives (Collins et al., 1995). It is important to observe that authors writing within frame 2 shoulder issues of institutional domination and material inequality in varied ways and degrees. For example, while West and colleagues (West & Fenstermaker, 1995; West & Zimmerman, 1987) offer an abstract account of institutional power, other authors provide more nuanced discussion of social and organizational structures that shape the discursive terrain (e.g., Faludi, 1998; Kondo, 1990; Mills, 1995; Mills & Chiaramonte, 1991). For the most part, however, organization emerges as a fairly firm stage—or sometimes, as a changing, unfinished set—that establishes preferences and boundaries for gender identity performance. Rarely does organization appear as an actor, or productive agent, in its own right.

Frame 3: Organizing (En)Genders Discourse

Frame 3 pulls organization out of the shadows, exposing a major figure minimized by frame 1 and 2's focus on individual identity. Building on insights from frame 2, frame 3 understands organization as a precarious social construction, more unfinished set than fixed stage. Not inert, organization—like gender identity—is a constant process of organizing, brought to life, sustained, and transformed by interaction among members (Weick, 1979). Simultaneously, organization guides interaction, predisposing and rewarding members to practice in particular ways (Barley & Tolbert, 1997; Giddens, 1979, 1984; J. R. Taylor, 1993; Taylor & Van Every, 2000). Thus, frame 3 theorizes organization as a gendering agent of sorts—a dynamic entity that actively (en)genders subjects, not just a sturdy backdrop. As this implies, individual identity becomes an organizational process and outcome, for our senses of self are inevitably fashioned in the context of organizational memberships and the multiple, even competing collective identities they entail. In short, "'context' precedes 'ourselves'"

(Mills & Chiaramonte, 1991, p. 385). Through the eyes of frame 3, then, organization is both a discursive product and producer. As in the second frame, discourse has two faces, but the focus shifts from micro to macro in frame 3. Authors in this frame emphasize discourse as a collective narrative of gender and power relations, which crystallizes into organizational form or design. Certainly, they also acknowledge discourse as a micro practice in which organizational forms become manifest and meaningful. But they stress the social construction of gender at the institutional and ideological level, where it carries abstract, symbolic, structural, and normative force that tends to cement systems of "advantage and disadvantage, exploitation and coercion, action and emotion, meaning and identity" (Acker, 1990, p. 146).

The radical idea that institutions, not simply individuals, may be gendered stems from feminist critiques of organization structure. As mentioned earlier, such critique—particularly that of bureaucracy—found wide circulation in activist and academic (not to artificially separate the two) feminist circles. In a classic review of the renowned Hawthorne studies, Acker and Van Houten (1974) were among the first scholars to consider the "sex structuring" of organization. They argued that organizations employ gender as a central control mechanism, generating—not merely reflecting—apparent gender variance in orga-nizational behavior. Likewise, Kanter (1975, 1977) redefined gender difference as a product of structural relations, not individual traits. Concentrated in the invisible and devalued infrastructure, or sprinkled as tokens near the top, women exist at a perpetual disadvantage. Gender enters as a maintenance tool for this imbalanced structure, supplying images of how roles should be enacted and by whom (for example, masculine ethics of authority and rationality). Ferguson (1984) significantly extended this work, depicting bureaucracy as a form of male domination that feminizes managers, workers, and clients by binding them in relations of subordination and dependence. Acker's (1990, 1992) influential work merged and developed these insights. She argued that gender does not stand apart from or simply assist organizational structure; it is not merely a metaphor or support-ing symbol for it. Rather, organizations are fundamentally gendered processes; that is, gender is a constitutive principle of organizing.

Structural critiques laid a foundation for the later, discourse-friendly claim that forms of organization offer abstract, narrative "maps" of ideal relations among gender, power, and work, which serve as resources that guide actual organizing processes. For example, Mills and Chiaramonte (1991) characterized organization as gendered metacommunication—a kind of running commentary on "appropriate" interaction and identity formation. Many authors have elaborated the gendered and, more precisely, "masculinist" character of conventional organization (Britton, 1997). Specifically, scholars have examined how bureaucratic discourse controls and excludes women and femininities with its commitment to hierarchical authority, impersonal relations, ostensibly objective yet already biased rules, and a discourse of rationality that suspects all things "private" (Britton, 1997; Grant & Tancred, 1992; Iannello, 1992; Morgan, 1996; Pierce, 1995; Pringle, 1989). Some authors have extended such criticism to newer organizational forms, like technocracy (e.g., Burris, 1996). Taken together, feminist critiques of organizational design considerably extend frame 1's generic recognition of the male-biased communicative culture of work, as well as frame 2's exposition of diverse ways in which localized identity performances entwine masculinity and work. Thus frame 3 reveals, first, how masculinities are subtly inscribed on specific organizational forms (Maier, 1999) and, second, how those forms tacitly direct member interaction (and therefore institutionalize gender inequality) and translate into tangible consequences for women and men (Acker, 1990).

Accompanying much of this scholarship is a call for alternative organizational forms that challenge oppressive configurations of gendered labor. As indicated in our introduction to this book, feminist organizations enjoy a long and rich history of responding to that call, and abundant research is dedicated to tracking their adventures (Ferree & Martin, 1995). Importantly, feminist communities cannot be reduced to the "feminine styles" or "women's ways" of organizing professed by frame 1. Indeed, for most scholars of feminist organization, "the feminine is not the feminist" (Jaggar, 1991, p. 92), nor can women claim intrinsic ownership of or a natural bent toward alternative organizing. Rather, oppositional forms comprise a political tactic for social change, which may be pursued by committed women and men (P. Y. Martin, 1993). Despite continued debate over what distinguishes "feminist" form (P. Y. Martin, 1990; Mayer, 1995; Riger, 1994), most studies highlight the structure of feminist communities and, specifically, their preference for collectivist, democratic, and other antibureaucratic, participatory designs (e.g., Ahrens, 1980; Baker, 1982; Rodriguez, 1988). However, one major conclusion of this research is the difficulty, if not impossibility, of sustaining such structures in practice (e.g., Mansbridge, 1973; Newman, 1980; Sealander & Smith, 1986). Countless studies concur that a fundamental contradiction between feminist ideology and the demands of organizing amid patriarchal capitalism erodes the best of egalitarian designs (e.g., Kleinman, 1996; Morgen, 1988, 1990; Murray, 1988; Pahl, 1985; Ristock, 1990; Seccombe-Eastland, 1988).

Recently, scholars have begun to reframe that dismal conclusion with a discourse-based model, which treats feminist organizations as "alternative discourse communities" that develop counterdiscourses of gender, power, and organizing amid cultural and material constraints (Fraser, 1989, 1990/91; Mumby, 1996). Mumby and Putnam (1992), for example, theorize a counterdiscourse of "bounded emotionality"—a feminist organizing pattern that reclaims marginalized elements of work experience, including "nurturance, caring, community, supportiveness, and interrelatedness" (p. 474). Notably, the discursive model rejects a fixed union between feminist organization and certain structures; it holds no hope for "pure" practice that neatly upholds revolutionary designs. Rather, it investigates how participants struggle to balance "the paradoxes and tensions that arise from enacting oppositional forms" (Poole, Putnam, & Seibold, 1997, p. 131) and to "maintain a complex set of ideals, obligations, regulations, and desires all within a social world that continuously makes demands upon them" (Maguire & Mohtar, 1994, p. 239). From this viewpoint, the ideology-practice contradiction becomes a situated web of dilemmas experienced by concrete organization members and piloted toward various ends.

A few scholars have begun to investigate the discursive tactics through which feminist organization members manage such tensions, as well as the macro discourses of organizing their tactics imply (Buzzanell et al., 1997; Gottfried & Weiss, 1994; Loseke, 1992; Maguire & Mohtar, 1994; Morgen, 1994). For example, Ashcraft (1998a, 2000, 2001) examines how the conflicted design of one feminist community posed acute tensions related to personalizing professional relationships, leading and following, practicing diversity, and formalizing rules. She argues that several ironic communication practices—such as the articulation of provisional policies in formal documents and the informal use of tentative language and humorous parody to simultaneously exercise and deny decisive influence—enabled members to navigate these tensions, ultimately generating a novel hybrid form that merged feminist and bureaucratic discourses. This project demonstrates how, by examining the dynamic interaction of organizational form and routine member talk, a discursive approach can reveal productive moments in the midst of ostensibly debilitating contradiction.

In sum, frame 3 hones our understanding of the gendered texture of organizational forms. Moving away from the usual focus on a priori structure, this frame increasingly treats organizational forms as discourse communities, guided by loosely shared narratives of gender and power relations that members enact and rewrite in mundane interaction (and that bear on members' individual identity formation). In particular, the discursive model of feminist organizing articulates a dynamic relation between macro and micro layers of discourse. Through this lens, structure is steady and shaky; practice is inventive and derivative; and organizational form is the productive, promiscuous, and fleeting site where structure and practice meet. In short, organization is subject and object of gendered discourse. As in frame 2, discourse performs a constitutive function, but frame 3 is more concerned with the sort of identities and interactions produced by institutionalized narratives about how people and labor should be arranged and carried out. And therein lies a crucial difference. That is, frame 3 accentuates what frame 2 is often said to minimize—the *re*productive function of discourse, with particular respect to power. Discourse creates and transforms, and among its chief "products" are ideologies that normalize particular relations of power. As ideology becomes institutionalized (for example, in organizational forms like bureaucracy or feminist collectivism), mundane interaction moves toward sedimentation and discursive alternatives get obscured and negated as a matter of course. Hence, whereas frame 2 usefully denies structural determinism, frame 3's institutional consciousness checks the reverse temptation to idealize the muscle of micro-level discourse, reminding us that—as critics of frame 2 caution—daily interaction is never free play.

Perhaps the most jarring implication of frame 3 is a practical one: It negates the popular image of sexist individuals discriminating in gender-neutral settings. Accordingly, it dispels the notion that training personnel for discursive sensitivity is sufficient to induce social change; it mandates daunting systemic overhaul. Mills and Chiaramonte (1991) explain that

> analysis of gendered acts cannot divorce the context of such acts from their interpersonal representations. It is theoretically inadequate to address gender discrimination *within* given public (e.g., organizational) or domestic (e.g., family) settings without taking into account the integral role of the setting itself. (p. 386)

In addition, frame 3 clarifies institutional forces at work in the production of gender difference and identity. Unlike studies of doing gender, however, scholarship that adopts frame 3 has scarcely considered the ways in which gendered organizational forms are also raced, classed, and so forth (Acker, 1990; Ashcraft & Allen, 2003; Cheney, 2000b; Nkomo, 1992).[3] And, as a closer look at the research reveals, frame 3 limits its scope to the work*place*. As it underscores the organization of physical sites where labor is performed, it obscures other discursive formations that also organize gender and work.

Frame 4: Discourse (En)Genders Organization

Frame 4 looks beyond discrete organizations—or, actual locations of work and related agencies (for example, labor unions and professional associations)—to parallel discursive arenas that interlace gender and labor. The macro face of discourse also takes precedence in frame 4 but turns away from narrow questions of organizational design. Instead, "a discourse" refers to a broader societal narrative embedded in systems of representation, which offer predictable yet elastic, lucid yet contradictory images of possible subjectivities, relations among them, and attendant disciplinary practices (Bederman, 1995; Connell, 1995; Foucault, 1977; Mouffe, 1995). Gender, organization, and power are mutually constituted in discourse. In other words, gender identities, their liaison with labor, and the resulting implications for being and action are a discursive product or effect. Manifold discourses (of gendered workers, for example) circulate and entwine at once, and those with greater institutional support tend to "look" and "feel" more persuasive than others (Hall, 1985, 1997; Laclau & Mouffe, 1985).

For the fourth frame, the notion of text becomes central in at least two ways. First, just as frame 3 viewed organization as a generative "map," so the fourth view sees larger societal narrative as a textual guide that directs the formation of identities (e.g., choices about self and career) and organizational forms (e.g., proclivity for bureaucracy). Second, frame 4 is concerned with how broad discursive formations find life in particular texts, in the more literal sense of the term. Specific social texts—such as those drawn from film, literature, museum, or scholarship—are conceived as narrative threads or fragments, partial and drifting representations that recite and elude larger discourses (McGee, 1990). Presumably, "real" people consume these representations, drawing upon and/or resisting them in the performances of everyday organizational life. At least to some extent, frame 4 depends on the assumption of this micro-level of discourse for its significance and legitimacy. Even so, micro practice tends to remain implicit in this perspective, as applied to gendered organization thus far.

This description raises the question, if organization as a specific site or context for social interaction is no longer the focus, in what sense does frame 4 examine organizational communication? First, the frame shifts attention from communication *in* organization to communication *about* organization, or how a larger society portrays and debates its institutions and the very notion of work. Second, and akin to other frames, frame 4 takes an interest in organization as the appearance and production of order amid chaos; simply put, it investigates the (dis)organization of gender and work. Rather than stress how this occurs at the site of labor, however, proponents of frame 4 emphasize the organizing properties of public discourse as it shapes available institutions, as well as how we participate in them and come to understand "work" endeavors.

While this perspective has begun to take root in organization studies (e.g., Carlone & Taylor, 1998; Czarniawska-Joerges & Monthoux, 1994; Jacques, 1996; B. C. Taylor, 1993a), its application to the study of gender and organization is comparatively recent. To date, scholars have directed most of their attention toward two broad discursive arenas, or representational sites, beyond the workplace: organization theory and popular culture.

Feminist authors often observe that organization scholarship rests on gendered premises, as the "concepts, explanations, modes of thought, and relevant questions used by organizational researchers are congruent with the everyday ways of thinking of managers" (Acker, 1992, p. 249). Scholars who hail from other frames have challenged these conceptual conditions—a trend that illustrates one of many overlapping interests across the perspectives identified in this chapter. For example, guided by a logic of difference reminiscent of frame 1, Marshall (1989) indicts the male bias of traditional career theory, which silences many women's work experiences and "female values" by normalizing upward, linear movement and cumulative development through a professional life without private interruption. Similarly, though suspicious of difference logic, Ashcraft (1999) contests the gendered base of executive succession theory, which erases the possibility of temporary succession implied by maternity leave. And Buzzanell (1994) proposes turn toward "feminine/feminist values"—such as community, connectedness, and integrative thinking—to confront dominant themes in organization theory and research. Across divergent lenses and motives, feminist critics concur that, at best, the discourse of organization theory unwittingly reflects the gender bias of its site of study.

Seen through frame 4, scholarly discourse becomes more culpable—a willing partner that actively preserves, promotes, and conceals gendered organization. A small but growing body of literature works to deconstruct and rewrite gender relations as constituted in organization theory. Indisputably, Marta Calás and Linda Smircich (1992b) have led this provocative effort, asking, "'Who is watching the watchers?' . . . Shouldn't we also focus our attention on the social consequences of our own practices—organizational research and theorizing?" (pp. 222–223). In a series of unsettling essays, one or both of these authors have taken classic organization and leadership texts to task (e.g., Calás, 1993; Calás & Smircich, 1988, 1992a), surfaced latent seduction therein (Calás & Smircich, 1991), and upended rhetorical devices of time, race, and voice that silence marginalized women in management research (Calás & Smircich, 1991). Typically, they follow textual deconstruction with radical alternatives for reconstructive writing.

Recently, several critics have converged on the discourse of "feminine leadership" (reviewed under frame 1), particularly as it traverses academic and popular management literature (e.g., Fletcher, 1994; Smith & Smits, 1994). For example, Calás & Smircich (1993) rightly note striking resemblances between contemporary fervor for feminine leadership and venerable tales of participative management, such as human resource theory. To weigh the significance and consequence of the gender label at this juncture, they juxtapose the feminine leadership literature against the simultaneous discourse of globalization in management studies. In tandem, these discourses replay a familiar cycle of power relations, wherein women's opportunity follows their instrumentality to masculinist aims. Put crudely, like Rosie-the-Riveter, the feminized manager tends the home fires so that "real" men can take part in the international battle of consequence. Conversely, Fondas (1997) contends that contemporary management texts on reengineering, team-based organization, and excellence embrace feminized management but deny its gendered origins, maintaining the guise of gender-neutral scholarship while standardizing feminization. In a similar analysis, May (1997) takes the hushed feminization of management as a sign that "the culture is deeply ambivalent about elevating the status of the female and femininity; doing so would call into question the entire system of gender relations that underpins most organization and management theory" (pp. 22–23). Jointly, such criticism demonstrates how scholarly practices construct and obscure power relations in complementary and conflicting ways, articulating and affirming dominant discourses yet spawning loopholes from which to challenge them. It also calls attention to another area of focus: representations of gender and work in popular culture.

A second area of study stems from the budding literature at the cusp of organization and cultural studies (Carlone & Taylor, 1998). Gender and organization scholars have begun to take part by attending to masculinities, femininities, and labor as depicted in popular culture. For instance, Shuler (2000) explores portrayals in the media of executive women; Ashcraft and Flores (in press) traces representations of a white-collar masculinity crisis across contemporary films; and Triece (1999) offers a historical analysis of working women as constructed in mail order magazines. Common across these efforts is an attempt to reconstruct larger societal discourses (i.e., social "texts," in the "map" sense) from the analysis of specific discourse fragments (i.e., seemingly discrete social "texts," such as books, films, and television shows). In an especially innovative project, Holmer Nadesan and Trethewey (2000) combine a critique of the self-help literature on women's workplace success with an analysis of in-depth interviews with professional women. After detailing the entrepreneurial discourse embedded in popular literature, they explored ways in which actual women internalize and resist this discourse as they mold their own professional identities. Among works that illustrate frame 4, this study is exceptional for its reach across dimensions and domains of discourse—macro and micro, popular literature and mundane interaction.

Particularly noteworthy in scholarship from frame 4 is the development of a more holistic and, specifically, historical perspective on gender discourse. As noted above, the debate over "feminine leadership" taps into historical context (e.g., Calás & Smircich, 1993), as do some studies of cultural representations of women and work (e.g., Triece, 1999). Masculinity scholars have taken especially significant steps in this regard. For instance, several authors have conducted extensive historical analyses that track widespread transformations in dominant discourses of manhood amid varied political economies (e.g., Connell, 1993, 1995; Kimmel, 1996). Similar to Holmer Nadesan and Trethewey's (2000) approach, a few of these projects evocatively span public and private discourse, examining how popular trends became manifest in personal writings from a given time period (e.g., Bederman, 1995; Rotundo, 1993). Although historical accounts of masculinity typically acknowledge that manly shifts are deeply entwined with changing labor arrangements, rarely is the intersection of masculinity and organization their explicit focus. As noted in the introduction, our analysis in Chapter 6 develops this neglected concentration. Based on Karen's study of U.S. airline pilots, we blend archival and interview data to investigate how airline pilot identity evolved across time and seemingly discrete spheres of organizing activity, such as popular culture, commercial aviation organizations, individual pilot experience, and so on. It is our intent that this analysis extend frame 4 (and the larger literature on gendered organization) by illuminating institutional collusion in the production of discourse and micro representational practices in which such discourse finds resonance, eventually gathering material weight. Through our historically informed analysis, we demonstrate that discourse can generate not only the meanings and subjects of work but also the political and economic standing of a profession.

Although in relative infancy, frame 4 already takes a vital step beyond the bounds of conventional organization scholarship. It calls attention to parallel and intersecting formations of gender and work, and it disrupts taken-for-granted understandings of what counts as organizational communication. It directs attention beyond "internal" organizational communication and "external" public relations messages to the organizing function of texts designed for public or popular consumption, such as news coverage, film, literature, museums, and so forth. In this sense, it has the capacity to reveal intertextuality across institutional messages, exposing discursive affiliations and tensions ordinarily outside the scope of organization analysis. Thus, it invites a more holistic approach to the study of organizing discourse and particularly encourages analyses situated in historical context. Of equal importance, it reminds us that "researchers and theorists are part of the relations of ruling" (Acker, 1992, p. 249). Put differently, frame 4 holds scholars accountable for their participation in gendering organization and, thus, shatters comfortable visions of scholarship as a mirror held up to organizational life (Calás & Smircich, 1992b). Thus far, frame 4 has generated analyses that tend to prioritize the textual over the material, macro over micro dimensions of discourse, and deconstruction over reconstruction. As such, it has minimized potential connections to actual people and the political, economic, and bodied conditions they inhabit; it has largely evaded tangible possibilities for resistance and social change (Cloud, 2001). Finally, frame 4 has focused on the formation of organizational subjectivities in popular culture, despite several other productive angles from which to explore the meeting of organization and culture (Carlone & Taylor, 1998). Recent empirical projects (e.g., Holmer Nadesan, 1996; Holmer Nadesan & Trethewey, 2000; Trethewey, 2001), including the original research we report in Chapter 6, suggest the ongoing and productive development of frame 4 and, specifically, its potential to hone our understanding of linkages among discourse, history, and material conditions.

❖ ACROSS THE FRAMES:
    THREADS OF ALLIANCE AND TENSION

Although the four frames articulated here appropriate constructs differently, they can also be configured in terms of overlap and alliance. As hinted earlier, several authors exhibit approaches that blend ways of seeing and thus blur the boundaries between them. For example, frames 2 and 4 intermingle when scholars examine how concrete identity performances invoke popular discourses of gender and work (e.g., Holmer Nadesan & Trethewey, 2000). Frames 1, 3, and 4 merge when gender difference theorists advocate organizational forms or theory founded on "female values" (e.g., Marshall, 1989, 1993). And studies of doing gender amid specific organizational forms integrate frames 2 and 3 (e.g., Alvesson, 1998; Britton, 1997; Sotirin & Gottfried, 1999).

Such projects suggest fluid borders between frames, as well as possibilities for collaboration and productive tension across frames, albeit within limits. Together, for example, the frames elucidate multiple ways in which discourse evokes and follows material conditions—environmental factors that shape socialization, economic and institutional changes, practices of bodily discipline, sexuality and violence, and so on. And, as they illuminate multiple layers, players, processes, functions, and products of discourse, the frames can assist one another with respective vulnerabilities. Despite the criticisms levied against it, for instance, frame 1 flags entrenched faith in gender dualisms and their persistent effects on the arrangement, practice, and interpretation of work. In this way, it usefully reins in the optimism that may follow frame 2, which, in turn, redresses the deterministic and apolitical tendencies of frame 1. In short, each frame generates moments of "truth" about gendered organization, which also obscure alternating and simultaneous truths. Accordingly, interplay among frames can reveal the complex, even contradictory realities of organizing gender and gendering organization.

Moreover, the literature as a whole represents a sustained effort to understand "difference" as a fundamental and consequential means of human organizing. In some way, all four frames are premised on the question, how is gender "a difference that makes a difference," and what exigencies—discursive, political, historical, material, organizational, and so forth—tend to mediate difference? How the frames answer this question depends largely on their account of relationships among key constructs and, hence, on their epistemological and ontological assumptions. But conceptual discord among frames cannot be reduced to arcane philosophical debate; such disagreements carry real consequences for how we pragmatically approach gendered organization. For example, frame 1 encourages us to train organizational members to appreciate gender communication styles. Conversely, frame 2 invites members to toy with those styles, maneuvering mundane interaction with innovative, disruptive identity performances. Frame 3 casts suspicion on both programs, pushing the need for systemic transformation through radical revisions of organizational form. Frame 4 implies that neither individual nor systemic change is entirely within reach of members, since they—and the kinds of community they can conceive of creating—are already shaped by social and political processes far beyond perceived organizational boundaries. To a significant extent, each frame's pragmatic consequences imply its principal insights and vulnerabilities. Frame 1 may be critiqued for rigid and decontextualized accounts of individual identity, whereas frame 2 becomes suspect for excessive faith in communicative flexibility. Frame 3 is susceptible to charges of overstressing the arrangement of work sites, while frame 4 risks detachment from such sites and the people who bring them to life.

As we begin to consider discord among frames, it becomes clear that the points of disagreement are not easily classified in relation to radical organization studies and, particularly, in terms of the critical modernist and postmodernist tensions outlined in the introduction to this book. Indeed, the frames attest to the diverse ways in which feminist organization scholarship draws upon and resists both strands of thought—an argument we develop by explicating the relationship between feminism and the discourses of modernism (Chapter 2) and postmodernism (Chapter 4). To set the stage for our argument, we conclude this chapter by highlighting how tensions between critical modernism and postmodernism infuse the frames articulated here. Four themes at the heart of this chapter organize the discussion: gender identity, power, discourse, and the micro-macro relation.

First, a concern for gender identity pervades the frames, though in varied and sometimes opposing ways. The first two frames, for example, share a guiding interest in identity and difference yet offer contrary accounts. Frame 1 views gender as a fairly stable identity that yields predictable discursive habits; frame 2 reverses the relationship, casting identity as a fragile effect of situated discourse. The contrast vividly reveals a primary tension across the frames between a conception of identity as (a) a fixed, coherent, relatively unified (albeit learned) set of individual traits and (b) an unstable, fragmented, often conflicted nexus of discursive activity. While frame 1 embraces the former conception, the remaining frames assume some version of the latter. Frame 2 envisions identity as a partial, precarious effect of discourse that is constituted through interaction. Frame 3 foregrounds the role of organization in that interaction, or how larger narratives of collective selves and relations influence the social construction of individual identity. And frame 4 situates identity—organizational and individual—as the effect of various societal-level narratives.

Second, each frame identifies power as central to the organization of gender relations. Frame 1 operates with perhaps the least sophisticated lens; as argued above, it pays scant notice to the serious political consequences of its own logic of difference. For this frame, the problem is not difference per se but, rather, hierarchical perceptions of difference that privilege one group at the expense of others. In many respects, frame 1 accepts not only a critical modernist conception of power as domination but also a liberal model of power, where access to once-forbidden realms and roles for women signals a shift in the institutional balance, from oppression to equality. Of the frames, frame 3 exhibits the most evident struggle between critical modernist and postmodernist accounts of power. Traditionally, for example, frame 3 entails a quest for organizational forms that challenge the oppressive relations intrinsic to bureaucracy with feminist alternatives free from coercion. From this view, emancipatory organization is that which promotes gender equality by erasing the destructive influence of power. In contrast, the more recent, discourse-based models of feminist organization reviewed above recognize that power is endemic to all organizational forms and, further, that the power relations any form will produce can only be realized in its situated applications. Similarly aligned with postmodern sensibilities, frames 2 and 4 hinge on a dynamic conception of power as a constitutive, productive element of gender and organizational discourse. Frame 2 emphasizes the organization of gender in mundane micro practice, where "doing gender" is the inherently political process of crafting identity amid situational resources and constraints. Frame 4 draws attention to the organization of gendered labor at the macro, societal level, where "grand narratives" of gender and work produce disciplined subjectivities and practices. In sum, frames 2 and 4—and more recent manifestations of frame 3— conceptualize power as an inevitable part of organizing individual and collective gender identities.

Third, the frames center discourse but define it in radically different ways. Across feminist organization studies, discourse carries at least four meanings: engrained personal communication habits, mundane interaction process, organizational form, and societal narrative. These definitions vary in the extent to which they treat communication as a dynamic, generative process. For the most part, frame 1 adopts a representational model of communication, wherein modes of discourse correspond to and reflect internal gender dispositions. The other three frames recognize communication as an ongoing process that constitutes identity and social reality. In frame 2, discourse as everyday communication continually (re)fashions individual identity. In frame 3, discourse as narrative of collective identity generates institutions that shape daily interaction, which, in turn, reifies and/or undermines those institutions. Discourse also serves constitutive functions in frame 4, which positions gendered selves and organizational forms as part of a larger, historically contingent, and ever-unfolding discursive field. Cultural narratives, or epistemological frames, become the primary focus, for they articulate the possibilities and preferences social actors (both academic and lay) invoke as they make sense of the connection between gender and organization.

As suggested by diverse definitions of discourse across the frames, a fourth and final axis around which the frames differ entails the extent to which they stress micro (i.e., situated, fluid communication practices) and macro (i.e., relatively stable institutional and social structures) dimensions of social life, as well as the relationship between them. Unearthing the frames' varied conceptions of organization provides one useful way to see the variation. Frames 1 and 2 treat organizations as a vital setting for the display of gender difference, but frame 1 accents the manifestation of difference and frame 2 stresses its production. In other words, the former presumes gendered selves that spill into organizational life, while the latter takes organization as a crucial site in which gendered selves are assembled. It is here that institutional influences on identity formation begin to gain visibility. Frame 3 elaborates this point, revealing organization as productive agent, not passive or neutral context. Organizations are seen as discourse communities in that their very design supplies subtly gendered scripts for identity formation and mundane interaction. Thus institutional discourse calls difference into being and generates possibilities for responding to it. Frame 4 once again displaces organizations from the spotlight, diminishing their agentic potential by rendering them at the mercy of other social processes.

Another way to understand the micro-macro tensions at stake involves putting the matter in terms of the "agency-structure" relationship, which lies at the heart of myriad scholarly attempts to capture the link between the knowledgeable behavior of social actors and the constraints institutional forces place on that behavior. For the most part, scholars have approached this relationship dualistically, privileging individual action to the neglect of social structure or bracketing agency to develop macro models of institutional behavior (for exceptions see, e.g., Giddens, 1979; Knights, 1990, 1997; Willmott, 1994). In the gender and organization literature, frame 1 illustrates a dualistic lens; namely, it investigates gender difference at the meeting of individual variance and interpersonal relations, while the larger social and institutional contexts that facilitate difference are held in abeyance or ignored altogether. Frame 2 attempts to overcome the dualism with a twofold conception of discourse as both dynamic daily interaction and the steady social scripts that guide such interaction. Early renditions of frame 3 simply reversed the dualism by stressing the gendered character of organizational structure and minimizing how structure plays out in practice. Increasingly, however, proponents of frame 3 remind us that organizational form directs, but by no means determines, members' mundane discursive practices (e.g., Ashcraft, 2000, 2001). Thus, frames two and three seek to balance interactional and institutional sides of discourse, although they reverse the relative emphasis. At the same time, and with notable exceptions (e.g., Kondo, 1990), there is often little or underdeveloped effort within these frames to unpack the dialectic between micro- and macro-level discursive processes.

Frame 4 generally excludes consideration of everyday identity construction, attending instead to societal discourses and texts—popular and academic—that (en)gender organization. In this sense, the frame broadens the scope of gendered organization studies, even as it tends to lose touch with actual bodies and organizations.

Although there are certainly other fissures across the frames, those identified here supply the core set of issues that occupy the next three chapters. To be sure, these issues are by no means exclusive to gender and organization studies, but our objective in this chapter has been to characterize the unique shape those struggles assume for feminist organization scholars. We have suggested that while the gender and organization literature reflects multiple efforts to manage metatheoretical conflicts, particularly in the conduct of empirical research, these tactics remain tacit and thus underdeveloped. This is the purpose to which we address the next several chapters: to call key metatheoretical tensions into the open and to articulate a model that usefully maneuvers them.

❖ CONCLUSION

Clearly, we view feminist organization scholarship as an interdisciplinary body of theory, research, and praxis that has its own agenda and momentum, which have uniquely contributed to our understanding of the relationships among gender, identity, power, organization, and discourse. Across this literature, discourse carries at least four meanings, which vary in their attention to micro and macro dimensions: (a) engrained personal communication habits, (b) mundane interaction process, (c) organizational form, and (d) societal narrative. The final three meanings best reflect the discursive turn in gender and organization scholarship, for, respectively, they address the constitutive power of micro (i.e., interactional), intermediate (i.e., institutional), and macro (i.e. societal) levels of discourse. Among other implications, the variable definitions and levels subsumed in *discourse* suggest a need to clarify applications of the term and its relation to *communication*—an issue to which we return as we develop our model in Chapter 5.

For now, we focus on critical problematics that characterize and exceed feminist organization studies: identity, power, discourse, and micro-macro relations. In the introduction to this book, we outlined key ways in which radical organization scholars also struggle with these metatheoretical matters. Indeed, the problematics sketched here represent centrally contested concepts that distinguish the larger movements of modernism and postmodernism. In the next three chapters, then, we explore in greater depth alliances and tensions among modernism, postmodernism, feminism, and organization studies. Our intent is to situate our argument and ensuing communicology model within the context of the major metatheoretical debates that have informed critical and feminist organization studies over the past few decades. As should be clear, we see these debates not merely as intellectual squabbles but as differences that are of immense practical and political consequence.

2

Feminism and the Discourses of Modernism

Articulating an Organizational Voice

❖ ❖ ❖

Thus far, we have argued that the feminist organization literature is not simply derivative of critical organization studies, nor does it merely address "sins of omission" committed by radical analyses. Rather, feminist organization scholarship engages directly with the critical tradition to provide unique and innovative possibilities for understanding organization as fundamentally gendered. In Chapter 1, we explicated four common frames through which feminist scholars tend to see relationships among discourse, identity, power, gender, and organization. In Chapters 2 through 4, we expand the scope of our argument by examining the relationship between feminism and organization studies from a broader, metatheoretical view. Given our earlier depiction of feminism as ambivalent toward theory and committed to praxis, one might well question this shift to a higher level of abstraction. Our answer is twofold.

First, our metatheoretical move is a temporary one, and we develop its implications for research and practice in Chapters 5 through 7. Second, we believe that such a shift is necessary because organization scholarship has become more self-reflexive in the last 20 years regarding its disciplinary assumptions (e.g., Burrell & Morgan, 1979; Deetz, 1994, 1996). Most of the debates that have emerged out of this self-reflexivity are primarily concerned with questions of epistemology and validity, and they have generally involved some version of the modernism-postmodernism opposition (e.g., Alvesson, 1995; L. Donaldson, 1995; Pfeffer, 1993; Van Maanen, 1995b).

And yet, feminist voices have remained mostly absent from this discussion. Lest we be misread to say that feminists have been silent with regard to the metatheoretical, let us clarify our point: To be sure, feminist scholars have participated in extensive metatheoretical debate. Many have directly conceptualized relationships among feminism, modernism, and postmodernism; their contributions infuse our discussion in this and the next two chapters. As we demonstrated in Chapter 1, however, metatheoretical matters remain largely implicit in feminist *organization* studies. Where feminist organization scholars have explicitly addressed metatheoretical concerns, their approach is usually deconstructive rather than reconstructive (e.g., Calás, 1993; Calás & Smircich, 1991; J. Martin, 2000), or else presents feminism as an *alternative* to mainstream organization studies (e.g., Calás & Smircich, 1992b, 1996). A key limitation of the literature, then, is its relative inability to influence questions asked by the field of organization studies from other than an "outsider within" perspective. Accordingly, the goal of the next three chapters is to suggest ways in which feminism can help to shape and shed light on disciplinary debates by articulating feminist metatheoretical contributions *in the specific context of organization theory and research.* Without such conceptual work, we would be hard-pressed to substantiate the claim that feminism is central to radical organization studies because it offers a guide through pressing contemporary tensions.

In this chapter, we focus on the relationship between feminism and modernism. Rather than present them as inimical to each other, we suggest that feminism and the various iterations of modernism function dialectically, presenting numerous possibilities for conceptualizing the relationship between gender and organization. This chapter is therefore an effort to articulate options for understanding gendered organization from within the discourse of modernism itself. In the first part of the chapter, we briefly outline what has become a fairly standard account of the relationship between feminism and the modernist project.

The remainder of the chapter develops a distinctively organizational voice on the matter, suggesting specific ways in which feminist organization theory has engaged with the multiple discourses of modernism. Given Chapter 1's attention to shifting meanings of "discourse," we should clarify that, in this chapter, we invoke the term in a Foucauldian sense, wherein it represents "systems of possibility" that enable and constrain what counts as "truth," as well as how subjects and objects of knowledge come into being (Foucault, 1980b).

❖ FEMINISM AND THE MODERNIST PROJECT: RECAPPING THE USUAL INTERPRETATION

There is no single, concise definition of or clear historical starting point for modernism. Here, we conceive of it as the period (beginning in the late 17th century) during which a confluence of developments across domains—intellectual, economic, technological, and spiritual—led to the emergence of a new conception of knowledge, progress, and human identity. Arguably, the very ideas of "the individual" and "progress" were modernist inventions (Foucault, 1973), fomenting the notion that the rational, systematic search for Truth leads to the betterment of the human condition. The source of such progress is neither God nor nature but the human, rational mind, best applied and developed through the deployment of systematic scientific procedures. Thus, ostensibly disparate developments—such as the beginnings of the industrial revolution in Britain in the late 1700s, the emergence of bureaucracies in Europe in the mid 19th century, and the creation of a "positive sociology" of human society by Auguste Comte in the mid 1800s—all have a common foundation in principles of reason, order, predictability, and progress toward an ideal human condition.

It is perhaps appropriate to characterize feminism as an "outsider within" the modernist project (Hill Collins, 1991). On the one hand, many feminist perspectives critique modernism as irredeemably patriarchal in its conception of knowledge, rationality, and progress, requiring the creation of alternative forms of knowledge and being (K. Ferguson, 1984; Ferree & Martin, 1995). In this view, modernism represents the systematic "othering" of women. Since the 19th century conception and treatment of the "hysterical woman" (Foucault, 1980a), women have literally embodied for modernism forms of excess that escape prediction and control; their bodies leak, they become emotional, and their minds—subordinated to their bodies—do not think systematically. In many respects, then, modernism is rooted in a set of binary oppositions such as mind-body, culture-nature, reason-emotion (Hekman, 1990), in which the first (masculine) element is privileged over the (feminine) second.

However, much feminist thought is inspired by and grounded in the ideals of the Enlightenment. For example, the "grand narrative" of feminism depicts the rational, systematic engagement with, and progressive breaking down of, patriarchal obstacles to women's advancement—economic, political, cultural, and linguistic. In this sense, feminism has frequently worked within modernism and appropriated its forms of knowledge and logic in order to transform it. Thus the history of feminism can be read as a struggle to make the emancipatory principles of the Enlightenment project more inclusive. In a number of ways, then, feminism simultaneously operates from within and critiques modernist thought.

A number of subplots have emerged within the larger narrative of feminism, with each situating itself differently in relationship to the modernist project (Tong, 1989). Liberal feminism, for example, perhaps most readily accepts the tenets of Enlightenment thought and the liberal political philosophy of Locke, Mill, and others. As such, it largely assumes a "sameness" model, arguing that women and men have similar abilities and potential for rational development, but that patriarchal laws and structures have limited women's access to social, political, and economic opportunities. In this sense, liberal feminism takes as relatively unproblematic the Enlightenment model of individuality and rationality, and it focuses on the need to create laws that will provide equal opportunities for individual women. From a liberal feminist view, organizations are not intrinsically gendered but, rather, embody differential access to power for men and women.

Other feminist perspectives present greater challenges to modernism while simultaneously sharing its ideals. Radical feminism, for example, rejects the accommodationist, "sameness" model of liberal feminism, instead articulating resistance to patriarchy from a "difference" perspective. Indeed, radical feminists argue that there is an essential biological difference between women and men, concluding that the only way for women to escape patriarchy is through the establishment of separate cultural, political, and even linguistic systems. However, even as radical feminists equate Enlightenment thought with patriarchy, they hold on to many of its epistemological, rational tenets. For example, writers such as Mary Daly (1978) assume a biological determinist position, in which the difference between men and women is conceived as "clear, absolute, and initially anatomical" (Morris, 1988, p. 47). Further, despite the fact that much of her writing deconstructs patriarchal linguistic systems (suggesting a social constructionist bent to her work), Daly's conception of meaning is heavily rooted in a representational model in which language is seen as the expression of an inner, coherent self. Finally, Daly assumes an objectivist epistemology that dichotomizes women's experience as articulating an authentic, foundational truth (particularly through gynocentric language), while patriarchy is false and distorts genuine experience.

Marxist feminism represents a third view that simultaneously draws much of its impetus from modernism and challenges some of its precepts (e.g., Barrett, 1988; Hartmann, 1979). Scholars adopting this perspective respond to the gender-blind character of classical Marxism and variously explore the relationship between capitalism and patriarchy. In particular, Marxist feminists decry classical Marxism for its "failure to connect the nearly universal division of labor in both public and private spheres with women's devalued status" (Steeves, 1987, p. 107). For example, Barrett (1988) shows how the nuclear family is a primary site of capitalist relations of domination through reinforcement of domestic roles and reproduction of capital-labor relations. Further, a number of Marxist feminists appropriate the insights of Marxist cultural studies to examine the processes through which women's identities are ideologically constructed in capitalist society. Again, some of this work is aimed at addressing the gender blindness of early cultural studies works—see, for example, McRobbie's (1981) rejoinder to Willis's (1977) analysis of a working class male adolescent subculture.

Finally, standpoint feminism has emerged as a more recent perspective that integrates both modern and postmodern approaches to gender issues (Harding, 1997; Hartsock, 1998; Hill Collins, 1991). Born of the recognition that many feminist approaches have tended to inappropriately treat women as a monolithic group, standpoint feminism acknowledges multiple women's voices and experiences while also recognizing women's shared experience of patriarchal oppression. Indeed, bell hooks's poignantly titled *Ain't I a Woman* (1981) simultaneously draws attention to the historical marginalization of African American women's experience of white patriarchy and demands the inclusion of African American women within the feminist movement *as women.* For example, hooks's writings have critiqued both liberal and Marxist feminism for their totalizing accounts of the role of the family in women's oppression (hooks, 1981, 1984, 1992). In contrast to the liberal feminist reading of the home as the source of women's lack of fulfillment, or the Marxist feminist analysis of the family as the nexus for the reproduction of capitalist relations of domination, hooks highlights the ways that, for black women, the home has historically been the source of a strong sense of identity in the face of a hostile world.

Together, these subplots bring home the point that the relationship of feminism to modernism is both critical and sympathetic and thus eludes easy characterization. For our purposes, one of the problems with this prevailing configuration of feminist perspectives (e.g., Tong, 1989) is that it has fairly limited application to the field of organization studies. We suggest that feminist metatheoretical discussion has had relatively little impact upon disciplinary debates partly because it is rarely framed in terms specific to organization studies. The remainder of the chapter works to redress this situation.

❖ FEMINISM AND THE DISCOURSES OF MODERNISM: DEVELOPING AN ORGANIZATIONAL VOICE

We begin by situating the feminism-modernism relationship in terms of the phenomenon of bureaucracy. In many respects, bureaucracy is the modernist institution par excellence. A prevailing form of organization, it serves as a vehicle for the modernist principles of rationality, objectivity, and instrumentalism (Weber, 1978). Perrow (1986) argues that the advent of bureaucracy signals an important shift from the traditional organizational form and its patrimonial structure toward a meritocracy premised on expertise and professionalism. As such, bureaucracy is the practical realization of modernist efforts to render society orderly, rational(ized), and predictable through systematic procedures. Concurrently, the bureaucratic form is evidence and enforcer of the patriarchal texture of modernism, in that it institutionalizes what we called earlier the "othering" of women and femininities. Numerous scholars have exposed the gendered functions of bureaucracy, for example, as it cultivates suspicion of things private and subjective as "chaotic" forces to be ruled out. Furthermore, the bureaucratic career historically emerged as intrinsically male (K. Ferguson, 1984; Pringle, 1989; Savage & Witz, 1992). As Witz and Savage (1992) explain, "The modern organization came into being depending on cheap female labour, and in turn helped define women as subordinate workers to men within emergent white collar labour markets" (p. 10).

From most feminist organizational perspectives, bureaucracy is a principal site of (and for some, a pivotal player in) gendered power struggle. As we explain below, the varied instantiations of contemporary feminism can be framed in terms of the ways in which they conceptualize the relationship among gender, bureaucracy, and power (Savage & Witz, 1992). Just as Weber's (1978) modernist sensibilities both valorized and problematized bureaucracy and its relationship to the human condition, so feminist perspectives have assessed the extent to which bureaucratic institutions embody patriarchal norms and structures and hence are inherently gendered. Feminist positions therefore are by no means straightforward; they vary along a continuum that, at one extreme, sees bureaucracy itself as a relatively gender-neutral context (e.g., Kanter, 1977) and, at the other, conceives of bureaucracy as intrinsically patriarchal in its structuring of gender and power relations (e.g., K. Ferguson, 1984; Pringle, 1989).

Below, we examine three modernist discourses, assessing each in terms of its impact on and appropriation by feminist organization studies: (a) post-positivism[4]—a discourse of explanation; (b) interpretivism—a discourse of understanding; and (c) critical theory—a discourse of suspicion. Each discourse, we suggest, adopts an increasingly transgressive stance toward what Benhabib (1992) calls the episteme of representation. In other words, each progressively problematizes any notion of a simple, representational connection between language and the world. As we shall see, questioning this relationship has important implications for the interconnections among communication, power, identity, and organizing.

Feminism and Post-Positivism: A Discourse of Explanation

There has been a widespread tendency among radical organization scholars to rather simplistically equate modernism and positivism. This seems particularly true in instances where the case is being made for a social constructionist approach to organization theory and research. Indeed, in the wake of the discursive turn it has been relatively easy (although not necessarily productive) for social constructionists of various persuasions to tar positivism and contemporary social science with the same brush in the rush to discredit the latter. However, contemporary social science has relatively little in common with either the 19th century classical positivism of Auguste Comte (1830–1842/ 1970) or the early 20th century logical positivism of the Vienna Circle (e.g., Ayer, 1960). While there are perhaps some social scientists in organization studies and other fields who believe in the radical separation of knower and known, subject and object, the possibility of a completely value-free epistemological stance, and the development of a neutral observation language, they are going the way of the dinosaurs—as far as we can tell, only Donaldson (1985, 1994) is a self-described positivist who inveighs against the challenge of social constructionism. For the most part, however, "positivism" has been used as an epithet to dismiss any form of social science research that does not adopt an avowedly social constructionist perspective. Of course, there is plenty to critique about contemporary social science research, but our point here is to provide a more thoughtful articulation of the relationship among contemporary social science, the so-called episteme of representation identified earlier, and gender and feminist organization studies.

We would argue that post-positivist social science discourse actually diverges from the representational model of knowledge and truth, and thus provides at least a partial or modified challenge to the realism and objectivism of early efforts to build the human sciences on a natural science model. Most significantly, post-positivist discourse questions— although does not completely overcome—the subject-object dualism foundational to Cartesian thought. How is this challenge manifest?

Most social scientists make commitments to an ontological position that resides somewhere between the social constructionism of many interpretivists and the hard realism of the early positivists (Miller, 2000, p. 58). This perspective assumes the existence of a real, material world that exists beyond the beliefs and interpretations of social actors, but it argues that this world is never fully accessible to us. Thus, social actors construct many different accounts of this obdurate reality—accounts to which social scientists can gain access through systematic analysis. Furthermore, many post-positivists would argue that their ontological stance is consistent with social constructionism in two other ways. First, people construct accounts of the world in relatively stable and predictable ways; hence, patterns of human sense-making can be established through careful analysis. Second, social actors frequently treat these humanly created patterns of behavior (e.g., organizations) as objective and reified, and as having a material existence independent from human behavior.

Moreover, as Miller (2000) has indicated, most social scientists have rejected the possibility of value-free knowledge claims in which there is a complete bifurcation of subject and object, knower and known. Instead, there is recognition among social scientists that they exist as part of a community of scholars that operates according to an intersubjective system of rules that guides the knowledge construction process. These rules constitute standards about what counts as an adequate knowledge claim, but they are not necessarily viewed as universal and immutable. As Phillips (1990) states,

> The ideal that is embraced seems to be this: Seekers after enlightenment in any field do the best that they can; they honestly seek evidence, they critically scrutinize it, they are (relatively) open to alternative viewpoints, they take criticism (fairly) seriously and try to profit from it, they play their hunches, they stick to their guns, but they also have a sense of when it is time to quit. (as cited in Miller, 2000, p. 61)

This position seems to differ quite radically from the various critiques of "social scientism" that appear in post-discursive turn writings in organization studies.

Finally, many contemporary social scientists argue that they are operating with a much more sophisticated conception of communication and discourse than their mid-20th century counterparts. Rather than adopting a simple transmission-based, conduit model of communication (Axley, 1984), a number of social scientists in organization studies would claim that their goal is the analysis of communication as a complex process that fundamentally shapes social actors' interpretations of the world. For example, much of the recent research in network analysis has shifted from a transmission model of communication, in which organizational networks are examined as relatively fixed conduits for the flow of information, to a much more explicit social constructionist position, in which networks are studied as complex, processual, humanly constructed communicative phenomena (Monge & Contractor, 2001). Many of these studies employ a mixture of quantitative and qualitative methods.

Much of the literature on gender and organizations both embodies and challenges this post-positivist orientation. On the one hand, much of this research assumes a variable-analytic approach that attempts to establish the existence of stable, enduring, and generalizable differences in the communication styles of men and women. As we saw in the first frame discussed in Chapter 1, there is widespread recognition that while gender differences are socially constructed, it is nevertheless possible to engage in rigorous social science research that provides empirical support for such differences. On the other hand, this body of research has challenged the discourse of post-positivism by introducing issues of voice into the equation, albeit in a relatively elementary manner. While the basic model of reason underlying modernism is that of the rational, independent, autonomous subject, a good deal of the gender and organizations literature has argued that such a model unnecessarily and arbitrarily privileges masculine ways of knowing and acting. In this sense, gender studies have—in a rather proto-feminist fashion—attempted to address questions of value, examining how certain forms of thinking and doing are privileged, while others are marginalized and devalued.

Similarly, the extensive literature on gender and leadership discussed in frame 1 adopts a post-positivist epistemological stance and challenges modernist discourse around the issue of voice. Much research has attempted to empirically establish whether women managers and executives adopt leadership and communication styles that differ radically from their male counterparts. At the same time, it is argued that such "women's ways" of communicating provide a fundamentally different set of value premises rooted in interconnectedness, participation, power sharing, and so forth. However, as we have also suggested, such research tends to operate according to a problematic (and deeply modernist) logic of difference in which men and women are assigned gender roles according to a rather simplistic binary model. From our perspective, such a model vastly oversimplifies the relationship between communication and identity, suggesting that a particular style is consistent with a certain gendered subjectivity. Furthermore, there is little effort in this research to problematize the bureaucratic structures within which such gendered forms of behavior unfold.

Kanter's (1977) classic study is an excellent example of feminist research that problematizes gender within the bureaucratic form, while leaving the form itself largely uninterrogated. Her major concern is the relative powerlessness of women in bureaucratic organizations. However, she explains this relative powerlessness not in terms of the intrinsically gendered character of bureaucracy but, rather, in terms of men's monopoly over bureaucratic power. Given the bureaucratic requirement of ordered, predictable behavior and decision-making,

Kanter argues that male homosociability serves as a crucial mechanism that reproduces male managers in their own image and thus facilitates ease of communication and rational decision-making. Once women enter bureaucracies in enough numbers and hence gain organizational power, such gender differences will become relatively insignificant. Thus Kanter views gender discrimination as an irrational element within the general rationality of bureaucratic life (Witz & Savage, 1992, p. 17).

Therefore, although Kanter conceives of gender as socially constructed through everyday organizational practices, her study does not really challenge the "episteme of representation" as it applies to the model of rationality underpinning the bureaucratic organizational form. Witz and Savage (1992) point out that Kanter appropriates the Weberian model of bureaucracy unproblematically, reading Weber in a degendered manner and generally taking for granted the basic principles of Weber's model. They argue that "Kanter may be seen as operating within a Weberian discourse of bureaucratic rationality, but without unpacking its gendered subtext" (Witz & Savage, 1992, p. 17). In other words, Kanter treats gender and bureaucracy as separate phenomena, rather than unpacking the ways in which they are interwoven historically, culturally, and economically.

Furthermore, the binary model that operates within much of "postpositivist feminism" risks essentializing both men and women, thus largely preserving extant relations of institutional power. It is one thing to argue for the valorization of so-called women's ways of communicating and organizing; it is quite another thing to change the ways in which institutional logics and systems of power make sense of such difference. Thus, if we take seriously the idea that power revolves around the ways in which systems of "difference that make a difference" are constructed, deployed, and made sense of, then the binary logic of the "gender difference" literature reifies such difference in a way that assigns men and women to largely inescapable roles. Difference, as such, becomes a potential means of organizational control in which men and women are assigned gender-appropriate organizational identities.

A further problem with much of this research is its preservation of the dichotomy of agency and structure that has dogged much of the post-positivist literature. With a focus on differences among individuals, organizations are conceived as static, stable, and mostly apolitical structures within which difference unfolds. Even Tannen's (1994) cultural analysis of the intersection of gender, power, and organization does little to suggest the ways in which organizations shape and control the gendered cultural identities that men and women bring to the workplace. As we showed in frames 2 and 3 in Chapter 1, and as we will see later in this chapter and the next, recent feminist organizational research has attempted to transcend this dichotomy through examination of the dialectics of resistance and control, agency and structure, hence placing the process of "doing gender" in a larger political context.

The discourse of explanation, then, represents a modified challenge to the representational paradigm that stands as the unrealizable ideal of 19th century modernism. However, its efforts to transcend the subject-object dichotomy of Cartesian thought are limited in a couple of respects. First, while it recognizes the active role of social actors in engaging the world through their interpretive abilities, it still appears to insist on dichotomizing beliefs about the world and the objectivity of the world itself; while ideas may be socially constructed, there is a true world to be discovered that lies beneath or behind those ideas. Ultimately, then, "post-positivism continues to operate under the same bias toward submitting theories and contested claims to the court of 'reality'" (Poole & Lynch, 2000, p. 214). Such a position reifies the distinction between the social and the material in a way that obscures the extent to which they exist in a reciprocal, dialectical relationship.

Second, while post-positivists claim to have rejected the *philosophy* that underlies positivism, there are still rhetorical and methodological elements of that philosophy that remain in contemporary social science. For example, the rhetoric of social science research preserves the separation of researcher and researched—published articles are written from a "God's eye," carefully detached perspective with the word *I* nowhere in sight. While social scientists may claim that they reject the possibility of value-free knowledge claims, they at least preserve that possibility in the rhetoric of their published research.

Finally, there is a relative disjuncture between the methods of social science and efforts to develop more complex, process-oriented views of the social world. For example, while network research in its current iteration is particularly interested in "semantic networks" (i.e., what people *perceive* as meaningful organizational connections), its "process" focus still relies heavily on methods that atomize the flow communicative practices in a reductionist manner. Such research may capture a "snapshot" of collective human behavior, but it has a much harder time evoking its dynamism.

Post-positivism thus modifies, but does not overcome, the subject-object dualism that lies at the heart of Cartesian modernism. Similarly, feminist and gendered approaches to organization studies both challenge and are implicated in the limitations of post-positivist modernism. While they challenge the tendency of post-positivist modernism to overlook gender as a significant "difference that makes a difference," they nevertheless fail to adequately challenge the forms of representation—in the sense of both voice and knowledge—that post-positivism assumes. In the next section, however, we address a modernist discourse that more directly confronts the representational assumptions that are embodied in the modernist subject-object dualism.

Feminism and Interpretivism: A Discourse of Understanding

Interpretive modernism—the discourse of understanding—provides an important alternative to positivism, challenging the latter's dichotomizing of subject and object. In this way, it offers some interesting possibilities for feminist studies, given its focus on dialogue and dialectics. As we will see, however, there are significant ways in which feminism and interpretivism are largely irreconcilable. This particular form of modernism has proliferated in the field of communication over the last 20 years or so, although the initial communication scholarship can be traced to the early 1970s to explorations of the relationships among hermeneutics, phenomenology, and communication studies (Deetz, 1973a, 1973b, 1978; Hawes, 1977). In organization studies, the principal legacy of interpretivism is the emergence of "organizational culture" as a viable and widely adopted approach to the study of organizing (Silverman, 1970; Smircich, 1983). From this perspective, communication is seen as constitutive of organizations. The study of stories, metaphors, rituals, and so forth is a way to explore the ontology of organizing as a collective communicative act (O'Connor, 1997; Pacanowsky & O'Donnell-Trujillo, 1982; Putnam, 1983; Putnam & Pacanowsky, 1983; Smith & Eisenberg, 1987; Trujillo, 1992; Trujillo & Dionisopoulos, 1987).

Common to all of the studies cited above is a conception of communication as a foundational ontology for human existence. Each study is predicated on the notion that community and identity are linguistically constructed. For example, according to Trujillo and Dionisopoulos (1987), engaging in "cop talk" through the telling of war stories is not the expression of an already fully formed, a priori identity (as a post-positivist conception of communication might claim); rather, it involves creating that identity in an ongoing and interactive manner.

Thus communication produces cop identity rather than merely expressing it. Similarly, Smith and Eisenberg's (1987) analysis of dominant root metaphors among employees at Disneyland shows that metaphors such as "Disney as Family" do not function as a way to describe an already fully formed organizational experience but, rather, shape the very possibility of experiencing life as a Disneyland employee. Their analysis of an industrial dispute between Disney management and employees shows how the conflict reflects different interpretations and thus experiences of Disney as a "corporate family."

The interpretive tradition coheres with several feminist concerns. First, it actively resists what post-positivism risks: the reification of gender as a static, binary variable available for measurement. Instead, the discourse of interpretivism renders gender as activity and accomplishment, process and product—a fluid meaning system perpetuated and contested through situated interaction (Gherardi, 1994; West & Fenstermaker, 1995; West & Zimmerman, 1987). In addition, interpretivist claims to the contextual and negotiated character of social reality complement feminist interest in gendered meaning as shaped by concrete social and organizational settings (Foss & Rogers, 1994; Reinharz, 1992) and question androcentric and feminist analyses that normalize and/or universalize gendered power relations (Alvesson & Billing, 1992; Rosaldo, 1987). Such claims also imply the potential for variation in and modification of gender relations, providing an epistemological and ontological grounding for the feminist quest for social change (Campbell, 1988; Dervin, 1987; Steeves, 1988; J. T. Wood, 1995).

Methodologically, the interpretive tradition facilitates feminist aims to understand women in their own terms by minimizing application of deductive categories, endorsing immersion in mundane settings, and preserving member voices through empathic narrative and collaborative authorship strategies (Reinharz, 1992; Taylor & Trujillo, 2001). Unlike post-positivism, the implementation, rhetoric, and semantics of interpretivist methods tend to explicitly acknowledge the researcher's role in constructing reality. Thus interpretivism supports feminist interest in how the links between knower and known influence the conduct of research and creation of knowledge (Calás & Smircich, 1992a; Carter & Spitzack, 1989); it also sits well with feminist claims to reduce or reject the researcher's capacity for objectivity, or detached "expert" knowing (Kauffman, 1991). In these ways, the discourse of interpretivism enables (but does not necessarily produce) more egalitarian relations between researcher and researched—a goal of many feminist scholars (e.g., Fine, 1988; Hawkins, 1989; Mies, 1983, 1991; Spitzack & Carter, 1988). Despite these meeting points, the philosophical fit of feminism and interpretivism is not complete; from a feminist viewpoint, interpretivists tend to don blinders that engender ideological and political denial.

The discourse of interpretivism has been widely criticized for its lack of attention to the political context in which the social construction process occurs. The research on organizational culture in the 1980s, for example, was largely devoid of any examination of the interests and power structures that lay behind the emergence of certain cultures (exceptions include Kunda, 1992; Rosen, 1985, 1988; Young, 1989). Such research was mostly content to treat culture as a relatively neutral system of meaning that emerged from the sense-making practices of its members (Bantz, 1993; Schein, 1992). While this work provided important insight into the links among discourse and organization, it failed to view culture as anything other than an integrative mechanism for the advancement of organizational cohesion (J. Martin, 1992). Furthermore, because of its apparent political neutrality, such interpretive work fell prey to co-optation by more functionalist, instrumental approaches to culture (e.g., Peters & Waterman, 1982). This led some organizational scholars to argue that the cultural approach was "dominant but dead" (Smircich & Calás, 1987).

A few feminist organization scholars have shown how the apparently gender-neutral character of organizational cultures is in fact premised on gendered constructions of meaning and organizational reality. Consistent with increased questioning of the episteme of representation, these scholars both examine gender as socially constructed and problematize the bureaucratic and organizational structures that shape these gendered constructions. Unlike Kanter's work discussed earlier, this research investigates how bureaucracies are enacted through gendered interpretive processes (e.g., Adkins, 1992; Ramsay & Parker, 1992). Rather than seeing bureaucracy as a neutral system of rationality within which gender relations unfold, scholars examine the contested, culturally mediated, and power-laden character of the bureaucratic form as it is realized in everyday organizational settings.

In addition to examining links between bureaucracy and culture, some authors take a broader approach to gendered organizing, examining how organizational discourses and meaning systems construct gendered cultures and employee identities (Alvesson, 1998; Alvesson & Billing, 1992, 1997; Billing & Alvesson, 1998). One of the interesting features of this work is that it only occasionally invokes feminism, choosing instead to speak of "gender studies." For example, Alvesson and Billing (1997) state explicitly that they "prefer the concept gender studies to feminist studies for several reasons. The most important is that gender relations can and should be investigated in ways other than strongly 'pro-female' ones" (p. 21). Of course, this represents a rather narrow, essentialist reading of feminism that conceives of it as "about women" and overlooks its exploration of the gendered dynamics of power and domination. Indeed, Alvesson and Billing's (1992, 1997) work is a good example of research on gender and organization that adopts what they describe as a "critical interpretive" perspective (1997:, p. 44) but that at the same time refuses political engagement in favor of a "doubting, skeptically committed" perspective (p. 45). Such a view seems to arise from their belief that much of feminist research politicizes gender issues, creating a simplistic dichotomy of women as victims and men as agents of domination. Certainly, among our goals in this book are both to avoid such simple dichotomies and to undermine the relatively narrow reading of feminism that Alvesson and Billing espouse.

One of the interesting qualities of feminist studies of organizational culture is that it has helped to shift the focus in organizational culture research from viewing culture either as something that an organization *has* (the so-called variable approach) or as something an organization *is* (the so-called root metaphor approach) to viewing culture as a *performance* by organization members (e.g., Bell & Forbes, 1994; Gherardi, 1994, 1995, 1996; Holmer Nadesan & Trethewey, 2000). Consistent with West and Zimmerman's (1987) notion of "doing gender," this work examines how the construction of gendered meanings and identities is a complex, ongoing, and ambiguous process that must be continuously negotiated. Adopting a symbolic approach, for example, Gherardi (1994) argues that

> The meaning of gender is constantly deferred and negotiated in discourse while we simultaneously acknowledge the deep symbolic order of gender. The thought and language that separates the female from the male underpins a symbolic order of gender which expresses experiences unique to each gender, and which embeds an episteme (Foucault, 1980a) of each gender in the culture. (pp. 592–593)

This conception of organizational culture is quite different from that employed in much of the culture research. Even in those studies where the "stuff" of culture (jokes, rituals, talk, symbols, etc.) is viewed as constitutive of organizing, there is often little sense of organization members "doing" culture in a dynamic and performative fashion (e.g., Smith & Eisenberg, 1987). Even in those studies where cultural performance is highlighted, we see a relatively static conception of performance as expression of particular dimensions of culture and symbolic forms (e.g., Trujillo & Dionisopoulos, 1987).

For example, Smith and Eisenberg's (1987) interpretive study of conflict at Disneyland presents the conflict as based in relatively stable and intransigent root metaphors that shape the experience and perception of the protagonists in oppositional ways. At no time do we get the sense that such metaphors are "constantly deferred" or negotiated in a dynamic and shifting manner. Similarly, Trujillo and Dionisopoulos's (1987) dramaturgical analysis of a police department presents the members of the organizational culture as playing out well-rehearsed and stable—albeit communicatively constructed—organizational roles. Interestingly enough, what the members of this (apparently all-male) culture seem to be performing is a particular form of hegemonic masculinity (Connell, 1987) that is rooted in the heroic depiction of otherwise mundane activity; the characterization of "the other" as scum, "dirtbags," and so forth; and the employment of rituals of male bonding and hazing. However, Trujillo and Dionisopoulos do not explore the gendered dimensions of this culture, evidence perhaps that gender is often only recognized as relevant or meaningful when the social actors studied are women.

In sum, the feminist study of "organizational culture" has helped to shift the focus away from the depiction of relatively stable, homogeneous cultures and toward a view of culture as dynamic, performative, and embodying gendered relations of power that are obscured through ceremonial and remedial work (Fletcher, 1998; Gherardi, 1995, 1996; J. Martin, 1992, 1994). For example, Gherardi's (1996) study of women's narratives in masculine organizational cultures illustrates how women are required to discursively position themselves in ways that accommodate a particular culture. Gherardi analyzes narratives through a typology that shows women discursively constructing themselves as, for example, a guest in a friendly culture, marginal in a hostile culture, a "holidaymaker" in a friendly culture, and so forth. As Gherardi (1996) illustrates, these narratives represent discursive positions that are already available in the masculine organizational cultures, and hence they suggest that "gender identity is partly constructed by linguistic registers diffused in the social order and that the symbolic order of gender is an integral part of the development of self" (p. 199).

The principal tension, then, between feminist organization studies and interpretive modernism is that while the latter tends to depoliticize the process of social construction, the former explicitly addresses the ways in which organizations are produced and reproduced through the intersection of discourses of gender, race, class, and so forth. In this sense, feminism addresses the political character of all social construction processes. In the next section of this chapter, we examine a third discourse—critical modernism—that takes precisely as its focus the discursive politics of meaning, exploring the connections among processes of representation, power, discourse, and organization. Again, our goal here is to note the ways in which feminist studies and critical modernism exist in tension, suggesting ways to radicalize the study of gendered organizing.

Feminism and Critical Modernism: A Discourse of Suspicion

While the tensions between feminism and the discourses of explanation and understanding are relatively clear, the relationship between feminism and critical modernism is more complex. As a response to the limitations of other modernist discourses, critical modernism examines representational practices as political. Meaning systems do not emerge simply through processes of dialogue and consensus but are viewed as the result of deep structure power relations that privilege particular political and economic interests over others. It is therefore with the critical modernist project that the issue of voice becomes much more central and complex; that is, meaning is conceived as a politically contested process in which different voices and interests compete for hegemony.

For much of its history, however, gender has been a blindspot for critical modernism. Certainly its two principal streams of thought—Western Marxism and Frankfurt School Critical Theory—historically have not addressed gender as a central problematic in the critique of capitalism. While Marxist feminism emerged beginning in the 1970s, the tensions between Marxism and feminism have often produced what Hartmann (1979) describes as an "unhappy marriage." Furthermore, even though Marxism is, by definition, a philosophy of praxis (Gramsci, 1971) oriented toward revolutionary social transformation, many feminists have historically been suspicious of its predilection for theorizing over concrete practices. In this sense, the emergence in the 1970s of women's collectives and alternative forms of organizing—while significant in its own right—can be read in part as a response to the perceived inability of male critical theorizing to address the everyday issues that women faced in a capitalist, patriarchal society. In addition, while critical organization studies began to develop a critical mass of scholarship in the mid-1980s, much of this work neglected gender as a constitutive element in the politics of everyday organizing.

In this section, then, we address the contributions of critical modernism to organization studies—focusing in particular on its critical analysis of communicative processes—and the ways in which feminist studies have engaged with critical scholarship in both a sympathetic and transgressive fashion.

As we suggested in the introduction to this book, critical organization studies constitutes a "discourse of suspicion" (Mumby, 1997a; Ricoeur, 1970), which assumes that surface level meanings and behaviors obscure deep structure conflicts, contradictions, and neuroses that limit the possibilities for the realization of a genuinely democratic society. From a critical modernist perspective, ideology shapes social actors' relationships to the world in ways that are not always apparent to the social actors themselves. Communication functions ideologically not by simply fixing or determining people's relationships to each other and to the wider society, but by mediating that relationship through social practice. In other words, ideology is not merely ideational but enacted and embodied in everyday practices. For example, gender and race are not just internal mental constructs through which people make sense of the world; they are enacted and realized in the moment-to-moment and in institutional contexts that do not necessarily give equal access to discursive, cultural, and political resources (Hill Collins, 1991; West & Fenstermaker, 1995; West & Zimmerman, 1987).

Critical organization studies is thus concerned with the process of ideological struggle, examining the ways in which organizing is produced, reproduced, resisted, and transformed through myriad discursive and material practices (Alvesson, 1985; Alvesson & Willmott, 1992a; Clegg, 1975; Deetz, 1992a; Deetz & Kersten, 1983; Forester, 1992; Mumby, 1988). In many respects, feminist organization studies has a similar agenda. Feminist scholars explore how gender, race, discourse, power, and organizing intersect to produce relations of dominance and resistance. However, as a number of feminist scholars have pointed out, critical organization studies frequently underplays or overlooks completely the gendered character of organizing processes.

In response, some feminist scholars have brought to light the gender-blind features of critical work, pointing out that such apparently gender-neutral analyses frequently adopt an incipient masculinist perspective (e.g., S. Benson, 1992; McRobbie, 1981). In Burawoy's (1979) classic study, for example, he even states explicitly that his decision not to consider gender in his analysis of the game of "making out" is based on the fact that there were only two women in the department where he conducted his study. Such a perspective clearly equates gender with women, but, perhaps more significantly, his critical analysis fails to address the extent to which worker efforts to control the labor process may be rooted in a strongly gendered, masculine identity.

A number of scholars have critiqued Burawoy's failure to adequately theorize subjectivity in his analysis (e.g., Collinson, 1992), and his failure to do so can be seen as a product both of his lack of a gendered analysis and of his implicit adoption of a reproduction model of control. Rather than view the workers' identities as constructed through the intersection of complex discourses of class and gender, he is content to construct the game of "making out" as an all-powerful ideological force that impels workers to reproduce the dominant relations of power. The limitations of Burawoy's analysis are suggested by Cockburn's (1984) feminist study of shopfloor workers at a printing press, where male workers use the ostensibly hard, physical nature of the work to justify systematic efforts to marginalize female workers. In addition, Gottfried and Graham's (1993) analysis of an automobile assembly plant suggests that even where bureaucracy has been replaced by post-Fordist decision-making structures (teams, decentralized decision-making, etc.), gendered power relations reassert themselves through the attachment of gendered meanings to particular activities and events. For example, workers feminize the experience of repetitive stress job injuries as a way to differentiate between those workers who are "up to" the work and those who are not. It is worth reminding ourselves of Acker's (1990) claim that even in contexts where gender is apparently not an explicit feature of the work context, "advantage and disadvantage . . . meaning and identity, are patterned through and in terms of a distinction between male and female, masculine and feminine" (p. 146). In this sense, feminist organization scholars have drawn attention to the blindspots of a number of critical analyses.

There is an important sense, however, in which feminist and critical studies face similar, contested issues regarding the relationship among discourse, power, and domination. Both perspectives, by definition, have drawn attention to the question of agency; that is, how social actors are able to make sense of organizing and perhaps "act otherwise" (Giddens, 1979) in the face of intractable institutional structures. Historically, critical scholars have theorized self-reflection and agency as a necessary and constitutive feature of emancipation and social transformation (e.g., Habermas, 1984; Lukács, 1971). Feminist scholars, on the other hand, have adopted a more pragmatic orientation toward issues of agency, often grounded in the activist efforts and lived experience of actual women.

As we discussed earlier, feminists have long situated the possibilities of agency in terms of women's attempts to create alternative forms of organization (Ferree & Martin, 1995). Since the late 1960s, feminist activists have founded communities designed to facilitate the consciousness and empowerment of women who are otherwise politically and economically disenfranchised. Increasingly, feminist organization scholars do not take these communities to reflect some sort of essential "women's way of organizing"—a binary and apolitical logic of difference more typical of post-positivist discourse. Rather, feminist organizations are more often viewed as a crucial component of feminist politics and praxis. This view rests on a critique of bureaucracy as an inherently masculinist form that precludes, or at least actively hinders, gender equality (Acker, 1990). In this sense, feminist organizations function as "subaltern counterpublics" (Fraser, 1990/91) that nurture marginalized voices with temporary insulation from the silencing effects of bureaucracy. Ultimately, these communities seek emancipatory social change, for example, by raising the public profile of once-privatized issues like domestic violence, sexual abuse, health care, and so forth. Recently, feminists have also located pragmatic possibilities in the epistemological privileging of women's standpoints, which arise from their differentially subordinated positions in the world. For example, Patricia Hill Collins (1991) articulates a Black feminist standpoint, the politics of which stem from "the dialectic of oppression and activism, the tension between the suppression of black women's ideas and our intellectual activism in the face of that suppression" (pp. 5–6).

However, both feminist and critical studies have struggled to adequately explore the agency-structure dialectic, particularly in connection with the development of useful and heuristic conceptions of agency. Indeed, we would argue that much of critical and feminist organization studies has adopted a "reproduction" approach to exploring the relationship between domination and resistance. Such a perspective argues that, for the most part, the dominant, institutionalized relations of power are produced and reproduced on a daily basis, with little possibility for resistance or transformation by the everyday social actor. Where resistance does occur, it is generally read as being implicated in the process of social reproduction itself (e.g., Burawoy, 1979; Willis, 1977). In particular, Gramsci's conception of hegemony has been appropriated in radical organization and feminist studies in a largely undialectical fashion, depicting social actors as meaning-makers who nevertheless tend to make sense of the world in ways that reproduce capitalist relations of power and production. For example, a special issue of *Administrative Science Quarterly* on organizational control, while not neglecting issues of resistance, generally examines "how societies control their members by clothing the iron fist of power in a velvet glove" (Jermier, 1998, p. 236).

Critical organization scholars have examined such discourse practices as storytelling (e.g., Helmer, 1993; Mumby, 1987; Witten, 1993), rites and rituals (e.g., Rosen, 1985, 1988), metaphors (e.g., Deetz & Mumby, 1990; Markham, 1996; Smith & Keyton, 2001), and everyday talk (e.g., Forester, 1992, 1993), in each case attempting to highlight the connection between the discursive enactment of organizing and the process of social control. In the research on organizational storytelling, for example, the focus generally is on how narrative functions ideologically to privilege certain interests and social realities over others. Again, consistent with a discourse of suspicion, a critical perspective suggests that organizational storytelling is a powerful vehicle for simultaneously reifying and obscuring deep structure power relations beneath everyday discourse. The reproduction of organizational control, then, is achieved because storytelling—as an endemic feature of organizational life—helps to produce and institutionalize forms of sense making.

Similarly, a number of feminist scholars have extended analyses of hegemonic processes in the workplace, addressing the intrinsically gendered character of organizational control (e.g., Buzzanell, 1995; Clair, 1993a; Cockburn, 1984; J. Fletcher, 1999; Gottfried & Graham, 1993). In such research, the emphasis is less on possibilities for women's resistance to patriarchal forms of oppression, and more on how the discursive construction of difference leads to the continued marginalization of women in organizations. For example, Clair's (1993b) analysis of women's narratives of sexual harassment stresses the ways in which women use discursive frames that limit possibilities for organizational change. She shows, for instance, how some women discursively construct harassment as a private, interpersonal matter. In another analysis, Clair (1993a) suggests how institutions become complicit in this sequestering process, formalizing sexual harassment policies that commodify, bureaucratize, and privatize sexual harassment behavior. In both studies, the principal focus is on sexual harassment discourses as they constitute the marginalization of women in the workplace. Fletcher's (1998, 1999) research similarly adopts a reproduction model of power, although she emphasizes the marginalization of women at the level of everyday interaction dynamics, as implied by the title of her 1999 book *Disappearing Acts.*

Even the feminist literature on alternative organizing strategies, which by its nature highlights the potential for human agency, ultimately diminishes possibilities for resistance. As we explained in Chapter 1, members of feminist organizations tend to face a core contradiction between their empowerment ideology and the political and economic demands that characterize their daily organizational lives. Most scholars have stressed how this tension chips away at the integrity of feminist practice and ultimately disables emancipatory outcomes (e.g., Kleinman, 1996; Morgen, 1988, 1990; Pahl, 1985; Ristock, 1990; Seccombe-Eastland, 1988). Consequently, we are left with an image of wishful but ill-fated utopias snuffed out by the regrettable human habit of reproducing dominant organizational forms. From this view, "real" feminist organization is all but impossible to achieve, thanks to the unbearable weight of larger structural and cultural forces.

An adequately dialectical approach, on the other hand, embodies a much stronger notion of agency that places greater emphasis on the dialectic of control and resistance, suggesting ways in which human action and identity emerge out of this dialectic (e.g., Collinson, 1992; Mumby, 1997b; Scheibel, 1996). At the same time, a dialectical approach examines the inherent tensions and contradictions between agency and structure, between the interpretive possibilities that exist in every discourse situation and institutional efforts to impose or fix meaning (J. K. Benson, 1977; Giddens, 1979; Papa, Auwal, & Singhal, 1995). In the last few years, critical and feminist organization studies have begun to explore this dialectical struggle in more rich and textured ways. Rather than viewing organizations as systems of domination concealed in velvet gloves, researchers have started to examine the complex struggles over meaning that simultaneously embody domination and resistance (e.g., Clair, 1994, 1998; Mumby, 1997b).

An excellent example of a gendered analysis is Collinson's (1988, 1992) critical ethnography of male shopfloor workers in a truck factory. He addresses some of the above questions by examining the relations among resistance, control, and gendered identity as they play out in various worker rituals and narrative performances. Such performances neither reproduce the dominant corporate culture in a simplistic manner nor do they represent pristine, authentic spaces of resistance to that culture. Instead, Collinson illustrates how rituals function to reproduce working class, hegemonic masculinity on the shopfloor and to resist management efforts to control the labor process. For example, hazing rituals both reproduce hegemonic masculinity and instill an ethos that resists management efforts to improve productivity.

Perhaps the most important dimension of Collinson's study is that he problematizes worker identity, viewing it as constituted through the contradictory discursive practices of the workplace. In this sense, identity is not simply linked to class or gender, or described in global terms as a manifestation of the culture; rather, it is explored as a shifting, tension-filled product of particular discursive articulations and sense-making practices. Consistent with a dialectical approach, Collinson examines discourse as communicative praxis (Schrag, 1986); that is, as the material, embodied performances through which social actors construct their identities in a dynamic, conflicted, and precarious fashion. From such a perspective, identities are produced, reproduced, and transformed through an ongoing process of struggle within systems of enablement and constraint (Deetz & Mumby, 1990).

A number of feminist researchers have moved beyond the reproduction model of organizational control, adopting a more dialectical approach to examining the intersection of gender, power, and organizing (Clair, 1994, 1998; Gottfried, 1994; Holmer Nadesan, 1996; Sotirin & Gottfried, 1999). Such studies focus on the tensions and contradictions that emerge in the gendered dynamics of organizing processes. Hegemony is conceived not as a simple system of control but as a site of struggle in which women and men construct sometimes competing, sometimes consonant conceptions of organizational reality. Some of this work bridges the gap between critical and postmodern approaches to power and will be addressed in detail in Chapter 4.

The more recent, discourse-based models of feminist organization reviewed in Chapter 1 also illustrate a dialectically minded feminist approach. This work begins by embracing the need for feasible systems that at once offer alternatives to patriarchal bureaucracies and recognize the limitations of operating within larger social, political, and economic contexts. No longer seen as an overdetermined force, the contradiction between ideology and practice becomes a web of situated tensions experienced by organization members, who respond to those tensions in various ways. Accordingly, scholars in this emerging line of research have begun to examine how members of feminist organizations nego-tiate the ideology-practice contradiction, as well as the evolving forms of organization they produce along the way (Buzzanell et al., 1997; Gottfried & Weiss, 1994; Loseke, 1992; Morgen, 1994). Ashcraft's (2000, 2001) study of a feminist domestic violence center demonstrates how, in the process of balancing paradoxical imperatives in practice, members generated a hybrid of feminist and bureaucratic organiza-tional forms. Similarly, Maguire and Mohtar's (1994) research of a battered women's shelter examines how members adapted externally directed discourse to meet pressures imposed by the varied communities (e.g., state funding agencies, local police) that comprised the organiza-tion's environment. Significant for the development of a dialectical perspective, such projects unearth resistant, transformative moments amid ostensibly debilitating structural and ideological contradiction.

The dialectical interest that increasingly characterizes critical and feminist studies is crucial to our own development of a feminist communicology of organization for several reasons. Among them, it positions mundane communication as a pivotal site where the dialectic of control and resistance resides and gender identities are made. Moreover, it attempts to recognize the ways in which institutions shape and are shaped by interaction. In this sense, dialectical arguments within critical modernism situate communication as an always ambiguous, constitutive yet constrained feature of organizing that can only be understood through contextual analyses.

❖ CONCLUSION

The purpose of this chapter has been to highlight key points of connection and conflict between feminist and modernist organization studies. Clearly, we are speaking here not of discrete bodies of litera-ture but, rather, of interconnected, overlapping, and yet tension-filled perspectives, agendas, and values. While feminism is, in many respects, a product of the modernist, Enlightenment project, it has also engaged with and challenged it in a number of ways. In this chapter, we attempted to nuance current views of modernism as an intellectual and practical project, and of feminism as an "outsider within" that project (Hill Collins, 1991), in the particular context of organization studies. Thus, while Chapter 1 addressed various ways in which gender and feminist research tacitly frames the discourse-organization relationship, this chapter explicated metatheoretical assumptions and representational practices that ground much of this research. We aimed to develop a distinctively organizational voice that both complicates and clarifies the relationship between feminism and modernism.

What, then, can we take from our examination of the connections and tensions between modernism and feminism? In brief, we see three important features that will be carried over into our development of a feminist communicology of organization. First, modernism treats organizations as enduring social structures that are produced, maintained, and reproduced across time and space. While we have highlighted some of the problems with a nondialectical, reproductive model of organizational power, we still wish to recognize that stable relations of power cannot simply be theorized out of existence by invoking actor agency and the possibilities for resistance to the status quo. One of the enduring lessons of feminism is that patriarchal power, while contestable and subject to transformation, is nevertheless a relatively persistent feature of social structures. For us, the trick is to acknowledge this empirical condition while theorizing the possibilities for a genuine dialectic of power and resistance.

Second, and related, the modernist tradition provides a way to recognize and explore the materiality of organizational structures. While this chapter invoked the crisis of representation and explained the limits of any correspondence theory of truth, we are concerned to maintain a connection between discourse and the material world without reducing one to the other. With many feminists, we argue that there *is* "something outside of the text," although this "something" is the material residue of discourse and can only be understood through discourse. As we will show in Chapter 6, discursive practices create the material world in distinct ways, but in turn this material world provides the social, political, and economic context in which discourse is produced by institutions and individuals. For us, the purpose of a feminist communicology is to explore how social actors take on competing gendered discourses and with what material consequences. Modernism, particularly in its critical form, provides a means by which to explore the connections among gender, social construction, and a "real" world.

Finally, both modernism and feminism share an ethic that calls for the development of just, coercion-free social and institutional contexts. For feminists, regardless of perspective, this ethic entails the elimination of patriarchy and the creation of institutions and political systems that respect and value difference. As a product of the Enlightenment, modernism is similarly concerned with issues of freedom and emancipation from oppressive relations of power. As communication scholars, we recognize that human communication creates possibilities for emancipatory dialogue and meaningful community. Thus, an ethic that values difference is built into the ontology of human communication. Indeed, critical communication scholars often study how the possibility of democracy gets foreclosed as communication privileges certain interests (Deetz, 1992a). We agree with Parker (2000) that the recent focus among critical organization scholars on the relation between epistemology and discourse has tended to marginalize the place of ethics in such debates. Accordingly, the feminist communicology of organization that we develop in Chapter 5 will give greater emphasis to normative questions.

But first, Chapters 3 and 4 continue to develop the argument that feminism plays a central role in radical organization studies by turning to the relationship between postmodern thought and, respectively, critical and feminist organization scholarship. In particular, we explore what the intersection of feminism and postmodernism suggests for the development of a communication-based model of gendered organizing.

3

Postmodernism and Organization Studies

Complicating the Conversation

❖ ❖ ❖

I n teasing out the varied intersections of feminism and modernism, we
have aimed to move beyond binary thinking, depicting a diverging
and converging relationship between feminist and modernist organization studies. We have argued that modernism is far from a monolithic
enterprise; in fact, the discourses that challenge the "episteme of representation" have diverse implications for the study of gendered organization. As will soon be evident, however, epistemological and political
challenges to the "episteme of representation" are more far-reaching
than we have acknowledged thus far.

The emergence of postmodern thought in the last 20 years has cast
doubt on the possibility of a set of foundational knowledge claims
about the social world. Postmodern scholarship has variously questioned the cherished assumptions and values of the modernist project.
In organization studies, postmodern discourse has begun to stimulate
scholarship that reflects an even sharper turn toward discursive
conceptions of organization. The last few years have witnessed the

rise of a veritable "cottage industry" devoted to such research, with numerous books and journal articles (even special issues) delineating the conceptual and empirical domains of this intensified discursive turn (Alvesson & Karreman, 2000a, 2000b; Grant, Keenoy, & Oswick, 1998; Keenoy, Marchak, Oswick, & Grant, 2000; Keenoy, Oswick, & Grant, 1997; Oswick, Keenoy, & Grant, 2000). Drawing on the writings of philosophers and social theorists such as Derrida, Foucault, and Lyotard, postmodern organization scholars complicate relations among discourse, power, and identity; in particular, they challenge mainstream conceptions of organizations as stable structures, question the distinction between researcher and subject/object of knowledge, and undermine lingering notions of a stable, objective truth awaiting discovery.

This chapter examines the emergence of the postmodern turn, assessing its impact on organization studies, as well as its potential (constraints) for radical scholars. We contend that postmodern thought provides essential critiques and extensions of critical organization scholarship, yet it also yields significant limitations for theorizing organization as gendered. Chapter 4 extends this argument by explaining how the juxtaposition of feminism and postmodernism can usefully ground a communication theory of gendered organization. To prepare for that endeavor, the present chapter unfolds as follows: We begin by considering the political and cultural terrain in which postmodernism has emerged; we then unpack some basic premises of postmodern thought. In the next section, we detail how radical organization scholars have taken up postmodernism in an effort to better understand the relationship between discourse and organizations. Finally, we address what we see as the most significant shortcomings of postmodern thought for the study of gendered organization.

❖ POSTMODERN ANXIETY

> *Postmodernism is what the French learned Americans were calling what they were thinking.*
>
> —Rajchman (1991, p. 120)

> *This word has no meaning. Use it as often as possible.*
>
> —Modern-day Dictionary of Received Ideas
> (quoted in Featherstone, 1988, p. 195)

The word pomo has no meaning. Use it as seldom as possible!

—Alvesson (1995, p. 1068)

In recent years, postmodernism has emerged as an important and controversial mode of understanding and deconstructing contemporary human experience. It is the subject of a huge and ever-expanding body of literature in both the humanities and social sciences (Bernstein, 1992; Best & Kellner, 1991, 1997; Callinicos, 1990; Harvey, 1989; Rosenau, 1992; Seidman, 1994). While the term itself gets defined and interpreted differently, "postmodern theory" has had a profound effect on the ways we think about human phenomena, including organizations (Alvesson & Deetz, 1996; Cooper & Burrell, 1988; Hancock & Tyler, 2001b; Hassard, 1993a). As that suggests, it is easier to declare the significance of postmodern thought than it is to describe and analyze it. As Foucault was moved to remark, "What are we calling post-modernity? I'm not up to date. . . . I do not understand what kind of problem is common to the people we call post-modern or post-structuralist" (Foucault, 1988b, pp. 33, 34).

Despite its apparent ineffability, "the specter of postmodernism has aroused widespread anxiety" (Kilduff & Mehra, 1997, p. 454) in the social sciences and in popular culture, and this anxiety transcends political boundaries. Among conservative critics, "pomophobia" (Byers, 1995, quoted in Gingrich-Philbrook, 1998, p. 215) appears in accusations that postmodernism undermines the basic values of Western society, creating the climate of moral relativism at fault for most current social ills, including falling educational standards, the demise of the nuclear family, and the emergence of rampant political correctness and Orwellian-style thought police on today's college campuses. Attacks from the left of the political spectrum tend to stress the perceived capitulation of postmodernists to the onslaught of global capitalism and to a generally conservative political and cultural climate. For example, one of the left's most visible representatives argues that

Critical Theory—or what passed itself off as such among postmodernists, post-structuralists, post-Marxists and kindred schools—amounted to a wholesale collapse of moral and intellectual nerve, a line of least resistance that effectively recycled the "end-of-ideology" rhetoric current in the late 1950s. (Norris, 1993, p. 1)

Interestingly, these critiques from opposite ends of the political spectrum are united in their perception that adherence to a postmodern worldview signifies moral failure. For conservatives, this moral failure originates from the decay of basic institutional structures (for example, the family) that are thought to ensure the continuity of bedrock societal values. For leftists, the moral bankruptcy of postmodernism lies in its abdication of the core, utopian value of collective emancipation from capitalist oppression through societal transformation. For both, postmodernism is a threat because it is irresponsible; that is, it abrogates a normative grounding from which to engage in social action and critique. Put colloquially, postmodernism wants to have its cake and eat it too.

Does postmodern thought warrant this kind of anxiety from so many quarters? We maintain that, like any perspective, postmodernism can be legitimately interrogated on several grounds, but much of the controversy surrounding it stems from the problematic tendency to paint modernism and postmodernism in monolithic strokes and then treat them as mutually exclusive opposites. For example, commentators often equate modernism exclusively with positivism (e.g., Albrecht & Bach, 1997; Redding & Tompkins, 1988; Tompkins, 1984) and postmodernism with a generic, social constructionist perspective on human behavior (Stewart, 1991, 1992).

Within organization studies, modernism and postmodernism have often been juxtaposed against each other under the aegis of the "incommensurability thesis," which holds that the two positions are "radically different systems of thought and logic" that "may be fundamentally irreconcilable" (Cooper & Burrell, 1988, p. 110). The sedimentation of such binary thinking often leads to a retrenchment of perspectives, with opposing positions assuming an almost siege-like mentality. Certainly, the well-known debate between Jeffrey Pfeffer and John Van Maanen seems more about staking out territory than seeking connection and dialogue (Pfeffer, 1993, 1995; Van Maanen, 1995a, 1995b). Their sword crossing reads like an academic "cold war" distinctly lacking in détente. Similarly, Donaldson's (1985, 1988, 1995) academic crusade against "anti-management" theories and "paradigm proliferation" appears more interested in establishing the sovereignty of his own perspective by setting up straw men to "rout" (his term) than in moving toward any kind of common ground. Common to such antagonism from "both sides" are caricatures of modernism and postmodernism and a strong sense of moralism about how social scientists ought to be studying other humans.

Fortunately, such binary logic does not exhaust the ways in which postmodernism has been engaged in organization studies. For example, Kilduff and Mehra (1997) respond to the "chorus of negativity" by treating postmodernism as a sensibility rather than as a set of predetermined epistemological and methodological criteria (p. 454). To their credit, they even refuse "to rule out any method or approach from the postmodernist's repertoire" and "champion the simultaneous availability of apparently incongruous research methods including laboratory experiments, deconstruction, ethnography, and sophisticated statistical analyses" (Kilduff and Mehra, 1997, p. 467). Their five "postmodern problematics" (i.e., problematizing normal science, truth, representation, writing, and generalizability) reflect a broad-based conception of postmodernism that acknowledges interplay with some strands of the modernist tradition. In a wide-ranging overview of critical theory and postmodernism, Alvesson and Deetz (1996) similarly explore continuities between the two perspectives, even as they highlight important differences.

Given the controversies that swirl around postmodernism, what is a useful way to frame the scholarship it has inspired? The next section identifies key concerns that tie together a loose amalgam of postmodern writers. Our goal is not, however, to provide a comprehensive overview of postmodern thought; as hinted above, such reviews are many and wide-ranging (Best & Kellner, 1991, 1997; Featherstone, 1988; Rosenau, 1992). By characterizing postmodernism as "a discourse of vulnerability," we aim to emphasize its connection with the previous chapter's analysis of the discourses of modernism as applied in organization studies. Our position is far from antimodernist; in other words, we present postmodern thought as an alternative to modernist logics, *not* as a vehicle for rejecting the latter. In particular, we see postmodernism as a crucial means for theorizing communication as a defining activity of organizational life at a time when what counts as "knowledge" is in a state of flux and transformation (see, e.g., DiMaggio, 1995; Parker, 1995; Weick, 1995).

❖ POSTMODERNISM AS A DISCOURSE OF VULNERABILITY

Postmodernism is defined, at least in part, in terms of its relationship to modernism—it both comes after modernism and is a response to and critique of modernist sensibilities. As such, "the postmodern" is frequently characterized as an epistemological break with "the modern" and as an historical break with the epoch of modernity (Cooper, 1989; Cooper & Burrell, 1988; Featherstone, 1988; Hassard, 1993a, 1993b). The distinction between an epistemological (modernism/ postmodernism) and epochal (modernity/postmodernity) view of the debate is manifest in the organization studies literature. Some scholars argue that the postmodern is a historical, ontological condition that demands new, postcapitalist, post-Fordist forms of organizing that are characterized by small economies of scale, flexible production capabilities, reintegration of the work process, and so forth (Bergquist, 1992; Clegg, 1990; Eisenberg & Goodall, 1997; Harvey, 1989). Other scholars pursue postmodern thought as a way to deconstruct the organization as a site of power that subjects members to various forms of disciplinary practice (Barker & Cheney, 1994; Burrell, 1988, 1992; Daudi, 1986; Deetz, 1992b; Kilduff & Mehra, 1997; Knights & Vurdubakis, 1994). We are more interested in the latter conception, given our concern with postmodernism as a sensibility that permits certain ways of understanding and critiquing social processes.

We adopt the phrase "a discourse of vulnerability" (Mumby, 1997a) as a way to describe postmodern thought insofar as it is here that the challenge to the "episteme of representation" reaches its apogee. While Jameson (1984) describes this challenge as one in which the notion of "a Truth" is radically undermined, its implications are more extensive than this. The phrase "a discourse of vulnerability" is intended to evoke how the postmodern intellectual gives up the "authority game" (J. Martin, 1992), exchanging a priori and elitist assumptions for a more emergent and context-bound notion of what counts as knowledge (Deetz, 1996). As Said (1994) puts it, such an intellectual is "unusually responsive to the traveler rather than the potentate, to the provisional and risky rather than to the habitual, to innovation and experiment rather than the authoritatively given status quo" (pp. 63–64).

In the last 20 years, much of the impetus for this perspective has come out of developments in postmodern anthropology, where the "poetics and politics" of fieldwork have come under close scrutiny (Clifford, 1988; Clifford & Marcus, 1986; Crawford, 1996; Jackson, 1989). Postmodern anthropology problematizes not only the notion of "a Truth" but also the idea that there are any standard, universal practices by which to articulate truth. Here, we focus on three specific postmodern challenges to the iterations of modernity discussed in

Chapter 2. First, the traditional image of the sovereign, knowing subject as a wellspring of knowledge is "decentered" and displaced. Where even Habermas's critical modernist project still places the reasoning, rational subject at the center of the theory (albeit in a transformed way through a linguistic model of rationality), postmodern thought deconstructs the idea of a coherent subject. While the modernist subject retains a certain autonomy and coherence, the postmodern subject is frequently portrayed as constructed and disciplined through discursive practices and knowledge structures. Foucault's (1979, 1980a, 1980b) work, for example, shows how "the individual" is an effect of various discourses that function to normalize and institutionalize our sense of autonomous subjectivity.

Second, the discourse of vulnerability destabilizes the common sense, correspondence model of the relationship between language and world. While the modernist discourses of understanding and suspicion question this relationship, postmodern scholars go further, attempting to sever completely the link between words and things. Stemming largely from Derrida's (1976) critique and radicalization of Saussure's (1960) structural model of language, such work contends that the reference point for discourse is other discourses, not some external reality. Derrida's (1976, p. 157) claim that there is "nothing outside of the text" suggests that the meanings of particular discourses are never fully present; instead, they are constantly deferred to other texts and discourses. The meaning of language therefore arises not only from a system of difference (as Saussure would have it) but from "différance"—the process of constant deferral and slippage through hierarchically arranged binary oppositions that play off of each other. Meaning only appears fixed because of a deceptively straightforward positive relationship between signifiers and signifieds. Derrida demonstrates the chimerical quality of this relationship by examining the play of presence and absence upon which textual meanings depend. In terms of the discourse of vulnerability, then, language is dethroned from its role as the neutral descriptor of a stable, unchanging world, and knowledge becomes a focus of deconstruction.

Finally, the discourse of vulnerability explicates the relationship between knowledge and power. Rather than conceive of the pursuit of knowledge as somehow separate from the exercise of power, postmodern scholars argue that knowledge production is, by definition, a political process. As hinted above, many contemporary ethnographers remind us that all knowledge claims position social actors in partial ways. Hence, questions of voice become especially acute, as researchers strive to be reflexive about the ways in which the "poetics and politics" of ethnographic work may unintentionally appropriate the voices of others (Clifford & Marcus, 1986; Conquergood, 1991; Jackson, 1989; Wolf, 1992). Deconstructing the poetics of ethnography exposes intimate connections between representational practices and knowledge claims (Van Maanen, 1988). At the same time, attention to the politics of ethnography reveals how modes of representation shape the "positioning" of those studied (Conquergood, 1991). Exposed is the myth of the "chameleon fieldworker" (Geertz, 1983) who seamlessly assimilates herself or himself into a culture and simply "writes up" what she or he "discovers." Indeed, the researcher's account may say as much about the researcher as it does about the social actors studied (e.g., Krizek, 1992). Such claims often lead postmodern scholars to refuse "grand narratives" of culture in favor of local, situated, and context-bound knowledge claims. In sum, postmodern thought destabilizes and politicizes taken-for-granted practices of knowledge production and representation.

For our purposes, these three elements sufficiently distinguish the discourse of vulnerability that threads through current postmodern writings. The next section considers how these elements have been taken up by organization scholars. Over the last 15 years or so, postmodernism has profoundly influenced organization theory and research, and we assess its impact with an eye for potential intersections of feminist and postmodern perspectives on organization.

❖ DISCOURSES OF VULNERABILITY
IN ORGANIZATION STUDIES

The multiple discourses discussed in Chapter 2 suggest that postmodern views of organization arose from a complex discursive terrain of modernist attempts to *consider itself* (Horkheimer & Adorno, 1988). Thus postmodernism did not emerge as a distinct, fully formed, and iconoclastic riposte to modernist organization studies; rather, it can be read as the continuation of a project begun within modernism. The central question therefore becomes how postmodernism has opened and closed opportunities for radical organization scholarship. Our intent here is not to provide a comprehensive review of postmodern organization theory and research, for such reviews are readily available (e.g., Alvesson & Deetz, 1996; Cooper & Burrell, 1988; Hancock & Tyler, 2001b; Hassard, 1993a). We narrow our focus to problematics of subjectivity, power, and discourse that stem from postmodern inquiry and resonate closely with our project.

Theorizing the Subject of Postmodern Organization Studies

Perhaps the most significant development in postmodern organization studies has been a more robust conception of subjectivity than that offered within modernism. This conception, arising particularly out of the work of the labor process theorists of the "Manchester School," takes seriously the concern that "subjectivity" has been under-theorized and lacks adequate empirical examination, even within radical organization studies (e.g., Knights & Morgan, 1991; Knights & Vurdubakis, 1994; Willmott, 1994; Wray-Bliss, 2002). It stems in part from a critique of 1970s labor process theory for its heavy focus on the structural, material aspects of capitalist workplaces to the neglect of how workers actually interpreted and experienced the labor process on a daily basis (Braverman, 1974; Burawoy, 1979, 1985). And, where subjective aspects of work *are* addressed within Marxism, postmodernists argue that the character of personal experience is essentialized or taken for granted. For example, critics have taken aim at Burawoy's (1979) efforts to address the subjective experience of work, arguing that he presumes rather than elucidates the construction of workplace subjectivity (see Collinson, 1992; Willmott, 1990, for a more detailed critique of Burawoy's conception of subjectivity). In response, contemporary labor process theorists build on the premise that the ordering of social practices and institutions is only possible through the reflexivity of human agents.

Much of postmodern organization scholarship is similarly concerned with theorizing human agency in a way that simultaneously attends to the determinative effects of power relations and the possibilities for human insight and resistance. Whereas critical modernists have either ascribed agency to social actors as an essential part of the human condition (Lukács, 1971) or conceptualized it as determined by class structure (Althusser, 1971), postmodernists have attempted to overcome this dualistic reading. They argue that both positions leave unanswered precisely that which demands explanation: namely, what are the discursive conditions under which human agency is even possible? What are the mechanisms by which subjectivity takes on certain forms in particular contexts? In such ways, postmodern organization scholars *problematize* subjectivity such that it becomes the focal point for theorizing power relations. As Hugh Willmott (1994) states, "In postdualistic analysis, the image and ideal of a unified subject is replaced by an understanding and experiencing of human agency as a complex, contradictory and shifting process that is open to many possible modes of being" (p. 117).

For a number of reasons, most postmodern efforts to explore workplace subjectivity reference the writings of Michel Foucault on disciplinary power and the subject (Foucault, 1979, 1980a, 1980b). First, Foucault deconstructs any sovereign notion of subjectivity, arguing that the subject is a product of intersecting discourses. Modern sexuality, for example, is not an essential human condition but a product of 19th century medical discourses that normalized particular sexual identities and practices (Foucault, 1980a). Likewise, the notion of "delinquency" is a historical discursive formation that serves to discipline certain forms of behavior (Foucault, 1979). Relatedly, Foucault replaces sovereign conceptions of power, which pervade most Marxist analyses, with a disciplinary model. As we described in our introduction, the former views power as a negative, coercive force imposed from above, while the latter embraces a positive, productive, and "ascending" view of power as distributed in a capillary manner throughout the social body. From the disciplinary view, power acts to produce certain meaning systems and modes of being; it fashions subjects in particular ways. Foucault's (1979) metaphor of the Panopticon captures well the claim that power embodies a strong sense of self-surveillance and self-discipline.

Roy Jacques's (1996) study of the history of management thought provides a compelling illustration of the point. He examines how management discourse has "manufactured" the employee as an identifiable, classifiable, and controllable subject; he argues that, in many ways, the success of capitalism rested on a paradigm shift from a "Federalist 'discourse of character' centered on the citizen as the ordinary subject in society" to "an industrial 'discourse of objectivity' whose subject was l'employé" (p. 96). Jacques (1996) demonstrates how this discourse of industrialism included the principle of observation such that "the worker had changed from being a *subject with* whom one shared knowledge to an *object about* whom one had knowledge" (p. 117). Indeed, this thesis is eerily redolent of Foucault's (1979) observation about the disciplinary, carceral institution: "The prisoner is always the object of information, never the subject in communication" (p. 192).

Perhaps the most important issue to grasp here is that Jacques conceives of management discourse not simply as oppressing and coercing workers and hence negating their "natural" sense of self and relation to the labor process (as Marxist theorists might argue). He shows instead how management discourse *produced* an identifiable subject—"the employee"—around which a particular system of possibilities and power/knowledge relations emerged. Thus, for example, employee identities are generated through the process of "textualizing observation," made manifest in the ubiquity of standardized tables, personnel files, and manuals: "The employee as file became the primary reality to which organizational relationships connect" (Jacques, 1996, p. 117). These discourses yield both management knowledge about the worker and worker self-knowledge regarding their identities as employees. Jacques's argument is supported by Holmer Nadesan's (1997) Foucauldian analysis of corporate personality testing as a disciplinary practice, one of the products of which is "a formalized discourse for self-knowledge" (p. 189).

In general, a postmodern, Foucauldian perspective treats the subject as the effect, not the origin, of discourses and forms of knowledge. This view destabilizes the coherent, unitary, and sovereign subject, supplanting it with a contradictory, fragmented, and destabilized identity. Despite Foucault's claims to the contrary, however, there has been a tendency to read his work as downplaying or perhaps eliminating a strong sense of agency that includes the potential for resistance to disciplinary practices. Indeed, even those Foucauldians within labor process theory debates contend that Foucault lacks an adequate conception of agency and resistance (Knights, 1990; Willmott, 1994). Knights and Vurdubakis (1994) summarize the principal concerns in terms of three types of critical questions: (a) location, (b) agency, and (c) justifiability. The question of location asks, "If power is, as Foucault argues, everywhere, then where does resistance reside?" Foucault paints a vivid picture of all-encompassing disciplinary mechanisms that pervade every nook and cranny of society, but such a picture seems to leave little or no room for moments of resistance. The question of agency asks, "If power constitutes subjectivity and agency, then who are the agents of resistance?" Foucault's argument that subjects are constituted as the effects of discourses appears to complicate claims to liberatory dimensions of agency. Finally, the question of justifiability asks, "Why fight?" (Habermas, 1987). Foucault's infamous refusal to root his analytics of power in a normative foundation seems to undercut any rationale for one course of critique or action over another. On what grounds does one even engage in resistance to power?

Answers to such questions are complex, and we will not review them in detail here. In brief, Knights and Vurdubakis (1994) suggest that many critiques of Foucault reflect false dualisms between power and resistance, as well as abstract conceptions of agency that fail to situate subjectivity as it plays out in specific social contexts. Indeed, our turn to feminism in Chapter 4 is motivated in part by recognition that several feminist scholars have critiqued and extended Foucault's account of subjectivity, conducting analyses that directly address the material circumstances in which specific gendered and raced identities emerge (e.g., Bederman, 1995; Bordo, 1999; Kondo, 1990).

In sum, postmodern organization scholars have been at pains to emphasize a discursive conception of subjectivity that highlights how the organizational subject is a product of various discursive processes (Holmer Nadesan, 1997; Townley, 1993). Most of this research is premised upon an account of the relationship among discourse, power, and organizing that differs significantly from a critical modernist rendering.

Theorizing Power in Postmodern Organization Studies

The prevailing conception of power in postmodern organization studies coheres with the Foucauldian, disciplinary model discussed above, which treats power as an endemic, defining feature of everyday life. Unlike critical modernist views, which tend to imply the possibility of a position free from power and ideology, postmodern perspectives argue that power and knowledge are mutually implicated. Foucault (1979) is very explicit about this relationship in the following famous quote:

Perhaps, too, we should abandon a whole tradition that allows us to imagine that knowledge can exist only where the power relations are suspended and that knowledge can develop only outside its injunctions, its demands and its interests. . . . We should admit rather that power produces knowledge . . . that power and knowledge directly imply one another; that there is no power relation without the correlative constitution of a field of knowledge, nor any knowledge that does not presuppose and constitute at the same time power relations. These "power-knowledge relations" are to be analysed, therefore, not on the basis of a subject of knowledge who is or is not free in relation to the power system, but, on the contrary, the subject who knows, the objects to be known and the modalities of knowledge must be regarded as so many effects of these fundamental implications of power-knowledge and their historical transformations. (pp. 27–28)

As mentioned earlier, this reworking of power is especially significant because it rejects the sovereign conception of power that has dominated political theory in favor of a productive conception of power. Put bluntly, power produces; it does not prohibit. Far from antithetical, power and knowledge are entwined, and their varied fusions generate the resources that enable social actors to develop coherent identities. Returning to examples from the previous section, the discourse of "l'employé" (Jacques, 1996) is not repressive; it enables a (relatively) stable worker identity, normalizing processes, further discourses and practices, and so forth. In a similar vein, Holmer Nadesan's (1997) Foucauldian analysis of personality-testing discourse shows how the tests articulate a subject who needs certain cognitive and emotional traits in order to excel in the organization. Such tests are normalizing in that they constitute "conditions of possibility" for organizational success.

Foucault's analytics of power has become particularly important in postmodern organization studies with the advent of the so-called post-Fordist organization (Clegg, 1990; Hall, 1991; Harvey, 1989). While there is some dispute about whether we are in fact living in a post-Fordist age—compare, for example, Thompson's (1993) negative response with Clegg's (1990) affirmative response to this question—a number of scholars have paid close attention to the new forms of organizational control that seem to have evolved alongside more flexible, decentralized organizational structures and control systems. For example, recent work on self-managing teams (Barker, 1993, 1999; Barker & Cheney, 1994; Mumby & Stohl, 1992; Sewell, 1998; Sewell & Wilkinson, 1992) illuminates how an ostensibly participative form of organizing intensifies self-discipline in "postbureaucratic" organizations. Barker (1993, 1999) shows how a shift from hierarchical, bureaucratic forms of control to "concertive control" (Tompkins & Cheney, 1985) is achieved through the establishment of work teams that basically engage in self-surveillance; power is produced from the bottom up through the everyday discursive practices that construct team members' identities. As one of Barker's informants states, "I don't have to sit around and look for the boss to be around; and if the boss is not around, I can sit there and talk to my neighbor or do what I want. Now the whole team is around me and the whole team is observing what I'm doing" (Barker, 1993, p. 408).

Similarly, Mumby and Stohl's (1992) analysis of work teams shows how absent members are discursively constructed as "deviant" by other team members and are required to provide an accounting of, or apology for, their deviant behavior. Both of these studies exemplify Foucault's conception of power as positive and productive rather than negative and repressive; they also reveal how post-Fordist discourses of power can yield more effective forms of control than bureaucratic discourses. In an insightful critique of such "empowerment" programs, Barker (1993) concludes that "The irony of the change in this postbureaucratic organization is that, instead of loosening, the iron cage of rule-based, rational control, as Max Weber called it, actually became tighter" (p. 408).

Much of the research on post-Fordist, postbureaucratic organization heavily emphasizes the disciplinary features of new forms of control, with particular emphasis on the process by which an "ascending" model of disciplinary power emerges. That is, while bureaucratic organizations employ a sovereign, top-down form of control that is largely imposed on employees, postbureaucratic organizations shift the locus of control to the employees, who intersubjectively construct a set of norms and values that functions as a means of self-surveillance. Thus, while the rhetoric of "pomo" popular management texts points to the empowering features of the new forms of organizing (e.g., Bergquist, 1992), the work of postmodern scholars emphasizes the ways in which the new disciplinary forms create systems of possibility that construct employee identity and workplace control in a much more insidious and panoptic fashion. As Sewell (1998) states in his Foucauldian study of an organizational team structure, "panopticism represents the desire, if not necessarily the ability, to identify and capture all knowledge of the subject by subsuming individuals under a totalizing instrumental rationalism" (p. 424).

While such studies certainly do not ignore the possibilities for employee agency and resistance to these disciplinary mechanisms, the prevailing tendency is to focus on the forms of control to which employees are subject. In this sense, Foucault's (1982) dual process of subjectification and objectification tends to be reduced in empirical studies to an examination of the process of objectification. Or, perhaps more accurately, most empirical studies focus on the process by which employees collaboratively construct forms of self-identity that objectify them through self-imposed disciplinary mechanisms. In this sense, despite the pleas of many labor process theorists for more adequate conceptualizations of the relationship between power and "the subject," there is still relatively little empirical work that adopts an appropriately dialectical approach to this relationship. Few studies actually explore the discursive and material complexities and contradictions that lie at the heart of process subjectivity as it unfolds in the context of disciplinary relations of power (for exceptions, see Collinson, 1992; Kondo, 1990). Accordingly, as we develop a feminist communicology in Chapter 5, we stress the organization of gender as a dialectical, fragmented, and contradictory process that simultaneously entails moments of resistance and control. Such a process can only be understood through an examination of specific discursive and nondiscursive mechanisms as they are manifest in particular historical, cultural, and power-knowledge contexts.

Discourse and Postmodern Organization Studies

The discourse of vulnerability is most apparent in organization studies in the ways in which postmodern scholars have engaged organizations as discursively constituted. In such work, organizations are depicted as complex, disciplinary, discursive apparatuses that are nevertheless vulnerable to the resistant micropractices of their members. In addition, postmodern organization scholars often embody a high degree of authorial self-reflexivity as they renounce their roles as the final arbiters of knowledge claims made in their writings. In many cases, these researchers eschew any pretense of engaging in traditional social science research, invoking fictional and poetic frameworks to construct accounts of organizational life (e.g., Banks & Banks, 1998; Boje, 1995; A. D. Brown, 1998; Pacanowsky, 1988)

One area of research in postmodern discourse studies that manages to capture both of these themes is that of the "storytelling organization" (Boje, 1991). Narrative as both metaphor and everyday organizational phenomenon is able, on the one hand, to capture the status of authorial knowledge claims as one story among many competing stories, and on the other hand, to recognize the multiple stories that constitute organizational life. Consistent with Lyotard's (1984) rejection of the grand narrative of modernity in favor of the "petit récits" (or little stories) of postmodernity, such work emphasizes the contingency of claims about knowledge and the ontology of organizing. The gap between researcher and researched is called into question, and power becomes both an endemic feature of everyday organizing and a constitutive element in the politics of theory and research.

Boje, Luhman, and Baack's (1999) ethnography of a choral company exemplifies both of these features of postmodern discourse analysis as they examine the ways in which members construct narrative accounts of their culture. However, rather than construct an account that reflects a consensual organizational reality, the authors stress the "polyphonic, polysemous, and infinitely intertextual" (p. 343) features of the "storied" organization. Furthermore, this intertextuality is not seen as politically neutral; instead, each member is characterized as having different motivations and investments in the organization, and as engaging in different legitimating and hegemonic moves in accounting for their organizational reality. For Boje and colleagues (1999), there is no such thing as telling "the whole story"; storytelling involves a process of "social choice and selective appropriation" (p. 343).

In a postmodern, deconstructive move, Boje and colleagues (1999) then turn this same view of narrative construction on themselves, expanding their analytic focus from the choral company to the researchers and the editor and reviewers of the journal in which the article is published. As they state, "We hope to unfold the microstories about the interactions of three specific storytelling organizations . . . as each constructs 'subject' positions of self and other within interactive, iterative, and negotiated stories" (p. 341). Furthermore, they invoke a move of "triple-reflectivity" that enables them to unpack the "micro-level hegemonic moves in this collective narrative" (p. 341):

> The first-level reflectivity is to tell what is happening with each of the stories. This involves questions of how to provoke and select stories in the voice of each teller, such as a researcher, a writer, a subject, a reviewer, or an editor. It is the level of story creation. The second-level reflectivity tells the story that is closest to each of us as a researcher, writer, subject, editor, and reviewer. It is the level

of the ethical movement within each story. The third and final level is how to reflect on the hegemony in stories, as acted out on the micro-level, without stepping into the pitfall of our own hegemony. (Boje et al., 1999, p. 341)

Boje and colleagues' analysis, then, fully embraces the discourse of vulnerability as it rejects the "authority game" (J. Martin, 1992) of the distanced researcher, refusing to privilege any of the narrative voices that make up their account. Such privileging, they argue, "is an act of narrative power, if not a Nietschian [sic] will to power" (p. 358). Can such privileging be avoided? We argue that it cannot, for the refusal to privilege any voice is itself a hegemonic move, in that it disguises the very real and material ways in which authors/researchers always play a privileged role in the construction of the final, published account.

Other postmodern discourse analyses center the problematic of voice in what we see as more promising ways. Trujillo and colleagues' (Communication Studies 298, 1997) ethnography of a theme bar is much more straightforward than Boje and colleagues' study, in the sense that it largely reflects the multiple voices of the research team members and their various experiences of the research site. The emphasis here is on the polyglot character of the ethnographic experience and the way in which contemporary postmodern cultural forms (here, the multi-theme bar) fragment personal identity. On the other hand, J. Martin's (1990) deconstruction of a CEO's story about a pregnant project manager's choice to give birth by caesarean section shows how different voices can be embedded in the same organizational text. Through a Derridian analysis of oppositional terms and moments of presence and absence, she shows how the story privileges a patriarchal reading of the relation between work and private life, simultaneously marginalizing alternative, woman-centered meanings. Martin's analysis captures well the intertextuality of organizational discourse and the ways in which discourse constructs organizational subject positions in particular ways; specifically, the role of "mother" is defined in terms of, and subordinated to, the corporate goal of project completion. We will return to this particular analysis in Chapter 4.

Generally speaking, postmodern organizational discourse analyses address power and subjectivity as exclusively discursive phenomena. Researchers analyze organizational subject positions as constructed through multiple, intersecting, and often contradictory discourses that constitute work reality. Organization members are thought to negotiate an unstable, fragmented discursive environment with numerous interpretive possibilities and shifting meanings. Given the assumption that the politics of everyday organizing is largely a *textual* politics, scholars tend to focus on how different organizational interest groups discursively construct meanings and subject positions that reproduce those interests. Similarly, forms of resistance are construed textually, as researchers unpack discursive tactics employed by members to construct alternative readings of organizing processes. For example, Bell and Forbes (1994) examine "office folklore"—the sayings and cartoons that secretaries display in their office spaces—as forms of resistance to bureaucratic control. Here, the authors do not suggest that such textual resistance might lead to collective action or organizational change; rather, their focus is exclusively on a kind of semiotic, individualized resistance. In such analyses, resistance is framed as playful, parodic, and highly localized.

Postmodern analyses of the relations among discourse, power, and subjectivity thus get played out almost exclusively in the realm of the textual. As we develop a feminist communicology of organization, we aim to move beyond "text positivism" to interrogate the dynamic, dialectical relationship among power, discourse, identity, and the materiality of organizing (including its political, economic, and historical context). In the next section, we identify some of our concerns with the current state of postmodern organization studies, establishing a context for our discussion in the following chapter of the relationship between feminism and postmodernism.

❖ POSTMODERN LIMITATIONS FOR UNDERSTANDING GENDERED ORGANIZATION

As should be clear, our intent is not to adopt a postmodern perspective uncritically but to engage in constructive dialogue that clarifies the potential and limitations of postmodernism for the study of gendered organization. Perhaps most significant for our purposes, a dearth of postmodern work directly addresses the intersection of gender and organizing. Certainly, there are several writers who examine the intersection of feminism and postmodernism in organization studies (e.g., Knights, 1997; Mumby, 1996), as well as feminist organizational scholars who have adopted a postmodern or poststructuralist orientation to their work (e.g., Calás & Smircich, 1991, 1992b; J. Martin, 1990). And yet, we see no sustained and thematic body of literature—particularly empirical work—that explores the intersection of power, discourse, identity, and organizing from a postmodern feminist perspective. Given the veritable explosion of postmodern writings and feminist writing in organization studies scholarship, this lacuna is somewhat surprising. Scholars such as Newton (1998) and Knights (1997) go so far as to advocate a turn to feminist scholarship as a way to provide redress for the limitations of postmodern analyses, but feminist studies are assigned a relatively peripheral role in their respective arguments. Interestingly, feminist scholars in the U.S.-based field of organizational communication seem to have been more successful in this regard than have their European colleagues (e.g., Holmer Nadesan, 1996; Holmer Nadesan & Trethewey, 2000; Jorgenson, 2002; Trethewey, 1997, 1999b, 2001), and their work is examined in more detail in Chapter 4.

In addition, much of the postmodern organization studies literature seems to operate—despite calls to the contrary—with a rather dualistic conception of the relationship between control and resistance. Most studies focus either on the disciplinary mechanisms that subordinate employees to organizational control (e.g., Barker, 1999; Sewell & Wilkinson, 1992) or on the strategies and tactics that employees use to create temporary spaces of resistance (Bell & Forbes, 1994; Murphy, 1998). While the former presents organizational control as a relatively seamless process with little room for agency and resistance, the latter often reduces agency to individual efforts to subvert the totalizing system of control; collective forms of resistance and possibilities for social transformation are markedly absent in such work. In contrast, we adopt a dialectical conception of control and resistance in which each is implicated in the other. Such a perspective requires that we examine subjectivity not as unitary and coherent—as either resistant or oppressed—but, rather, as formed at the intersection of frequently competing discourses. Such a view of "process subjectivity" (Weedon, 1987) necessitates examination of the specific context in which forms of subjectivity emerge (e.g., Kondo, 1990).

Relatedly, the conception of subjectivity and identity proffered by postmodern scholarship remains relatively anemic. Indeed, Newton (1998) suggests that efforts to develop a postdualistic theory of organizing have actually resulted in the downplaying of agentic subjectivity rather than in an elision of the agency-structure dichotomy, and he attributes this failure to the Foucauldian analytics on which much of this research rests (e.g., Knights, 1990; Knights & Morgan, 1991;

Willmott, 1990, 1994). Newton argues that Foucault tends to present institutional discourse as subjectless, and—despite his claims that because power is everywhere, resistance is everywhere—to depict subjectivity as simply the effect of discourses. Missing from such analyses is an explication of the actual social processes through which the organization of identity occurs. While there are some exceptions to this tendency (e.g., Kondo, 1990), postmodern scholars have largely neglected the specific practices and processes of identity construction (Newton, 1998). For example, in studies where the focus is on particular management discourses and their normalization effects (e.g., Holmer Nadesan, 1997; Townley, 1993), there is often little or no effort to understand how members appropriate and experience such discourses. Likewise, when the agency of organization members assumes center stage, seldom are resistance tactics situated within the larger political economy and history of the workplace. Along with Newton, we maintain that efforts to develop a more robust conception of agency and identity do not require a return to some sort of essentialist theory of subjectivity but, instead, suggest a focus on "the social processes through which people actively manoeuvre in relation to discursive processes" (Newton, 1998, p. 426).

Finally, and consistent with this claim, we argue that one of the unfortunate consequences of the postmodern version of the "discursive turn" is a lack of concern for the materiality of organizing. While it is a fruitful and powerful move to examine organizations as discursive constructions, an epistemological blindspot has evolved wherein the extent to which organizations exert tangible effects on real, flesh-and-blood people gets frequently overlooked. We do not mean to regress to some revisionist form of positivism; ours is a call to attenuate the kind of "text positivism" in which many postmodernists engage. Sure, one can argue that there is "nothing outside of the text," but a reduction of organizations to pure text/discourse sidesteps the material consequences of organizational life for its members. Hence, Chapter 5 develops a position that examines how organizational discourse has profoundly real effects—how it constructs the material world. For example, we take interest in how organization members' bodies are discursively constructed and with what palpable consequences (Bordo, 1992, 1999; Hassard, Holliday, & Willmott, 2000). In this way, we aim to recognize relatively stable features of identity that exist in tension with the contingent, precarious features of agency.

❖ CONCLUSION

This chapter addressed the implications of postmodern theory for radical organization studies. The emergence of postmodern thought in the last 20 years has had a significant bearing on the development of organization theory and research, particularly on our understanding of organizations as discursively constructed. And yet, as we have shown in the last two chapters, the so-called discursive turn emerged out of modernist and postmodern social theory. While postmodern thought presents radical challenges to the modernist project, it can also be seen as an extension of that project—an effort to engage in modernism by other means.

Thus, just as modernism in its multiple strands provided us with important, constitutive features of a feminist communicology, so postmodern thought suggests amendments to that emerging framework. In particular, the postmodern conception of a discourse-based subjectivity that is complex, contradictory, and processual has significant implications for our conceptualization of communication and human identity formation. Moreover, the postmodern shift away from a sovereign model of power as domination to a productive model of power as discipline yields innovative approaches to the relationship among power, resistance, and gendered organizing.

Of course, conspicuous by its absence from this chapter is discussion of the relationship between feminism and postmodernism. Chapter 4 explores this intersection. There, we argue that feminist scholarship indicates several ways in which the limitations of postmodern thought—observed in the final section of this chapter—can be addressed.

4

Organizing at the Intersection of Feminism and Postmodernism

❖ ❖ ❖

Despite an understandable attraction to the (apparently) logical, orderly world of the Enlightenment, feminist theory more properly belongs in the terrain of postmodern philosophy. Feminist notions of self, knowledge, and truth are too contradictory to those of the Enlightenment to be contained within its categories.

—Flax (1990, p. 183)

Postmodernism is a masculine ideology based on a notion of consciousness as hostile, and an epistemology of negation which is one of separation, discontinuity and dismemberment. Narcissistic and romantic, these idéologues (late Enlightenment nominalists) imitate divine process. They are engaged in a process of disengagement. As such, it is not possible to reclaim or rehabilitate postmodernism for feminist uses.

—Brodribb (1992, pp. 19–20)

I n the previous two chapters, we examined the complex relationships among feminism, modernism, postmodernism, and organization studies. We argued that the modernist project is much more complex than commentators frequently make out, and that the relationship between modernism and feminism is full of tensions that both enable and constrain critical organization studies. Furthermore, we suggested that while the development of a postmodern turn in critical organization studies has advanced our understanding of organizations as discursive phenomena, such a turn has also limited critical efforts to understand organizing as material (albeit socially constructed) and constituted through dialectics of power and resistance.

This chapter examines these issues from a different angle by taking up the rather contested relationship between feminism and postmodernism. If the challenge to the "episteme of representation" concerns the relationship between voice and knowledge claims—who gets to make claims about whom using which epistemological frame—then we have to consider carefully the ways in which postmodernism and feminism intersect. Indeed, as the quotations that open this chapter suggest, there is no unified position among feminists regarding the relationship of feminism to postmodernism. One might even characterize feminism as negotiating a relationship between the emancipatory ideals of the modernist, Enlightenment grand narrative on the one hand, and postmodern appeals to local knowledge and multiple voices and truths on the other. Both present powerful yet ostensibly incommensurable trajectories for feminist praxis. However, we intend to show that articulating feminism and postmodernism together does not inevitably lead to a marginalizing of feminist voices; rather, it creates additional possibilities for their expression. Simultaneously, we suggest that postmodern thought is by no means some grand panacea for the difficulties that feminism confronts in its efforts to articulate strong political and epistemological voices.

How, then, might one bring feminism and postmodernism together in a productive manner? How do we both retain the insights of postmodern thought and suggest possibilities for the systematic critique of structures of power and domination? Below, we develop the beginnings of an answer to these questions by mapping the contours of the principal arguments made in favor of and against postmodern feminism. Does the attempt to bring together feminism and postmodernism provide a more powerful form of social critique, or are postmodernists simply manifesting "a neurotic symptom and scene of repression of women's claims for truth and justice" (Brodribb, 1992, p. 20) and, hence, appropriating feminism into the masculine "order of things"?

❖ FEMINISM AND POSTMODERNISM: CONVERGENCES AND DIVERGENCES

As Anne Balsamo (1987) has pointed out, there are certain affinities between feminism and postmodernism, in part because feminism has already challenged modernism on many of the same grounds as has postmodernism. For example, the postmodern "incredulity toward metanarratives" (Lyotard, 1984) has precedence in the feminist challenge to patriarchy as a "master narrative" (Balsamo, 1987). Similarly, the postmodern rejection of grand theorizing finds resonance in the feminist critique of the "totalizing vision of the male perspective" (Balsamo, 1987; see also Beauvoir, 1973).

At the same time, many feminists remain suspicious of postmodernism partly because of its apparent radical break with modernism and the articulation of a condition of "crisis." Balsamo (1987) encapsulates this sense of unease when she states,

> From a feminist perspective, the crises which preoccupy postmodernism do not appear as such, largely because the break between modernism and postmodernism is indistinct and arbitrary; patriarchal relations of domination have continued undeterred. Women's voices are still actively suppressed. Can we interpret postmodernism as an instance of patriarchy valorizing its own epistemological crises as a new cultural and historical age? (p. 69)

To what extent are these two positions incommensurable? Is it possible *both* to be highly suspicious of postmodernism and its efforts to undermine any notion of grand theorizing *and* at the same time to see it as providing possibilities for feminist critique and praxis? Here, we spend some time laying out both arguments, starting with the work of feminist theorists who proclaim a strong affinity to postmodern thought.

Postmodern Feminism

Postmodern feminism has emerged in the last 20 years in part as a response to some of the perceived limitations of second wave feminism.

In particular, postmodern feminists have seriously addressed the problems associated with the idea that to be a viable force for political and social change, feminism must be rooted in a homogeneous, singular notion of "woman." From the latter perspective, feminism's revolutionary potential is derived from a universal conception of women's shared experiences of domination in a patriarchal society. Such a perspective is exclusionary in its elision of difference and in its assumption of a single, monolithic feminine subjectivity rooted in a white, middle class conception of the world. Postmodern feminists have attempted to undermine the rather naive conception of knowledge and consciousness rooted in this essentialist perspective (Balsamo, 1987; Fraser & Nicholson, 1990; Lovibond, 1989; Nicholson, 1994a, 1994b; J. W. Scott, 1988). Indeed, Jane Flax (1992) has argued that postmodernism "calls into question the belief (or hope) that there is some form of innocent knowledge to be had" (p. 447). Echoing this sentiment, Linda Nicholson (1994a) states that "what postmodernism adds to feminism is an expansion of the widely held feminist dictum 'The personal is political' to include the dictum 'The epistemic is political,' as well" (p. 85).

In this sense, postmodern feminism calls into question the apparent complicity of the feminist movement with white, Western, patriarchal ways of knowing. As Flax's statement quoted at the beginning of this chapter suggests, Enlightenment thought and feminist studies are too contradictory for the latter to be able to articulate a coherent critique of patriarchy from within the former. Postmodern feminism thus represents an important challenge to feminism from within its own body of discourse. At its root, postmodern feminism as represented by writers such as Flax (1990, 1992), Butler (1990, 1991), and Nicholson (1990, 1994a, 1994b) challenges feminism to give up the "grandiose [Enlightenment] fantasies that have brought us to the brink of annihilation" (Flax, 1992, p. 460).

What, then, are some of the principal features of a postmodern feminism? Some feminist theorists argue that the conjuncture of feminism and postmodernism has allowed for an expansion of feminist concerns beyond issues of political practice and consciousness and into the realm of epistemology. Fraser and Nicholson (1990), for example, argue that the relationship between feminism and postmodernism is useful for both enterprises because each mitigates the other's respective weaknesses. Thus, postmodern thought has paid particularly close attention to the critique of foundational, metaphysical tendencies of much of Western philosophy, but without grounding such critique in political practice, while feminist thought has tended to privilege politics and social transformation, but with an attendant suspicion of arcane philosophical debates and grand theorizing. At a most general level, then, feminism and postmodernism provide counterbalances to tendencies in each to neglect the relationship between theory and politics. In short, postmodern feminism represents the intersection of politics and epistemology.

One way to explore the tension between feminism and postmodernism is to take up a central theme of postmodern discourse, variously referred to as the "death of man," or the "decentering of the subject." As we saw in Chapter 3, for postmodernism, the notion of an essential, natural human being that can be defined a priori is a humanist fiction that obscures how human identity is constructed through various discourses of power and knowledge. For someone like Foucault (1973), "man" is a fictive character who exists only through the functioning of certain epistemes that define objects of knowledge.

This theme of decentering of the subject has become a central(!) one for postmodern feminists. In particular, the notion of "woman" as a category that describes a stable, coherent, female identity has been critiqued extensively. Such a notion is seen as problematic for two reasons. First, it positions women as defined in terms of and subordinated to men and thus as "the second sex" (Beauvoir, 1973). Second, the notion of a stable category of woman suggests a universal basis for feminism, invoking an identity politics that is exclusionary in its vision of resistance and empowerment. Thus, postmodern feminists argue that any feminism built upon an essentialist, Enlightenment conception of subjectivity inevitability reproduces the attendant limitations of such thinking. For example, second wave feminism—with its strongly middle class, white, heterosexual conception of women's liberation— is built upon the acceptance of patriarchal definitions of identity, autonomy, and participation in the good life.

If the notion of a centered, rational, autonomous subjectivity is problematic for postmodern feminists, what alternatives do they suggest? Judith Butler (1991) argues that the idea of decentering the subject is not the same thing as completely negating the very concept and possibility of a subject. She suggests that postmodern feminism focus on the processes by which particular forms of subjectivity are privileged; that is, whose interests are served by the construction of one form of subjectivity over another? Butler (1991) asserts that

> To deconstruct the subject of feminism is not . . . to censure its usage, but, on the contrary, to release the term into a future of multiple significations, to emancipate it from the maternal and racialist ontologies to which it has been restricted, and to give it play as a site where unanticipated meanings may come to bear. (p. 160)

Postmodern feminism therefore does not reject the category of the subject but, rather, interrogates its foundation. Such a move is clearly consistent with Derrida's attempt to situate rather than destroy the subject. For feminists like Flax, decentering the subject leads to a fundamental shift in thinking about the feminist project. Rather than locating emancipation in a grand narrative like "mothering," or in some unitary notion of "woman," Flax contends that feminism should be concerned more appropriately with gender relations and the processes through which masculine and feminine subjectivities are jointly constructed through gendered relations of power. This framing of the feminist project is central to our feminist communicology, as we explain in Chapter 5, and Chapter 6 examines the co-construction of feminine and masculine subjectivities in the airline industry. In this sense, we draw attention to the ways in which both women and men are "prisoners of gender" in their subordination to patriarchal constructions of subjectivities (Flax, 1990, pp. 179–183).

Flax therefore sees the principal goal of feminism as one of introducing more instability, complexity, and disorderliness into our conceptions of reality than currently exist. In this way, we can begin to unfreeze the stability of the gender categories that, postmodern feminists argue, are articulated through patriarchal discourses that shape our understanding of difference. Like Butler, Flax does not view the feminist project as one of the complete negation of the category of the subject. Instead, Flax (1990) suggests that feminist theorists

> have a special interest in constructing concepts of self that do justice to the full complexity of subjectivity and the spaces in which it is likely to find itself. It is possible and more desirable to construct such concepts of subjectivity than to 'repress our intuitions of it' or abandon the subject altogether. (p. 219)

Postmodern feminism puts into crisis the notion of a centered, stable subject within the larger context of the interrogation of Western models of truth, power, and knowledge. In recent years, a number of feminist scholars have explored the possibilities for the development of a Foucauldian feminism that investigates and critiques the gendered character of such models (Diamond & Quinby, 1988; B. Martin, 1982; McNay, 1992; Sawicki, 1991). Diamond and Quinby (1988) identify four points of convergence of feminist theory and research and Foucault's genealogical project. First, both identify the body as a site of power through which a docile subject is constituted. Second, both focus on the local and micro-level operations of power rather than on the supreme power of the state. Third, both foreground the role of discourse and its connection to hegemonic systems of power, as well as the possibilities for the challenges to such power that exist in marginalized discourses. Finally, both critique the ways in which Western humanist thought has privileged the knowledge claims of the Western masculine elite and its universal notions of truth, freedom, and human nature (Diamond & Quinby, 1988, p. x).

This interest in Foucault among feminists has emerged partly in response to the oversimplification of the relationship between patriarchy and capitalism suggested by much feminist work (B. Martin, 1982). In effect, Foucauldian feminism critiques the unreflective appropriation of the sovereign model of power that, Foucault suggests, is reflected in Marxist theories of the state. While Marxist models of power tend to treat the state and capital as the origin of a negative, coercive form of power imposed from above, Foucault argues that political theory should "cut off the head of the sovereign," developing in its place a productive, micro model that explores the various sites of power that emerge from below.

For feminism, a Foucauldian analytics provides a way to examine gender, the body, and sexuality as the products of discursive practices that construct docile individuals. For example, Foucault's (1980a) genealogy of discourses on sexuality does not search out the "truth" about sex, but shows how, particularly in the 19th century, sexuality becomes an object of study and thus subject to a particular game of truth. The key question is therefore what is at stake in the construction of the body as a regulatable machine and the concomitant development of a biopolitics that governs acceptable sexual behavior.

For a number of feminist theorists, Foucault's analytics of power provides important insights into the processes through which Western epistemology is linked intimately to the historical disciplining of women as subject effects. In Foucault's sense, the creation of a disciplinary, panoptical society produces various apparatuses (both discursive and nondiscursive) that position women as "the object of information, never a subject in communication" (Foucault, 1979, p. 200). At the same time, however, the coming together of feminism and postmodernism represents a place of resistance from which to undermine the homocentrism and hierarchy of Western thought and to rewrite the relations among gender, knowledge, and power.

Susan Hekman (1990, 1997) takes up precisely this task in her articulation of a postmodern feminism. Hekman views feminism and postmodernism as the only contemporary theories that provide a radical alternative to Enlightenment thought. In fact, she claims that a feminist perspective that retains any of the basic principles of modernism will inevitably reproduce the hierarchical, masculinist epistemologies upon which the Enlightenment was founded. Modernist thought, she argues, is structured around the dichotomous pairs of rational/irrational, culture/nature, and subject/object. In each case, masculine ways of knowing and being are associated with the former term, while feminine ways of knowing and being are associated with the latter term. Any modernist feminism is faced with the choice either of accepting these masculinist dichotomies and attempting to open up the privileged term to women (as with liberal feminism) or of reversing the valence of the dichotomies and valorizing the previously marginalized term (as with radical feminism). As Hekman and others have argued, both strategies reproduce the dichotomous modes of thinking that structured women's oppression in the first place. Thus, for example, radical feminism's appeal to an essentialist, universal feminine nature (e.g., Daly, 1978) privileges the biological superiority of women, hence reifying the culture/nature dichotomy upon which patriarchy is partially based.

Hekman's third, postmodern alternative is to abandon altogether epistemology in the traditional sense of the term. By deconstructing the basic dichotomies of humanist, Enlightenment thought, it becomes possible to explore the ways in which women's oppression is rooted in discourse. From her perspective, there are three dimensions to the postmodern feminist critique of male discourses of domination (Hekman, 1990, p. 187). First, Hekman argues that we need to understand how the feminine has been constituted in the first place as inferior. Thus, following Foucault, she suggests the development of a "critical ontology of ourselves [i.e., women]" (p. 187) that aids in the disruption of the accepted categories. In many respects, this has been a major and ongoing project within feminism, as feminist scholars seek to recuperate those feminine voices that have been assigned to the margins of history (e.g., Campbell, 1989; Spitzack & Carter, 1987).

Second, Hekman advocates an exploration of the limits of male discourses and the discursive terrain beyond them. Here, the role of postmodern feminism is to explore the silences and ambiguities of discourse and to revise accepted truths. In organization studies, for example, the deconstructive work of Calás and Smircich (Calás, 1992; Calás & Smircich, 1991, 1992a, 1993) explores the limits of androcentric theorizing. The point is to show that the discourse of organization theory has, for the most part, articulated a single, monolithic grand narrative that privileges a rational, neutral, masculine voice.

Finally, Hekman argues for the articulation of feminist discourses that constitute femininity, masculinity, and sexuality in different ways. Certainly, this project is in its nascent state in feminist studies, but there are nevertheless some scholars who are pursuing such work. For example, Butler's (1990) model of gender as "performative" suggests how sexuality and identity can be reconceptualized. Furthermore, masculinity research has both critiqued and deconstructed the idea of "hegemonic masculinity" and considered how masculinity itself can be rethought (e.g., Connell, 1993, 1995; Hearn, 1996; Hearn & Collinson, 1994).

In sum, many feminists recognize postmodern thought as a powerful epistemological and political framework that provides a much-needed corrective to feminist theory and research that is still constrained by the limitations of Enlightenment thought. The "view from nowhere" that characterizes much of modernist theorizing is replaced with a radical interrogation of systems of rationality that attempt to root knowledge in foundational principles. In addition, the refusal of a stable, taken-for-granted subjectivity opens up the possibilities for rethinking the relations among gender, identity, power, and knowledge. Postmodern feminists see revolutionary potential in the multiplicity of voices that emerge through decentering the (male) subject of reason that Enlightenment thought valorizes and reifies. Jana Sawicki (1991) sums up the possibilities of a postmodern (particularly a Foucauldian) feminism in the following manner:

Women are produced by patriarchal power at the same time that they resist it. There are good reasons to be ambivalent about the liberatory possibilities of appealing to "reason," "motherhood," or the "feminine" when they have also been the source of our oppression. Even the recent history of feminism in the late twentieth century suggests that feminism has often been blind to the dominating tendencies of its own theories and to the broader social forces that undermine and redirect its agendas. (pp. 101–102)

However, the attempt to develop a postmodern feminism has not been taken up with great alacrity by all feminists. As we noted earlier, postmodern efforts to undermine the modernist proclivity for normative foundations have been met by often-intense criticism from various quarters (e.g., Benhabib, 1990, 1991; Brodribb, 1992; Callinicos, 1990; Eagleton, 1995; Ebert, 1996; Stabile, 1995; E. M. Wood, 1995). Many theorists have seriously questioned the ability of postmodernism to provide a coherent, normative, and sustainable agenda for feminist theory and politics. We now turn to a closer examination of these concerns.

Feminism Contra Postmodernism

As we suggested in Chapter 3, a number of writers argue that postmodern theory represents a capitulation to capitalism in its neglect of the material, historical grounding for systems of oppression. The shift away from systemic analyses of the connections among capitalism, power, poverty, and the possibilities for collective, revolutionary action has led to "a deep epistemological skepticism and a profound political defeatism" on the part of postmodernists (E. M. Wood, 1995, p. 9). Some Marxists claim that the postmodern rejection of "totalizing" narratives and collective emancipatory politics allows capitalism to be unproblematically reproduced (Callinicos, 1990; Eagleton, 1995; Stabile, 1995). The postmodern refusal to oppose systematic oppression with methodical, materially grounded analysis forecloses ways to think against capitalism. Moreover, Ellen Wood (1995) argues that much of postmodern thought reflects a basic contradiction; namely, the declaration of epochal novelty coupled with the denial of a fundamental historical reality—"that all the ruptures of the twentieth century have been bound together in a single historical unity by the logic . . . of capitalism, the system that dies a thousand deaths" (1995, p. 4).

From a feminist perspective, postmodernism becomes suspect for undermining a coherent feminist politics based in claims about equality and justice. Stabile (1995), for example, argues that postmodernism culminates in a "lifestyle" politics of consumption and individualism, negating any politics grounded in common interests and collective struggle. By abstracting "rights" from their historical, political, and economic contexts, postmodernism has weakened feminist struggle, fostering the suspicion that it serves only narrow interests. Stabile proposes instead a feminist perspective anchored in historical materialism—a position that declares women's liberation incompatible with capitalism. According to Stabile, a historical materialist perspective

> offers the possibility of coalitions based on a broader understanding of the exploitative nature of capitalist relations of production, enlisting women and men in struggles against family violence, further cuts to already severely diminished social programs, and moreover, against the system that benefits from these ills. (Stabile, 1995, p. 104)

A second critique centers on the putative postmodern "death of the subject." As we mentioned earlier, several feminists are disturbed by the fact that just as women seem to be gaining a strong sense of agency, subjectivity, and collective identity, along come (male) postmodernists to declare that there's no such thing as the subject after all (Hartsock, 1996). Seyla Benhabib (1990, 1991, 1992) offers one of the most coherent accounts of incompatibility between the "death of the subject" thesis and the goals of feminism. Describing the relationship between feminism and postmodernism as "an uneasy alliance," Benhabib (1991) argues that, while she concedes the structuring of subjectivity through language and symbols, the leap from this idea to the notion that subjectivity is the *effect* of discourse is highly problematic for feminists. Criticizing Butler's (1990) performative model of gender, Benhabib (1991) asks,

> If we are no more than the sum total of the gendered expressions we perform, is there ever any chance to stop the performance for a while, to pull the curtain down, and only let it rise if one can have a say in the production of the play itself? Isn't this what the struggle over gender is all about? (p. 140)

In this way, Benhabib turns Butler's own performativity metaphor against her to stress the importance of agency and autonomy for feminism. In Benhabib's eyes, Butler is replacing an engendered (i.e., agentic) subjectivity with one that is fractured and opaque. This denial of coherence elides "the doer behind the deed" and makes a virtue out of a necessity. In other words, it is precisely because women have so often had their histories written for them by men, and because women have so rarely controlled the conditions of their own existence, that postmodern visions of fragmented, discursive, subjects-as-effects makes feminists like Benhabib uneasy.

Ultimately, Benhabib (1992) argues, postmodernism signals for feminism a "retreat from utopia" (p. 229). While postmodernism has usefully demonstrated how foundational thinking and utopianism can go wrong, as well as how consensus can yield its own form of terror (Lyotard, 1984), such critique should not lead to the wholesale rejection of all metanarratives. The key question then becomes, can feminism ally with postmodernism and still remain emancipatory? Can the celebration of fragmentation, difference, and local, situated knowledge be something other than parochial and always subject to the recuperative powers of commodity capitalism (Bordo, 1992, p. 172)?

Susan Bordo (1993) offers a spin on the issue that is critical of the sort of "gender skepticism" that characterizes the work of Butler and other postmodern theorists. Like Benhabib, Bordo is sympathetic to the premise that gender is discursively constructed and exists in complex, unstable relationships to race and class; at the same time, she expresses concern that gender as an analytic category is losing its potential for critique and transformation. That is, the postmodern shift toward difference and ceaseless textual play tends to forget that such difference (and the forms of resistance that emerge from it) is embedded in actual material and historical circumstances. Critiquing the "text positivism" discussed in the previous chapter, Bordo (1993) suggests that, "intoxicated with the interpretive and creative *possibilities* of cultural analysis, [postmodernists] neglect to ask themselves what is actually going on in the culture around them" (p. 295).

In regard to Butler's work, for example, Bordo (1993) argues that her world "is one in which language swallows everything up, voraciously, a theoretical pasta machine through which the categories of competing frameworks are pressed and reprocessed as 'tropes'" (p. 291). From this perspective, according to Bordo, the daily social practices in which people engage are neglected. The body (the focus of Bordo's scholarship), for instance, is not an abstract text that is purely linguistic in its performativity—any "difference" that it displays occurs in the context of social dynamics that shape meaning, power, and resistance. Thus Bordo (1993) writes, "The pleasure and power of 'difference,' I would once again insist against postmodern theorists, is hard-won; it does not bloom freely, insistently nudging its way through the cracks of dominant forms" (p. 299).

In the critiques of scholars like Benhabib and Bordo, then, we see tensions between modernist notions of identity and postmodern conceptions of difference. For Benhabib and Bordo alike, the celebration of difference and resulting gender skepticism give rise to ahistorical analyses that obscure how women's identities and resistance tactics have been forged out of specific, material systems of power. Ironically, Bordo (1993) suggests, the postmodern effort to honor multiple voices and to undermine the Cartesian conception of truth as a "view from nowhere" has resulted in an equally transcendent "view from everywhere," in which an "infinitely perspectival, destabilized world" (p. 226) is the norm. From within such a framework, postmodernists "refuse to assume a shape for which they must take responsibility" (p. 228) and with which one can dialogue. Transformative knowledge becomes completely fluid and limitless in its multiplicity and, hence, perhaps meaningless.

A third feminist critique of postmodern thought hinges on a concern that postmodern feminism reduces feminism to a focus on questions of knowledge and epistemology rather than those of power and justice. The concern is captured well in an exchange in the feminist journal *Signs* between Susan Hekman and a number of feminist standpoint scholars. Hekman (1997) criticizes feminist standpoint theory, contending that it rests on an objectivist conception of the world, which depicts women as having "truer" access to reality than do men. Such a theory roots women's epistemologically privileged position in their experience of oppression in a patriarchal society—a move Hekman thinks is untenable for several reasons. First, it creates a dichotomy between "reality" (women's world) and "concepts" (men's world), which it then resolves by embracing the former and rejecting the latter. Hekman finds this position self-defeating, given the interdependence of both; that is, embracing one means acknowledging the epistemological validity of the other. Second, Hekman claims that the world is discursively constructed, and that any attempt to assert direct access to the truth about this world ignores the processes through which all "truths"—masculine and feminine—are mediated by discourse. Finally, if standpoint theory, in response to criticisms from feminists of color, recognizes the multiplicity of women's positionality, does this mean that there are multiple truths (theoretically, as many truths as women to articulate these truths)? It follows that standpoint theory potentially undermines the possibility of a coherent, cohesive feminist politics (Hekman, 1997, p. 349).

Consistent with her earlier work (Hekman, 1990), Hekman (1997) recasts feminist standpoint theory in a postmodern frame. She argues that, despite its limitations, postmodernism "represents the beginning of a paradigm shift in the concept of knowledge, a shift that is transforming not only feminist theory but also epistemology itself" (p. 342). Hekman (1997) claims that we should use a Kuhnian rather than a Marxist framework to make sense of standpoint theory, since it amounts to an epistemological break with modernism: "Feminist standpoint theory defines knowledge as particular rather than universal; it jettisons the neutral observer of modernist epistemology; it defines subjects as constructed by relational forces rather than as transcendent" (p. 356). Ultimately, Hekman (1997) argues, the point of feminism is to change "the language game of politics" (p. 363), and reading feminist standpoint theory from a postmodern perspective aids in this goal by articulating a counter-hegemonic discourse at once engaged and situated.

Although there are a number of responses to Hekman's article (Harding, 1997; Hartsock, 1997; Hill Collins, 1997; D. Smith, 1997), we limit our attention here to those that are most relevant. In one such response, Nancy Hartsock (1997) expresses discomfort with Hekman's focus on matters of truth and epistemology. The point of standpoint theory, she argues, is to understand power relations, particularly those "centered on the development of capitalism and the commodification of increasingly greater areas of human experience (p. 370). In this light, Marx's critique of capitalism remains extremely germane to late 20th-century social conditions. By appropriating Marxism as a global theory through which to frame issues of truth, subjectivity, and privileged knowledge claims, the focus shifts from individual standpoints to macroprocesses of power and their role in the construction of truth and subjectivity. Accordingly, the bases for valuing some knowledge claims over others (i.e., particular standpoints) shift from epistemological to ethical and political criteria. Hence, Hartsock (1997) claims, some forms of knowledge can be privileged over others (a decidedly nonpostmodern notion in itself) because they "offer possibilities for envisioning more just social relations," as well as transforming individuals into "resistant, oppositional, and collective subjects" (p. 373).

Patricia Hill Collins is equally critical of Hekman's "epistemological" reading of standpoint theory. Again focusing on Hekman's elision of power as a central issue, Hill Collins argues that the attempt to identify criteria for the "truest" standpoint obscures the fact that standpoint theory concerns itself with historically shared group experiences. As Hill Collins (1997) states,

> Bracketing the question of power and restricting argument solely to the question of truth certainly reveals the limitations of using epistemological criteria in defense of privileged standpoints. But within the reality of hierarchical power relations, the standpoint of some groups are most certainly privileged over others. The amount of privilege granted to a particular standpoint lies less in its internal criteria in being truthful, the terrain in which Hekman situates her discussion, and more in the power of a group in making its standpoint prevail over other equally plausible perspectives. (p. 381)

For Hill Collins (1997), any attempt to extract knowledge claims from the power relations out of which they emerge undercuts the basic purpose of standpoint theory: to explicate the configuration of power relations that result in privileging certain forms of knowledge and thus to create possibilities for alternative knowledge forms and "cultures of resistance" (p. 381).

Principally, Hekman draws criticism for reducing the primary impetus of feminist standpoint theory to issues of epistemology. Interestingly, Harding (1997) accuses Hekman of an "administrator perspective" that tries to adjudicate between "culturally local people, with their conflicting perspectives, claims, and demands" (p. 387). And ironically, such an attempt at adjudication seems an intrinsically modernist move. As Harding (1997) asks rhetorically, "Whose locations, interests, discourses, and ways of organizing the production of knowledge are silenced and suppressed by taking the administrative standpoint on standpoint theory that Hekman centers?" (p. 389).

Having sketched broad points of convergence and divergence in the relationship between feminism and postmodernism, we are ready to delve further into that relationship as manifest in the context of organization studies. The next section explores the question, how does postmodern feminist organization studies engage and problematize the relationships among gender, discourse, power, and organization? We are particularly interested in how this work approaches identity as discursively constructed in mundane contexts and routine performances of power, resistance, and organizing.

❖ ORGANIZING GENDER:
A POSTMODERN FEMINIST PERSPECTIVE

One of the basic premises underlying this book is that gender is not simply one feature of organizing that may be addressed or ignored; rather, it is a basic, constitutive feature of organization. As we explained in Chapter 1 (see especially our discussion of frames 2 and 3), organization members "do" gender, thus creating "gendered organizations" in the moment-to-moment (Gherardi, 1994). As one iteration of this perspective, postmodern feminism represents a political and epistemological effort to shape our thinking about organizational life. Epistemologically, postmodern feminism is an attempt to break the last few bonds of a foundationalist position that seeks to discover the truth about organizational life generally, or about gender specifically. With postmodern feminism, gender is both constitutive of organizing and a contingent condition that has no essence. Scholars in this vein "play" with and deconstruct gender, adopting it as a strategic construct to reveal certain truth effects, which emanate from the construction of gender as a difference that shapes lives in meaningful ways.

Politically, postmodern feminism explores how discourses of difference create and are created by certain forms of power-knowledge. Not neutral, the discursive construction of gendered identities positions people within networks of power, privileging some identities and marginalizing others. One of the goals of postmodern feminist scholarship is to destabilize, through deconstructive efforts, the sedimentation of forms of difference that fashion women as "other" within this network of power. As accepted forms of gender identity become disrupted, possibilities for alternative, and perhaps more liberatory, conceptions of self come open. This move is meant not to replace one dominant system with another but, rather, to render troublesome *any* attempt at a foundational way of thinking about gender and organizations. The process of deconstructing gender involves "stepping back from the opposition of male and female in order to loosen the hold of gender on life and meaning and [thus] rendering gender more fragile, more tenuous, and less salient both as an explanatory and as an evaluative category" (Ferguson, 1993, p. 4).

Ferguson's words summarize quite succinctly much of the postmodern feminist research in organization studies to date. Some of this work operates at a metatheoretical level, aiming to destabilize extant organization theory on the grounds that, under the guise of scientific objectivity and neutrality, it typically smuggles in patriarchal conceptions of knowledge that privilege masculinist worldviews (e.g., Calás & Smircich, 1991, 1992a, 1993). Other work politicizes the workplace itself, variously illustrating how gendered identities are assembled at the nexus of discursive relations of power and resistance (Bell & Forbes, 1994; Holmer Nadesan, 1996; J. Martin, 1990; Trethewey, 1997, 1999b).

In addition, some researchers have examined specific corporate discourses to expose how they function as forms of knowledge and discipline that shape organization members' gendered identities in ever more subtle ways. Postmodern analyses of personality testing (Holmer Nadesan, 1997), human resource management (Townley, 1993), and discourses of consumerism and entrepreneurialism (Holmer Nadesan, 1999; Holmer Nadesan & Trethewey, 2000) address the ways in which such discourses (en)gender subjects that are more amenable to capitalist forms of control.

Finally, postmodern feminist organization scholars have focused on the body and sexuality as an important and contested "terrain" of organizing. The shift to a focus on the body is an effort to transcend the Cartesian mind-body dualism, theorizing both gendered organization as embodied practice and workers' bodies as gendered social constructions (e.g., Brewis, Hampton, & Linstead, 1997; Dale, 2001; Hassard, Holliday, & Willmott, 2000; Trethewey, 1999a, 2001). This work, for example, examines the intersection of gender and sexuality and challenges the modernist idea that organizations banish the erotic from daily life (Burrell, 1992; Gherardi, 1995). Organizations are read as sites of control where sexuality and the erotic are never quite fully disciplined and suppressed by modernist forms of bureaucratic rationality (e.g., Pringle, 1989).

In broad terms, postmodern feminist organizational scholarship addresses the intersection of power, discourse, and the construction of gendered organizational identities. Research focuses on how organizational discourse produces gendered subject effects in the workplace. Such discourses may originate in particular workplaces or, as explained in Chapter 1's discussion of frame 4, may be part of broader cultural or academic discourses that shape identities both at and beyond the workplace (Fletcher, 1998, 1999; J. Martin, 1990; Martin, Knopoff, & Beckman, 1998; Townsley & Geist, 2000; Trethewey, 1997). Much of this work has a strongly Foucauldian flavor to it, with considerable emphasis on illustrating a disciplinary, productive conception of power.

A tricky issue in much of this work is the question of agency. While Foucauldian-inspired research makes a strong link between discourse and the production of subject identities, the tendency is to theorize such identities as the effects of discourse, with little room for human agency. A central concern for us is the extent to which postmodern feminist organization scholarship is able to articulate a discursive conception of identity and power, while at the same time avoiding the pitfalls of Foucauldian analytics and its rather anemic conception of human agency. Regardless of the feminist perspective adopted, the elision of an adequate theory of agency appears to obviate its worth as a mode of feminist praxis, given the raison d'être of feminism.

In the remainder of this section, we address more systematically the growing body of postmodern feminist organization research and consider its contribution to our understanding of organization as gendered. We also critique key limitations of this work in preparing to articulate a feminist communicology of organization in Chapter 5.

Postmodern Feminist Critiques of Mainstream Organization Theory

At the outset of Chapter 2, we stated that feminist organization scholars have rarely explicitly engaged in the metatheoretical debates that have characterized the field of organization studies for the last 20 years. We now clarify that argument somewhat. In one sense at least, feminist scholars have entered that debate via the deconstruction of existing research, focusing on theories and constructs that have played a significant role in shaping the landscape of management and organization studies (Calás, 1992; Calás & Smircich, 1991, 1992a; K. Ferguson, 1994; Leonard, 2002; Mumby & Putnam, 1992; Putnam & Mumby, 1993). Such work tends to operate largely as a response to the current scholarly terrain, with little sustained effort to rework that terrain. In broad terms, these deconstructions show how the rhetorical/theoretical practices of organization theory and research are closely connected to the representational practices of organizational decision making and behavior. The underlying premise holds that how scholarship gets done significantly affects whose voices are heard in the workplace. In feminist terms, deconstructive analyses address the gendered character of the relationship between the representational practices of scholarship and those of the corporation. In Chapter 1's discussion of frame 4, we introduced writings of this sort; here, we briefly return to those feminist analyses of scholarly discourse for a few illustrative examples.

The work of Marta Calás and Linda Smircich (1991, 1992a, 1992b) explores how extant organizational theory and knowledge can be critiqued and rewritten from feminist perspectives. Through deconstructive analyses, they explore how gender is systematically written into organizational theorizing, even in theory or research contexts where gender issues are not explicitly identified. Their strategy is both to problematize gender and to demonstrate the ways in which it is represented, suppressed, and marginalized through the process of theory and research. For example, in their deconstruction of organizational leadership texts, Calás and Smircich (1991) juxtapose the idea of seduction against the construct of leadership. By providing "seductive" readings of leadership models (through the rhetorical device of a split page), they "analyze the dependency of supposedly opposite concepts on one another and [show] how rhetoric and cultural conditions work together to conceal this dependency" (p. 569). In this way, they are able to "question the limits that may have been imposed on discourses of knowledge, and [open] the possibility of enacting other, different, discourses" (p. 569).

Mumby and Putnam (1992; Putnam & Mumby, 1993) pursue a similarly deconstructive route in their analysis of Herbert Simon's (1976) concept of "bounded rationality." In this instance, deconstruction is employed to illustrate how the concept of bounded rationality—despite its efforts to mitigate the modernist notion of organizations as purely rational structures—draws on heavily gendered notions that privilege particular organizational forms and structures and marginalize others. Specifically, hierarchy, means-end chains of decision making, instrumental reasoning, fragmentation of labor, and mind-body dualisms are shown to underpin Simon's construct. Mumby and Putnam conduct this deconstruction by juxtaposing against "bounded rationality" the notion of "bounded emotionality"—an invented term used in a strategic manner to generate a "play of difference." By placing these two concepts in a dialectical relationship, the analysis accomplishes two things: (1) It makes visible the hidden, deferred meanings upon which the definition of bounded rationality depends; and (2) it highlights possibilities for an alternative mode of organizing based on the construction of intersubjective meanings, an integration of mind and body, work as community, tolerance of ambiguity, and nonhierarchical goals and values. Importantly, Mumby and Putnam deconstruct the polarity of rationality and emotionality, illustrating how concepts can be conceived as interdependent and dialectical rather than oppositional.

Postmodern feminist deconstructions of mainstream organization theory provide important insight into the politics of theory and epistemology, revealing the ways in which theory development is grounded in frequently unexamined and gendered assumptions about the character of knowledge claims. And yet, while useful, such analyses offer only a limited starting point for the sort of communication model in which we are interested. As we noted above, deconstructive work tends to respond to existing theory, engaging metatheoretical debates reactively. Little of this early work attempts to proactively construct alternative metatheoretical and theoretical standpoints. In contrast, we argue that feminist organization studies is sufficiently developed to articulate its own metatheoretical voice(s) and to develop new conceptual stances. The chief goal of our project is to do precisely that by articulating a feminist communicology of organization. Moreover, because they generally operate at an exclusively metatheoretical level, feminist deconstructions are only indirectly related to the ongoing practices of daily organizational life. While they destabilize the ways in which such life is theorized and implicitly *represented*, it takes a considerable leap to make claims about the impact of such theorizing on the actual experiences of organization members.

In addition, there is little or no sense of human agency in most feminist deconstructions. Although the analyses enhance understanding of the politics of theorizing, they cannot shed light on how real people engage with theory as it becomes manifest in concrete organizational settings. For example, while theoretical models of leadership are available for deconstruction by academics, and may indeed be masculinist in their assumptions, (how) are such theories appropriated by managers and other employees? Is there some kind of inevitable (causal?) connection between the tacit assumptions of management theories and the ways in which they are taken up in organizational practice?

Finally, deconstructive analyses are generally guilty of the "text positivism" described in Chapter 3. That is, they treat organization as exclusively textual, taking seriously Derrida's proposition that there is "nothing outside of the text." Once again, it is difficult to imagine how text translates into the organizing process, since textual analyses treat theories and constructs in a rather static, desiccated form. For example, in practice, might there be overlap or slippage between Mumby and

Putnam's theoretical conception of "bounded emotionality" and the corporate practice of emotional labor and rationalization of feelings that Hochschild (1983) critiques (see Ashcraft, 2000; J. Martin et al., 1998)?

In sum, while feminist deconstructions of mainstream organization theory compellingly demonstrate the close connection between power and knowledge, they are unable to provide more than a kind of structural analysis of the ways in which particular power-knowledge discourses are configured. In the next section, we address postmodern feminist analyses that are concerned explicitly with the relationships among discourse, power, and identity as they are enacted in the organizing process.

Power, Discourse, and Organizational Identity

In the last few years, postmodern feminist research has moved beyond metatheoretical deconstructions to the empirical examination of gendered organizing processes. While it is not our intent to treat this work monolithically, we do wish to mark certain features that recur across different interests and empirical foci. First, given their rejection of epistemological foundationalism, postmodern feminist researchers seek not to discover truths about gendered organizing but to show how gender is constructed in particular ways with partial truth effects. Second, because gender is regarded as having no essence, postmodern feminists attempt to understand how gender is constructed through intersecting mechanisms of discourse, power, and organizing. Relatedly, postmodern feminist scholars assume that the discursive process of gender construction is beset by complexities and contradictions that undermine coherent, unitary, and fixed identities. Finally, postmodern feminists focus on the dynamics of discourse, power, and resistance as they articulate organizational realities and identities; the analytic goal is to destabilize gender as a construct in an effort to better understand its role in disciplinary systems of difference and power. Following Britton (2000), the goal of such research is to move beyond the claim that organizations are inherently gendered and to deepen what it means to make such a claim; in short, what are the dynamics of the gendered organization?

One of the earliest examples of a feminist postmodern analysis is Martin's (1990) deconstruction of a single organizational story. Her focus is on narrative as a political resource that constructs gendered identities in ways that reproduce extant relations of (patriarchal) power. The story itself—told by the CEO of a multinational corporation at a conference on the relationship between corporations and social problems—is as follows:

> We have a young woman who is extraordinarily important to the launching of a major new (product). We will be talking about it next Tuesday in its first world wide introduction. She has arranged to have her Caesarean yesterday in order to be prepared for this event, so you—We have insisted that she stay home and this is going to be televised in a closed circuit television, so we're having this done by TV for her, and she is staying home three months and we are finding ways of filling in to create this void for us because we think it's an important thing for her to do. (J. Martin, 1990, p. 339)

Interestingly, the CEO tells this story as an example of his company's sensitivity to gender issues. Martin's method is deconstructive, examining the play of presence and absence in the story as text. Her intent is to show that the meaning of the story (and hence its configuration of gendered meanings) is not simply self-evident and fully present but, instead, relies on a complex interplay between present and absent terms. Through deconstructive techniques such as dismantling dichotomies that are embedded in the story (e.g., between the public and private realms), examining silences (e.g., exclusions implicit in the use of "we"), and attending to narrative disruptions (e.g., "filling in to create this void"), Martin illustrates how—far from illustrating the beneficence of the company's policies toward women employees—the story contains reactionary understandings of the gendered workplace by suppressing gender conflicts that might otherwise enable a rethinking of extant organizational power relations.

Martin's deconstruction is an important effort to unpack the complex relationships among narrative, gendered identity, power, and organizing. Indeed, the analysis is able to demonstrate the power of everyday storytelling to produce and reproduce a discursive reality that fixes identities and meanings in mundane ways. Power is perhaps most insidiously (and innocently) exercised in this banal manner. However, Martin's analysis can also be read to practice the sort of text positivism to which we referred above. Although her focus is an actual organizational story, the story itself is analyzed as a static organizational artifact—as pure text—ripped from its narrative and organizational context. Interestingly, in a short appendix, Martin provides a transcript of the conference facilitator's comments that immediately preceded the telling of the story, and then she states that the story itself elicited in the audience a mixture of approving nods and hisses of disgust. However, she makes no attempt to incorporate this observation into her analysis. This is unfortunate because, as we all intuitively grasp, stories are dynamic, living discursive phenomena that are told and heard by real, flesh-and-blood bodies who make sense of them in diverse ways. Through their diverse reactions, in fact, members of the conference audience seemed to confirm what Martin's analysis suggests (albeit in a more complex fashion)—that stories can be understood and appropriated in different ways, some of which reproduce the status quo, and some of which challenge and even transform it. Unwittingly, then, Martin demonstrates the "absent presence" in her own analysis— namely, the recipients of the story who variously make sense of it in the context of lived relations of power and meaning (i.e., a conference at a major university, with a powerful CEO given a forum to speak to a relatively passive audience of academics and practitioners). Unfortunately, the deconstructive method employed means that we only get to hear the voice of the author as she makes sense of a text stripped of its narrative and social context. Any sense of agency is confined to the author and to the CEO's heavy-handed efforts to position his company as humanitarian in its attitudes toward women employees.

More recent feminist postmodern analyses have been more successful in their efforts to capture the dynamics of gendered organizing as it unfolds around questions of discourse, identity, and power (e.g., Gregg, 1993; Jorgenson, 2002; Kondo, 1990; J. Martin et al., 1998; Sotirin & Gottfried, 1999; Townsley & Geist, 2000; Trethewey, 1997, 1999b, 2001). Much of this work focuses on the dialectical relationships between processes of organizational control and acts of resistance, as well as efforts by women workers to maintain and reproduce a coherent sense of self in the interstices of this dialectic. From a postmodern perspective, such efforts involve the ongoing construction of identities through the situated appropriation of gendered discourses in ways that reproduce and resist prevailing narratives of gendered organization. Far from fixed sets of meaning, then, identities are local, contingent, and frequently constructed out of contradictory discourses.

Thus, for postmodern feminist researchers, a principal aim is to deconstruct how women's identities are crafted both through and in opposition to the discursive resources that are available to them. This perspective eschews any notion of essential identity or womanhood as the source of agency, and instead positions agency as the ability to take up available discourses in particular, perhaps even innovative, ways. Agency gets defined in terms of certain articulatory practices; that is, moments in which discourses—that are often disparate and contradictory—are configured together to yield meanings that reify and/or subvert dominant narratives of gendered labor.

For example, Sotirin and Gottfried's (1999) analysis of "bitching" among secretaries shows how that discourse both draws on and challenges gendered stereotypes. The mundane communication practice of bitching does not simply represent a stable "secretarial identity" that captures "the meaning" of pink-collar culture; rather, this discourse gets played out in an "ambivalent dynamics" of accommodation and resistance. "Bitching" therefore functions in contradictory ways to *simultaneously* reproduce and challenge normative gendered practices. Whereas a standard interpretive study of "gendered organizational culture" might focus on the ways in which bitching—as a feminized discursive practice—creates coherence and unity among secretarial pool members through the promotion of shared values, Sotirin and Gottfried (1999) suggest a more complex reading, wherein bitching entails "an ambivalent struggle within and against the prevailing orders of power, meaning, and pleasure" (p. 64). It is both emancipatory and accommodative; it reproduces a feminized identity, even as it unravels the premises on which that identity is based.

Much of the extant postmodern feminist research draws on interview studies as the principal way of examining the discursive construction of gendered identities (e.g., Jorgenson, 2002; Townsley & Geist, 2000; Trethewey, 1999a, 2001). In most of these projects, scholars examine how women take up discourses in order to construct and/or perform certain identities in relation to the researcher. In this sense, postmodern feminist researchers treat the interview context not as a neutral vehicle through which women express an inner, coherent sense of identity but, rather, as a political and performative context for the co-construction of interviewer and interviewee subjectivities (Kauffman, 1991).

In her interview study of women engineers, for example, Jorgenson (2002) argues that "How one positions oneself vis-à-vis the interviewer or audience . . . is a critical element in the performative construction of identity" (p. 359). Jorgenson adopts the notion of "discursive positioning" to explore how women engineers performatively negotiate their gendered identities in a predominantly masculine professional field. Arguing that "gendered subjectivity is the site of multiple and contradictory effects," Jorgenson (2002) suggests that the women in her study draw on five different discourses to position and construct themselves as engineers (p. 358). These five discourses position the self as career-identified, organizationally adept, nonfeminist, good mother, and singular individual. Jorgenson explores how the ironies and contradictions among these modes of discursive positioning require a quite complex process of sense making by these women. Perhaps Jorgenson's most interesting reading of her data is that the women's positioning of themselves as "nonfeminist" reflects less a lack of self-reflection regarding the hegemony of patriarchy in their profession and the wider society and more a rejection of the researcher's framing of the study as "about" women engineers (thus positioning them in a special, "marked" category). In this sense, the women engineers' self-positioning as "nonfeminist" is a political move rooted in their performance for the researcher.

Women engineers are also the central protagonists in Fletcher's (1998, 1999) postmodern feminist analysis of workplace practices. Fletcher combines a poststructuralist analytic framework with feminist standpoint theory ("relational theory") to examine how a group of women engineers in a predominantly male work environment make sense of their work. She argues that the women engineers adopt a mode of "relational practice" in the workplace that involves "preserving" (protecting the well-being of work projects), "mutual empowering" (empowering others to contribute to projects), "achieving" (empowering oneself to achieve goals), and "creating team" (building collectives to create positive work outcomes). Fletcher contends that this mode of relational practice embodies a deliberate, strategic attempt by the women engineers to bring to the organization an alternative orientation to work practice traditionally associated with the private and feminine spheres of society. However, despite the women engineers' resistance to traditional, masculine modes of work practice, Fletcher shows that the dominant culture of the organization results in this alternative orientation to work "getting disappeared." In other words, the women engineers' commitment to relational practice is subsumed beneath the dominant "rules of truth" for what counts as appropriate workplace behavior. Fletcher (1998) contends that there was "a dynamic process in operation in which relational practice got disappeared as work and got constructed as something other than work" (p. 178).

Although Fletcher's analysis illuminates how gendered workplace identities are discursively constructed in the context of organizational power relations, there are a few noteworthy limitations to her study.

First, the combination of a poststructuralist analytic framework and the standpoint model of relational practice seem strangely at odds. Although standpoint theory and poststructuralism are not inherently incompatible, Fletcher appears to ontologize and essentialize the elements of the model of relational practice, suggesting that they reflect an intrinsically woman's way of being that is largely incompatible with the dominant workplace culture. Rather than viewing the woman engineers' identities as constructed through the mundane activities of organizing, she views those identities in an a priori manner as relatively unitary, stable, and simply reflected through communication practice.

Furthermore, Fletcher's concept of "getting disappeared" seems to confirm this view of meaning and identity as relatively stable, consistent, and unchanging. The concept suggests that the women's relational practices are simply silenced or obscured by the dominant masculine culture; the practices themselves remain pristine and authentic expressions of women's work culture. An alternative reading is that the women's relational practices are not "disappeared" but, rather, are appropriated, reconfigured, or reframed by the dominant culture. This reading repositions the relational model as a set of discursive practices that are "up for grabs" within the dialectic of organizational meaning construction. Perhaps practices such as "mutual empowering" are not "disappeared" as such but, instead, are reconfigured to fit within the dominant system of workplace meanings. In this latter sense, certain gendered practices are not seen as intrinsically part of a particular "women's culture"; they are viewed as the medium and expression of a dialectical struggle among competing interests, identities, and discourses.

Other postmodern feminist scholars, particularly those in the field of organizational communication, have begun to develop a strong corpus of work that takes seriously this nonessentialist view of gendered identity and comes to grips with the ways in which gender, discourse, power, and resistance are articulated together through the organizing process (Gregg, 1993; Holmer Nadesan, 1996; Holmer Nadesan & Trethewey, 2000; Trethewey, 1997, 1999b, 2001). For example, in her analysis of two separate efforts by women workers to organize politically, Gregg (1993) eschews a simple "identity politics" as a way to explain their organizing efforts, arguing instead for a "politics of location." The latter provides a way to better explore how the women workers invoke several discourses that, articulated together, both enable and constrain their abilities to organize effectively. A politics of location suggests a process of negotiation among various discursively and materially created subject positions on which the women draw. Thus, rather than the relatively stable female identity suggested by Fletcher (1998), Gregg (1993) argues that

> Subjective experience is understood . . . as both the sites where individuals 'inhabit' numerous discursive positions simultaneously, and those places in which established everyday discourses— those of class, race, gender, age, ethnicity, and sexuality, for example—give meaning to subjective experience by suggesting appropriate positions from which to make sense of one's life. Acting from a constellation of subject positions, individuals engage in practices that reproduce, reconstitute, and contest those meanings. (p. 5)

This notion of subjectivity preserves the possibilities for agency and political praxis, while stepping beyond the simplistic equation of women with particular feelings, experiences, or dispositions from which a collective identity is generated. Gregg's position thus enables a much more textured framework for examining the limits, possibilities, and contradictions that organize gendered identities.

Other feminist organizational communication scholars have contributed to such a project through their examination of the relations among discourse, identity, and organizing. Trethewey's (1997, 1999a, 1999b, 2001) studies, for example, examine women's identities as constructed in complex ways—both reproducing and resisting available subject positions—through the appropriation of various discourses. For example, her recent work on professional women's bodies suggests how the construction of a professional image/identity within a dominant, masculine culture involves the articulation together of discourses of aging, sexuality, race, and entreprencurialism in ways that reproduce and resist dominant narratives of women's place in the workforce. Importantly, such research moves beyond the confines of the organization as physical site to examine the effects of larger, cultural discourses (e.g., of entrepreneurialism and body image) on women's identities.

Holmer Nadesan's (1996, 1999; Holmer Nadesan & Trethewey, 2000) research has combined the study of various cultural and administrative discourses with investigation of agentic responses to those discourses. For example, Holmer Nadesan's (1996) study of female custodians uses Daudi's (1986) concept of "space of action" to examine how the custodians appropriated administrative discourse in ways that both resisted and reproduced their administratively ascribed organizational identities as "service workers." On the other hand, her analyses of the discourse of entrepreneurialism (Holmer Nadesan, 1999; Holmer Nadesan & Trethewey, 2000) illustrate how conceptions of agency are always already situated within larger, cultural discourses that shape and discipline available possibilities for meaning construction and action.

In sum, recent postmodern feminist organization studies have begun to develop a significant body of work that explores the relations among discourse, gendered identities, power relations, and organizing. Such work treats identity as a complex and contradictory discursive construction that occurs through dialectics of resistance and control. The next chapter builds on this work by developing a feminist communicology of organization, which simultaneously draws on postmodern feminist insights and endeavors to redress key limitations of such work.

❖ CONCLUSION

In the first half of this chapter, we addressed in some detail the relationship between feminism and postmodernism. We laid out cases for and against the intersection of feminist and postmodern thought, suggesting its epistemological and political implications. The second half of the chapter concentrated on the ways in which critical and feminist organization scholars have taken up postmodern feminist thought. While the study of organizations as gendered has produced a significant body of research, the development of a postmodern feminist perspective represents a particular intervention in this effort. Specifically, in important ways, it problematizes current conceptions of identity, knowledge, power, and organizing. Far from simply reducing issues of identity to Foucauldian disciplinary "subject effects," postmodern feminist organization studies has begun to articulate ways in which subject identities can be discursively positioned *and* agentic, beset by contradiction *and* coherent.

Next, we take on the question of what such a theory might look like. As we develop basic premises of a feminist communicology, our purpose is to propose a conceptual and analytic framework that accounts for gender as discursive and performative, situated in material relations of power, and unfolding in the everyday lives of real people. As this suggests, we seek a framework that cannot be easily categorized as "critical" or "postmodern." Indeed, we argue that a feminist communicology begins to transcend such dichotomies, theorizing gendered organization across critical and postmodern analytics.

5

A Feminist Communicology of Organization

❖ ❖ ❖

A number of goals motivated our efforts to address the relationships among feminism, modernism, postmodernism, and organization studies. First, we wanted to make sense of the complex epistemological and political terrain that results from bringing together these wide-ranging discourses. Second, we saw it as important to position feminist studies as an active rather than marginal shaper of this terrain. Finally, we were engaged in laying the groundwork for the development of a theory of gendered organization that brings to the fore issues of communication, power, resistance, and identity.

In this chapter, we explicate key features of this conceptual framework. In doing so, we wish to contribute to the growing body of literature that situates gendered organizing as a discursive, communicative process, but we want to do this in a particular way. Rather than adopting a position "for" postmodernism and "against" modernism, we wish to articulate a feminist communicology that is positioned at the intersection of these discourses. On the one hand, we wish to preserve the modernist insights discussed in Chapter 2, which recognize the material character of oppression and enduring, gendered structures of power and dominance. Seen as a modernist, emancipatory discourse, feminism has long explored the abiding, institutional features of patri- archy. On the other hand, we draw on a postmodern conception of relationships among discourse, identity, power, and organizing—a view that moves beyond essentialism and toward irony and contradiction. In sum, we want to bring to the debate on discourse and organization a sensitivity to the materiality of discourse, as well as a sense of the every- day communication processes that constitute gendered organization (see, e.g., Chia, 2000; M. Parker, 2000; Reed, 2000; Tsoukas, 2000, for a recent instantiation of the discourse-materiality debate).

In proposing what we call a "feminist communicology of organiza- tion," our purpose is to articulate a heuristic framework that provides a point of convergence for critical and feminist studies of organization. In part, this framework represents an effort to respond to recent concerns about the fragmented character of gendered organization studies (e.g., Martin & Collinson, 2002). We suggest that our own field of organiza- tional communication provides a useful site for disciplinary integration, for communication scholars have long emphasized discourse as central to understanding the human condition and, specifically, have theorized how communication constitutes organizing (Cooren, 2000; J. R. Taylor, 1995; Taylor, Cooren, Giroux, & Robichaud, 1996). Our field embraces communication as the ontological condition for human being and situates communicative praxis as the material, constitutive condition of human agency and identity (Schrag, 1986). Such premises do not essentialize communication; they problematize it as that which requires investigation.

To provide a backdrop for our model, we begin the chapter with a brief description of the field of organizational communication, situat- ing it in relationship to gendered organization studies. We then articu- late the premises of a feminist communicology, suggesting its viability as a framework for the study of gendered organizing. In Chapter 6, we extend this argument by applying the elements of this framework to an analysis of the professional identity of airline pilots.

❖ ORGANIZATIONAL COMMUNICATION AND GENDERED ORGANIZATION

The development of a feminist communicology of organization takes its impetus from our own disciplinary location in the field of organizational communication. Arguably, the discursive turn of the last 20 years in organization studies places the field of organizational communication in a pivotal position with respect to a critical mass of scholarship that treats organizations as discursively constructed. Indeed, there is a huge body of work in our field—addressed at different points in earlier chapters—that examines "organizations as discourse" from a variety of perspectives, including interpretive (e.g., Cheney, 2000a; Pacanowsky & O'Donnell-Trujillo, 1982; Putnam, 1983; Putnam & Pacanowsky, 1983; Trujillo, 1992; Trujillo & Dionisopoulos, 1987), rhetorical (e.g., Bullis & Tompkins, 1989; Cheney, 1983, 1991; B. C. Taylor, 1993b, 2002; Tompkins & Cheney, 1985), critical (e.g., Deetz, 1982, 1985, 1992a; Helmer, 1993; Howard & Geist, 1995; Mumby, 1987, 1988), postmodern (e.g., Barker, 1993; Holmer Nadesan, 1996, 1999), and feminist perspectives (e.g., Ashcraft, 2000, 2001; Ashcraft & Pacanowsky, 1996; Buzzanell, 1994, 1995, 2000; Clair, 1998; Gregg, 1993; Mumby, 1996; Trethewey, 1997, 1999b).

In their recent analysis of gendered organization as a fragmented area of study, Martin and Collinson (2002) claim that scholars of gender and organization should "strike out" on their own, since "a new field has fewer conventions to limit risk-taking and enforce orthodoxy" (p. 256). In some ways, this account of a "new field" fairly well describes the case of organizational communication. Having tested and stretched the bounds of orthodoxy in the early 1980s (an "orthodoxy" that had only been around for 20 years, anyway), we have developed into a field of study that values epistemological, ontological, and methodological pluralism, in which no single perspective or group of researchers functions as the arbiter of good scholarship. We would even argue that our field embodies a productive tension between integration and divergence, exhibiting simultaneous loose and tight properties, to invoke a Weickian notion. On the one hand, we witness efforts to characterize the field as coalescing around a broad set of core issues and problematics (e.g., Corman & Poole, 2000; Mumby & Stohl, 1996). While, on the other hand, we have a large group of scholars, engaging in diverse research agendas—from social science driven network research (e.g., Monge & Contractor, 2001) to feminist deconstructions of university sexual harassment policies (e.g., Clair, 1993a)—who are happy to see their field as inherently transdisciplinary and methodologically ecumenical.

But what about research on gender and organizing? It is certainly true that the field of organizational communication was late on the scene in making a significant contribution to the study of organizations as gendered. While our field has always recognized the importance of studying "gender in organizations," the shift to studying "gendered organizing" is a relatively recent occurrence. However, in the last 10 years or so, this dearth of research has been replaced by a dynamic and innovative body of scholarship that has systematically examined the connections among gender, communication, power, and organizing. Feminist organizational communication scholars have "struck out" in innovative and improvisational ways to examine the communicative/ discursive features of sexual harassment (Clair, 1993a, 1993b; Townsley & Geist, 2000); alternative organizational forms (Ashcraft, 2000, 2001; Edley, 2000); masculinity and organizing (Ashcraft & Flores, in press; Ashcraft & Mumby, in press; Gibson & Papa, 2000; Gibson & Schullery, 2000; Mumby, 1998); the intersection of race, gender, and organizing (Allen, 1995, 1996, 1998; Ashcraft & Allen, 2003; Grimes, 2001, 2002); gender, control, and organizational resistance (Holmer Nadesan, 1996; A. G. Murphy, 1998; Sotirin & Gottfried, 1999; Trethewey, 1997, 1999b); gender, Post-Fordism, and globalization (Holmer Nadesan, 2001); the development of feminist theories of organizing (Bullis, 1993; Buzzanell, 1994, 1995, 2000; Mumby, 1993, 1996); and a host of other topics.

Tying all of this work together is a focus on the ways in which communication practices constitute subjectivities amid routine, situated, and systemic relations of power. In general, this body of work rejects the subject-object dualism implicit in "subjectivist" or "objectivist" approaches to organizing processes (e.g., Burrell & Morgan, 1979). As Deetz (1996) has shown in his critique of Burrell and Morgan's (1979) widely cited sociological framework, their positing of subjectivist (interpretive, meaning centered) versus objectivist (functionalist, positivist) approaches actually preserves the hegemony of functionalism-positivism by framing meaning-centered research as subjective and ideational and thus subordinate to research on "real" social structures. A communicative model, however, overcomes this dualism by examining how communication *constitutes* the very possibility for a subject-object, self-world relationship. Adopting a framework embedded in a communication perspective does not, therefore, involve the examination of how social actors subjectively (i.e., cognitively) make sense out of an already created material world. Rather, it requires examination of how—through interactive processes—social actors *intersubjectively* construct identities and social structures.

Thus, a communication-based framework undermines the dichotomy of an "inner" and "outer" world by examining the ways in which agency/identity and structure are co-constructed. As it vitiates the subject-object dualism, such a framework reveals possibilities for the development of a feminist perspective that resists the modernist-postmodernist dichotomy. Put simply, we do not have to choose between a rather essentialist focus on the enduring, material conditions of oppression and a discursive, textual interest in unstable systems of meaning. Adopting a communicative frame means exploring the dialectical relationship between these possibilities.

Part of our argument, then, is that the tendency among critical-feminist organization scholars to overlook organizational communication research inadvertently blocks a fruitful avenue for the development of rich, interdisciplinary theories of gendered organization. Next, we lay out basic premises of one such interdisciplinary model, grounding our approach in a disciplinary tradition that prioritizes communication.

❖ ARTICULATING A FEMINIST COMMUNICOLOGY OF ORGANIZATION: INITIAL PREMISES

Our feminist communicology of organization starts with the assumption that gender is a complex, ongoing, and contradictory accomplishment, unfolding at the nexus of communication and organization. Thus we take gender as situated, embodied communicative praxis (Schrag, 1986), enacted in an intricate field of discursive and nondiscursive relations of power, accommodation, and resistance (Jermier, Knights, & Nord, 1994). From this beginning point, our communicological framework is aimed at examining the dialectical tensions between mundane micro-level social practices and macro-level institutional processes of reproduction and transformation.

What, then, is the significance of a *communicology* of gendered organizing (as opposed to, for example, a *discursive* model)? First, as suggested by our critique in Chapter 3, we want to distance ourselves somewhat from (although not completely reject) the Foucauldian conception of discourse that has come to dominate critical organization studies in the wake of the discursive turn (Foucault, 1979, 1980a, 1980b; Knights & Morgan, 1991; McKinlay & Starkey, 1998). While Foucault's analytics provide powerful conceptions of the disciplinary mechanisms through which human subjectivity is constructed, it also affords little room for the flesh-and-blood speaking subject, either as a purveyor of these disciplinary practices or as their object (Newton, 1998).

Our notion of communicology represents an effort to rehabilitate the performing subject and to examine what Calvin Schrag (1997) calls the "who" of discourse—the embodied, speaking subject who engages in agentic communicative praxis. Thus we are interested in discourse not simply as text or symbolism but as invoked by social actors who engage with a real—albeit socially constructed—world. This conception of a speaking subject does not regress to a form of Cartesian essentialism or existential authenticity; it is an effort to show subjectivity as both stable and in flux, coherent and contradictory.

Second, and related, the notion of communicology draws on our own disciplinary tradition and its focus on the rhetorical, performative aspects of communication. As the medium and product of everyday life, communication is never disembodied or context free; it is always constitutive of the dynamic and ongoing process of making meaning (Putnam & Pacanowsky, 1983; J. R. Taylor et al., 1996). Gendered organizations thus do not "exist" as such; rather, they are performed moment by moment through the communicative practices of their members (Scheibel, 1992). While such performances usually do not unfold capriciously but, rather, follow well-established scripts, it is still only in the doing—the performing—that such scripts are produced, reproduced, resisted, and transformed.

Such a performative, communicological perspective moves beyond the realm of the discursive and textual to include the body as a constitutive and constituted element in the construction of subjectivity (Bordo, 1993, 1000; Conquergood, 1991; Hancock & Tyler, 2001a; Hassard et al., 2000; Trethewey, 1999a). Put differently, gendered organizing is "mobilized" and enacted through "em-bodied" communicative practices (P. Y. Martin, 2001). It is in this sense that our feminist communicological perspective resists efforts to reproduce the modernist mind-body dualism, in which the mind is seen as the repository and source of knowledge, culture, and rationality, while the body is relegated to the status of the uncontrollable, irrational, and emotional (i.e., feminine) other.

Based on these initial claims, we conceive of *communication* as *the dynamic, situated, embodied, and contested process of creating systems of gendered meanings and identities by invoking, articulating, and/or transforming available discourses.* From such a perspective, communication is not a mere cipher or conduit for the enactment of larger discourses; rather, it is the process through which those selves and settings are constituted. In other words, it is in the act of communicative praxis that identities and meaning structures are enacted, maintained, and transformed within the context of organized relations of power and resistance (Schrag, 1986, 1997). Communication is therefore inherently political, due to the ways in which social actors and groups struggle to "fix" and articulate meanings in particular ways via contexts ranging from mundane interaction to the public and mediated messages of popular culture (Deetz, 1992a). In the following chapter, for example, we will explore how various media and institutional discourses struggled to shape and fix the identity of (male) professional airline pilots in the face of public concern about the safety of flight. The shift in the pilot's identity from "intrepid birdman" and "barnstormer" to coolly competent and laconic professional was not a seamless process; it occurred amid a number of gendered discourses that competed to institutionalize the role of both men and women in commercial flight.

In the remainder of this chapter, we flesh out these initial assumptions through the development of six theoretical premises: (1) Subjectivity is unstable, fragmented, and constructed in an ongoing and dynamic manner through various communicative practices; (2) The relationship between power and resistance is dialectical and mutually defining; (3) Analysis of historical context is crucial to understanding the ongoing dynamics of gendered organizing; (4) The relationship between discourse and the material world is dialectical— discourse is fundamentally material, while the material world is dis- cursively constructed; (5) The analysis of masculine and feminine identities requires a focus on the dialectics of gender relations and the co-construction of masculinities/femininities; and (6) The examination of the relationships among gender, power, and organizing requires a normative, ethical moment that explores both the consequences of particular configurations of power for human identity and meaning formation and possibilities for praxis.

Communication and Gendered Subjectivity

In articulating a theory of gendered subjectivity, our feminist communicology of organization draws on the analysis conducted in the previous chapters, particularly the effort to situate feminism in relationship to modernism and postmodernism. We do not see feminism as reducible to either; rather, we see feminism as existing in a productive tension with these two discourses, which generates possi- bilities for innovative theorizing. Our perspective thus attempts to avoid the pitfalls of the endlessly deferred, textualized, and decentered subject of postmodernism and of the essentialism and monadic auton-omy of Cartesian modernism. The juxtaposition of feminist concerns for agency and identity with a postmodern concern to "decenter the subject" actually enables a conception of the "speaking subject" of communication as contingent, fragmented, and yet teeming with agen-tic possibilities (Holmer Nadesan, 1996; Kondo, 1990). In this sense, the "subject" of communication is precisely what is problematized and scrutinized rather than accepted as given. Our goal here is to overcome the "subjectless" character of many postmodern analyses, while avoid-ing any reinscription of the agency-structure dualism that has plagued labor process theory for so long (see, e.g., Braverman, 1974; Burawoy, 1979; Knights, 1990; Newton, 1998; Willmott, 1994). However, rather than drawing on the rather anemic Foucauldian model of agency and its attendant limitations, we are interested in articulating a more adequate speaking subject of discourse.

This shift requires that we examine communication not as text but as unfolding, dynamic, and embodied everyday practice that draws on—not simply reflects—larger discourses. Thus, we retain Foucault's concept of discourse as "conditions of possibility"—temporarily fixed (i.e., predictable but not determined), coherent (though also conflicted), abstract and dispersed social narratives about people, objects, and events (Laclau & Mouffe, 1985)—but we are interested in how such "conditions of possibility" actually get played out in material, every-day circumstances. Although it is clear that multiple discourses (e.g., of masculinity, race, and sexuality) circulate and intersect at once, and some enjoy greater institutional support than others, this recognition does not necessarily provide insight into how particular communicative practices enact, resist, and/or transform such discourses.

For example, despite the importance of Jacques's (1996) analysis of the emergence of "l'employé" (see Chapter 3), his focus on macro-level discourse provides us with little sense of how social actors might engage with this larger managerial discourse at an everyday, commu-nicative level. Real employees enact the discourse of "the employee" in reproductive, resistant, and accommodative ways in actual social contexts. Holmer Nadesan's (1996) analysis of the relationship between organizational identity and "space of action" suggests a variety of ways that employees appropriate hegemonic managerial discourses. Such appropriations cannot simply be predicted by the character of the dominant discourse but, rather, are shaped heavily by particular dynamics of race, class and gender, the communicative contexts at hand, and the material conditions under which the employees work (in this instance, engaging in custodial work in a university dormitory).

Feminist communicology thus demands a close examination of the mundane dynamics of organizing in order to gain insight into the contextual features of the gendered identity-construction process. Such a model invokes a sense of "process subjectivity" (Weedon, 1987), in which identity is viewed as both stable and precarious, coherent and contradictory. Neither of these conditions is pre-eminent, functioning in dialectical tension as social actors negotiate the interpretive ambiguities of everyday life. Most important, a communicological perspective recognizes that "process subjectivity" involves an agentic, communicative engagement with the social world. Subjects produce and reproduce themselves as they appropriate, accommodate, resist, and ironically adopt available discourses. Hence, we recognize the degree to which social actors—as communicative beings—actively and reflexively navigate institutionalized and sedimented social structures. In this sense, we see no contradiction between viewing people both as decentered selves who are the product of multiple discourses and as agents who engage the social world in an active and meaningful way.

A Dialectic of Power and Resistance

Of course, the construction of gendered identity does not take place in a political vacuum. Accordingly, a feminist communicology embodies a dialectical approach to the relationships among power, resistance, and organizing (Benson, 1977; Kondo, 1990). Despite Benson's (1977) call for a dialectical approach to the study of organization, much critically oriented research continues to operate largely from a functional framework, in which either domination or resistance is privileged as the primary explanatory mechanism for organizational behavior. A domination perspective views mechanisms of organizational control as functionally reproducing hegemonic interests and relations of power (e.g., Burawoy, 1979; Jermier, 1998; Witten, 1993). While the possibility for employee resistance is often acknowledged and perhaps explored, it is generally interpreted as ultimately reproducing the dominant mechanisms of control (Willis, 1977). A resistance perspective tends to privilege and frequently essentialize social actors' ability to "penetrate" (speaking of gendered terms!) the prevailing system of domination. In this work, marginalized actors and social groups are frequently credited with an epistemologically privileged and "authentic" level of insight into conditions of oppression (e.g., Scott, 1990). This position is equally functionalist in that it largely presumes rather than explains the subjectivities and conditions that make such resistance possible.

There are two problems that these positions share. First, each operates with a model of power as domination. Whether control or resistance is the primary focus, the assumption is that power is a repressive, negative force that must be overcome. Second, by bifurcating power and resistance, each position overlooks relations of power as simultaneous processes of resistance, reproduction, and transformation. Social actors are neither completely subject to power formations nor occupying pristine spaces of resistance that are free from power.

In contrast, our dialectical approach to power and resistance requires attention to dynamic power relations as they are played out in disjunctive and contradictory ways through everyday communication (Collinson, 1992; Kondo, 1990; Mumby, 1997b). Framed in this manner, discourses are neither inherently dominant nor resistant but become part of complex struggles among different interest groups. Conceived dialectically, hegemony is seen as a dynamic process of discursive struggle in which various groups compete to secure meanings in conflictual contexts (Mumby, 1997b). Kondo (1990) puts this dialectical perspective best when she states that

> Rather than positing these categories [of power and resistance] as foundational and thus invoking a metaphysics of closure and presence, we might examine the unexpected, subtle, and paradoxical twists in actors' discursive strategies, following out the ways meanings are reappropriated and launched again in continuous struggles over meaning. For perhaps it is not a matter of some utopian space of resistance as such . . . but of the complicated web of contradictions and ironies which bind us and which we in turn fabricate as we live out our lives. (p. 225)

Accordingly, a dialectical stance draws attention to irony, ambiguity, and contradiction in gender-work relations and examines them through the connections between micro-level communicative processes and macro-level discursive, political, and economic forces (Kondo, 1990; Trethewey, 1999b). Our analysis of the social construction of airline pilots' identities will take up this dialectic, drawing attention to the intricate struggles over meaning that characterize the development of specific communication practices and of a larger societal culture of flight. This emergent process suggests no simple teleology; it requires an analysis that refuses a simple reading of the relationship among identities, meanings, and power relations as uniform, coherent, and causal.

Historical Context

While by no means a causal force, embedded relations of power generate tangible (i.e., "real" and perceived) conditions with which human discourse wrestles. Yet, these material, contested contexts tend to fade from collective memory as discourse takes root in social consciousness. In response, a feminist communicology of organization attends to historical context. It seeks to build a diachronic perspective on gender and work, couching organizational communication processes within the political economy of the day. Our purpose here is to say more than that gendered organizing processes change over time; more fundamentally, a historical analysis brings to light the radical ruptures and contradictions of organizational change (Mills, 2002). In Foucault's (1979) sense, historicizing organizational analysis means writing the "history of the present," bringing to light the ways that current organizational realities reflect the hegemony of particular, historically emergent discourses. Furthermore, in contrast to "Whiggish" histories that accept modernist narratives of linear progress, we view histories as discontinuous, with newly emergent dominant discourses rewriting prior history in order to maintain continuity. In this sense, we agree with Mills's (2002) view of history as discursive constructions that embody the reality of dominant interest groups. Few writers have adopted a historical perspective to examine the gendered assumptions of management thought (for exceptions, see Acker & Van Houten, 1974; Banta, 1993; S. Benson, 1992; Child, 1995). However, some scholars have begun to address how dominant discourses arise out of particular historical exigencies (e.g., Jacques, 1996; O'Connor, 1999).

For us, the historicizing of organizational discourse and the concomitant view of history as discursively constructed adds significant texture to the conception of the speaking subject articulated above. In addition to conceptualizing the identity of social actors as agentic and rooted in everyday communicative practice, it is also important to view larger historical, institutional discourses as the work of particular agents. Such agents are not necessarily individual social actors; they can be institutions, groups, social movements, and so forth. Hence, analyses of disciplinary mechanisms and discourses are enhanced by considering how disciplinary forms arise out of concrete struggles among identifiable groups.

Reed (1988) has similarly argued for the need to focus on the relations among agency, institutional structures, and historical change:

> The problem of human agency . . . must be approached in historical terms so that the relationship between action and structure can be reconceptualized as 'a matter of process in time' (Abrams, 1982: ix). This requires that the analytical focus of organizational studies be directed on those social practices through which social structures are created, maintained and transformed over time. Such an approach stands in sharp contrast to those treating the latter as entities or objects that evolve according to a hidden developmental logic in which human agency is conspicuous by its absence. (p. 42)

One goal of examining history as discourse, then, is to understand how dominant groups and institutions mobilize particular meaning systems by drawing on and articulating together existing cultural discourses. Furthermore, we can examine how dominant groups respond to the emergence of oppositional discourses that challenge the hegemony of institutionalized meanings. As we hinted at the outset of this section, dominant discourses, once established, frequently take on a self-reproducing, autopoetic quality and become detached from their original site of production (Deetz, 1992a). A historical perspective can bring back into focus precise moments of political, economic, and/or cultural crisis, in which opportunities for change and transformation opened up. In such moments, the ambiguity of meanings and identities becomes particularly acute, and the struggle to fix such meanings and identities is sharply contested.

Thus, from a feminist communicological perspective, we are interested in (a) how macro-level institutional agents (and the cultural and political discourses on which they draw) articulate certain gendered identities; and (b) how social actors reproduce and/or resist these articulations at the level of everyday praxis and interaction. In short, we engage in "the engendering of historical narrative" (Benhabib, 1992, p. 212), displacing the idea of history as uniform, homogeneous, and linear, in order to examine how the relationship among gender, identity, and work is subject to shifting and frequently contradictory cultural, political, and economic forces. In this sense, the very form of a particular discourse arises out of a complex, ongoing struggle among various interest groups and in competition with other, already established discourses. In the next chapter, for example, we situate airline pilot identity at the historical intersection of competing discourses of masculinity, femininity, and professionalism.

A Dialectic of Discourse and Materiality

Throughout the book thus far, we have argued for a dialectical relationship between discourse and the material, "objective" world. Certainly in the wake of the discursive turn in organization studies, scholars have debated for some time the relative merits of a "realist" (e.g., Reed, 2000) versus a social constructionist (e.g., Chia, 2000; Gergen, 1992) view of organizations. Within critical scholarship itself, there is considerable debate over the relationship between discourse and world; some critical scholars privilege the discursive/textual over the material (Calás & Smircich, 1991, 1993; Chia, 2000), while others prioritize the materiality of organizing (Cloud, 2001; Reed, 2000; Thompson, 1993). In contrast, we propose a communicological approach that examines the reciprocal, dialectical, and mutually defining character of the symbolic/discursive and material conditions of organizing. By "material," we refer not only to "macro" economic and political arrangements but also to "micro" practices, including those relative to the body and sexuality (Bordo, 1992, 1999). We consider this discursive-material dialectic important for several reasons.

First, against the postmodern predilection for seeing the social world as in flux and unstable, we maintain the importance of recognizing and exploring abiding features of social structures. As we indicated earlier, part of the raison d'être of feminism is to explore, critique, and transform the enduring and material features of patriarchy that continue to oppress women and men. Thus, there is no contradiction between arguing for a material and durable social world on the one hand, and claiming that such a world is socially constructed on the other. Social actors produce (gendered) realities that become sedimented and naturalized over time, reflecting the ability of the powerful to shape such realities in terms of their own interests and values.

Second, we view communication itself as a material act. Framed materially, communication constitutes the day-to-day practices of social actors. Performatively speaking, social actors take up discourses (e.g., of race, class, gender, sexuality, etc.) and enact them in varied social contexts. That is to say, people "do" identity and difference in concrete situations (Fenstermaker & West, 2002; West & Fenstermaker, 1995; West & Zimmerman, 1987). For example, Scheibel's (1992) analysis of the communicative performance of a "fake ID" by underage female students attempting to gain entrance to a bar illustrates well how identity is a choreographed, situational, and perhaps even fleeting phenomenon (needing only to survive the scrutiny of the bouncer at the door). In addition, discourse is material in its interpellation of social actors (Althusser, 1971), creating the very possibility of particular subject positions. In Althusser's (1971) terms, people recognize themselves as subjects by virtue of the process of interpellation—or hailing—through various discursive forms. Organizational narratives, for example, do more than inform members about appropriate or inappropriate behavior; they provide fundamental organizing frames that people take on, accommodate, resist, and transform (Ehrenhaus, 1993; Helmer, 1993; Mumby, 1987).

Third, the symbolic/material dialectic is important in that it allows us to explore how the material world itself is subject to and defined by human discursive possibilities. Discourse frames the materiality of the world for us in particular ways. For example, the concrete, material reality of an organizational meeting has substance only insofar as there is a discourse that enables us to participate in and interpret such an event *as* meaningful. Everything of substance about an organization—parking lots, offices, desks, restrooms, people, and so forth—is always already meaningful within an interpretive frame that shapes the conditions of possibility and constraint for organization members' sense making and behavior. Discourse, then, makes possible and even enacts material changes in the world.

A Dialectic of Gender Relations

Guided by a dialectical sensibility, our feminist communicology also involves an effort to move beyond a "separate spheres" approach to gender. While research on gendered organizing has come to recognize the importance of studying both femininities and masculinities, a pronounced scholarly division of labor typifies this research. On the one hand, abundant scholarship examines the social construction of women's identities in the workplace (e.g., Bell & Forbes, 1994;

Buzzanell, 2000; Gregg, 1993; Holmer Nadesan, 1996; Maguire & Mohtar, 1994; Sotirin & Gottfried, 1999; Trethewey, 1997). Much of this work explores women's engagement in diverse forms of agentic, collective behavior amid patriarchal relations of power. On the other hand, as noted earlier, a growing body of research on masculinity and organization has expanded the study of gendered organizing processes and identities (Collinson & Hearn, 1994, 1996a, 1996b; Gibson & Papa, 2000; Gibson & Schullery, 2000; Hearn, 1994, 1996). Emerging partly in response to the tendency of gender and organization research to associate gender with women, and partly through the influence of feminist studies, this work has usefully destabilized the normalized status of men and masculinity in organizations. As the title of Hearn's (1996) essay suggests, the focus on organizational masculinity(s) reflects an effort to "deconstruct the dominant" and to "make the 'one' the 'other,'" submitting masculinity to the same kind of scrutiny as femininity.

While such attempts to "make 'the one' the 'other'" are significant, they also serve to sustain and reproduce dichotomous ways of framing gender. All forms of masculinity and femininity are produced in the broader context of gendered discourses of identity. In this sense, even studies that are ostensibly about the social construction of masculinity presume conceptions of the feminine against which particular forms of masculinity are situated. For example, in Willis's (1977) ethnography of working class adolescent masculinity, "the lads" construct a particular discourse of femininity (occupied by the "ear'oles," mothers, and girl-friends) against which their sense of masculinity is measured. However, Willis fails to treat the lads' masculinity dialectically in that the voices of the ear'oles, mothers, and girlfriends are absent. The lads' masculinities are thus constructed monologically.

In contrast, we argue that the social construction of gender identity is a dialectical, ongoing, and highly interdependent and interactive process, and we take seriously the idea that masculine and feminine gendered identities are coconstructed. This position is consistent with Flax's (1990) argument, discussed in Chapter 4, which views feminine and masculine subjectivities as jointly constructed in the context of gendered relations of power. Such an orientation requires not only the examination of masculinities/femininities as they are constructed in the course of everyday organizing processes but also the study of macro-level discourses of femininity and masculinity that get articulated together in particular ways.

Certainly, there are some researchers who have examined this dynamic. For example, Gherardi's (1994, 1995) discussion of women's "remedial work," which occurs in the wake of violations of the separate spheres of the masculine and the feminine, presumes an interactive framework. Similarly, Fletcher's (1998, 1999) analysis of the phenomenon of "getting disappeared," discussed earlier, suggests how women engineers' identities are tied to the dynamics of male-female interaction in the workplace. In addition, Alvesson's (1998) study of gender relations in an advertising firm captures well the coproduction of masculine and feminine work identities. Finally, Kondo's (1990) feminist ethnography of a Japanese pastry factory explores the complex dynamics of home-work relations, masculine and feminine work identities, and class. Such studies, however, are relatively few and far between.

The implications of the general lack of attention to the dialectic of masculinity and femininity can be illustrated by juxtaposing Kondo's ethnography against Collinson's (1992) critical ethnography of working class masculine shopfloor identities. While Collinson paints a fascinating and textured picture of the complex and often contradictory discursive production of shopfloor masculinities, we get little sense of the how the shopfloor dynamics are connected to the men's other spheres, particularly their home life. Certainly the identities of the (exclusively male) respondents are heavily invested in their roles as breadwinners and strongly heterosexual beings, but we get no sense of how these identities play out in the gendered dynamics of the private and public spheres away from the workplace, other than as reported by the men themselves. The voices of the women who are so objectified by many of the shopfloor workers are conspicuous by their absence. Thus, although Collinson problematizes and explores masculine working class subjectivities in a way that goes beyond earlier studies (e.g., Burawoy, 1979; Willis, 1977), the workplace itself appears as a strangely closed system that admits of no "outside" discourses or voices. Given Collinson's focus on how the various masculine subjectivities emerge out of a search for a secure and stable identity in an unstable political and economic environment, it would have been interesting to explore how the workers' "critical narcissism" is contested and/or reproduced in other spheres, such as the home.

By contrast, Kondo's (1990) analysis of workplace subjectivities is particularly sensitive to the gendered dynamics and interconnectedness of various spheres, including work, home, and public spaces.

In other words, she fully recognizes and explores the *contextuality* of gendered identity construction, showing how the performance of identity changes markedly across contexts. Furthermore, the dynamics of masculine and feminine performances on the shopfloor are central to her analysis. Thus, while the young male artisans who produce the elegantly crafted confectioneries express their masculine work prowess in interview situations, this strong sense of masculine, artisanal identity is mitigated in their relationship to the older women on the shopfloor, who adopt a very maternal relationship to the young men. Although the women are clearly subordinate to the male artisans in terms of workplace hierarchy, other gendered discursive spheres—such as home—destabilize the apparent coherence of the masculine work discourse. Kondo's analysis therefore suggests the difficulty of adequately theorizing subjectivities without recourse to the larger network of discourses out of which they emerge.

Through a feminist communicology of organization, we view identity construction not simply as discursive but, more important, as an in situ, communicative process where various discourses of identity compete, intersect, are appropriated, and engage in resistance. Thus, while discourses of gender, sexuality, race, and so forth precede the subject positions of social actors, such discourses are realized only through their instantiation in everyday communication, which ranges from mundane interaction to formal institutional documents.

Communicology as a Feminist Ethic

Recently a number of critical and feminist scholars have turned their attention to developing ethical frames for examining organizing processes (Ferguson, 1997; Haas & Deetz, 2000; M. Parker, 1998, 1999, 2000). For the most part, this scholarship moves beyond a "business ethics" approach that seeks to distinguish ethical from unethical practices (Redding, 1996) and instead shifts to a concern with the relationships among discourse, theory, power, and organizational democracy. Similarly, our feminist communicology entails the articulation of an ethical stance regarding the relationships among gender, power, and organization. We articulate a feminist ethic that is grounded in a conception of communication that rejects both the moral absolutism of some feminist standpoints (Brewis, 1998) and the moral relativism—the "let difference be" approach—of postmodern feminism (Ferguson, 1997). In other words, we view a feminist communicological ethic as an effort to unpack the relationships between power and truth, and to reveal the moral and ethical consequences of privileging certain power-knowledge relations over others (Brewis, 1998; Foucault, 1988a). Furthermore, we suggest that the conception of communication with which we operate offers the possibility of a "nonfoundational foundation" for a feminist ethic of organizing. We explicate this below.

First, we suggest that all theorizing—but especially critical, dialectical theorizing—embodies a particular ethic and, hence, an orientation toward and commitment to praxis. Benson (1977) describes the relationship among theory, ethics, and praxis in the following manner:

> The commitment to praxis is both a description—that is, that people under some circumstances can become active agents reconstructing their own social relations and ultimately themselves on the basis of rational analysis—and an ethical commitment—that is, that social science should contribute to the process of reconstruction, to the liberation of human potential through the production of new social formations.
>
> Dialectical analysis contributes to this process in part by dereifying established social patterns and structures—points out their arbitrary character, undermines their sense of inevitability, uncovers the contradictions and limits of the present order, and reveals the mechanisms of transformation. (pp. 5–6)

Accordingly, we see our feminist communicology as a politically engaged project that examines the processes and consequences of gendered organizing. In other words, we are concerned with addressing in whose interests particular knowledge claims are made and who gets to benefit from the maintenance and reproduction of certain social structures. In part, our project is intended to "dereify" gendered structures and relations of power and to reveal potential "mechanisms of transformation" through the opening up of other ways of thinking about the world. Such a project inevitably foregrounds ethical questions in that it makes judgments about the preference for one set of conditions over another or, at the very least, suggests that a conversation about such preferences is important.

However, such an ethic does not derive from some kind of Archimedian point of absolute moral judgment regarding certain social structures and gendered forms of power. A feminist communicology suggests the possibility of a normatively grounded ethical orientation that simultaneously rejects any absolute foundation from which to render ethical judgments. In this sense, our ethic does not derive from a sort of feminist essentialism that makes moral claims rooted in women's epistemologically privileged position (such a position would be especially odd given that one of us is male). At the same time, we challenge the kind of postmodern relativist ethic mentioned above that suggests we "let difference be" (Ferguson, 1997). We do not argue against highlighting difference per se; indeed, we embrace such an orientation in its efforts to "unsettle the settled contours of knowledge and power in order to make way for disunities and misfits" (Ferguson, 1997, p. 89). Yet, Ferguson's postmodern feminist ethic implies an ontologizing move that underplays the ongoing, discursive construction of differences. A move *beyond* "letting difference be," then, involves *engaging* difference. This move is communicative in that it enables differences to enter into dialogue, raising the possibility for new meanings and ways of being.

Consistent with the view of subjectivity we presented earlier, we invoke Deetz's (1992a) notion of communication as involving the destruction of self by overcoming one's fixed subjectivity and giving oneself up to the play of possibilities in the engagement with (different) others. This position is rooted in precepts intrinsic to the communication process itself. Communicative engagement with another demands the recognition of difference and the giving of oneself over to a dialectic that may produce a shift in one's sense of self. This move takes us beyond rooting a feminist ethic in the notion of letting difference be, because it recognizes that some differences are constituted precisely as a way to marginalize some groups and privilege others. As we will see in the next chapter, the creation of the "lady-flier" in airline industry discourse functioned both to constitute an identity that was different from that of the male flier and to privilege the latter in a manner that ultimately eliminated the "lady-flier" as a legitimate identity. The real issue, then, is not to "let difference be" but, rather, to examine how differences are actively constituted and to examine the ethical dimensions of this constitution process.

The goal of a feminist communicological ethic, then, is to draw attention to how particular communication practices privilege some interests and forms of difference over others, and to examine the consequences of such processes of privilege. We need to ask, what or whose interests and values are served through the communicative construction of certain (gendered) realities and identities, and in what ways does this construction process limit agentic possibilities for certain groups? Thus we see communication as unethical to the degree that it engages in "discursive closure" (Deetz, 1992a) and systematically limits the participation of groups and individuals in the construction of a meaningful social world in which their particular interests and values are represented.

❖ CONCLUSION

The principal goal of this chapter has been to articulate a feminist communicology of organization that sits at the intersection of modernist and postmodernist conceptions of discourse, power, identity, and organization. While earlier chapters laid out the complex connections and tensions among feminist, modernist, and postmodernist approaches to organizing, this chapter has presented one possible point of articulation for those connection and tensions. The six principles developed in this chapter attempt to navigate a course between postmodern fragmentation, instability, and flux and the modernist proclivity for stability, materiality, and coherence. By thematizing the notion of communicology, we conceive of discourse as textual and material, subjectivity as decentered and agentic, and power and resistance as mutually constitutive. In addition, we have shown how one might contextualize the discursive analysis of gender relations, framing discursive constructions of gendered identities within larger institutional and historically specific systems of meaning. Finally, we suggested how our perspective presumes an ethic that draws attention to questions of organizational values and democracy.

In the next chapter, we illustrate and further develop our feminist communicology of organization through empirical application. Drawing on archival and interview data from Karen's ongoing research project, we analyze the discursive construction of commercial airline pilot identity. Specifically, we detail how the consequential "fact" of pilot professionalism evolved from competing gendered discourses, which arose in response to specific economic, cultural, and political exigencies. The analysis adds flesh to our model of gendered organization as a complex, historically situated, and ongoing process of negotiating meanings, identities, and power relations.

6

A Feminist Communicology of the Airline Pilot

*Gender and the Organization
of Professional Identity*

❖ ❖ ❖

Oh! I have slipped the surly bonds of earth
And danced the skies on laughter-silvered wings;
Sunward I've climbed, and joined the tumbling mirth
Of sun-split clouds and done a hundred things
You have not dreamed of—wheeled and soared and swung
High in the sunlit silence. Hov'ring there,
I've chased the shouting wind along, and flung
My eager craft through footless halls of air.
Up, up, up the long, delirious, burning blue
I've topped the wind-swept heights with easy grace
Where never Lark, or even Eagle flew—
And while with silent lifting mind, I've trod

> The high untrespassed sanctity of space,
> Put out my hand and touched the face of God.
>
> —John Gillespie Magee, Jr.

*H*igh Flight, written by John Gillespie Magee on the back of a personal letter in 1941, surfaced time and again across the research reported here. The poem rhapsodizes the romantic, even spiritual experience of flight. But how did flight capture the social imagination, and how did we come to know and admire those who make it their livelihood? How did the aviator become symbolically and materially nestled in a white male body, and how did he secure unprecedented professional standing? How do contemporary airline pilots invoke and rework this discursive legacy? The empirical analysis we present in this chapter is part of Karen's ongoing study that addresses these questions. The larger project explores how U.S. airline pilot identity evolved across spheres of organizing activity and, more specifically, how this romanticized profession became entangled with gender, race, and class formations. Thus, in the spirit of the fourth way of framing discussed in Chapter 1, the project shifts the usual meaning of *organization*, looking beyond particular physical sites to the formation of professional identity across public and private arenas of practice, such as popular culture, commercial aviation organizations, and individual pilot experience. This chapter is not meant to offer a comprehensive analysis of the study data, which span museum exhibits, archival texts and film, and in-depth interviews with contemporary pilots. Instead, our intent is to provide an exemplar that illustrates the application and promise of the feminist communicology approach outlined in Chapter 5.[5]

Consistent with a communicology perspective, we take the idealized identity and professional status of airline pilots as a provisional product of shifting, competing, and historical discourses, which have been (dis)organized through communication across various social arenas. Relevant institutional contexts may include, for example, commercial airlines, labor unions, federal interventions and regulatory agencies, military organizations, civilian training and certification programs, air and space museums, Hollywood films, and career socialization in families. In particular, this chapter draws attention to representational patterns that cut across early popular and trade discourses of the pilot, as well as contemporary airline pilots' interpersonal efforts to represent themselves. With an eye for common threads and tensions, we examine how institutions and individuals (have) work(ed) to secure the status of airline pilots as venerated professionals, as well as the extent to which gender has figured as the medium and outcome of that process. Our focus on gender emphasizes the co-evolution of masculinity and femininity, as well as how these discursive formations intersect with other aspects of identity and thus are always partial.

In the first section of this chapter, we set the stage for our analysis by reviewing historical images of the pilot and identifying key vulnerabilities they posed to aviation and aviators. The second section examines how the "lady-flier," or "lipstick pilot," functioned in the 1920s and 1930s to assuage public fears about aviation safety and to demystify pilots' work. The third section considers a public relations campaign to concurrently ease public anxiety and attract passengers—namely, the efforts of commercial transport lines and the burgeoning airline pilot union to (re)mystify the airline pilot as an elite professional. In the fourth section, we investigate what happened when these two discursive formations, the "lady-flier" and the "professional airline pilot," collided in the case of the first U.S. woman to "fly the line." The fifth section explores the contemporary legacy of the airline pilot's gendered dialectic of class, wherein female fliers continue to represent an imminent threat to elite professional standing. Speaking directly to the tenets of our feminist communicology model, we argue that the communication of gendered symbolism served as a crucial mechanism for producing such material outcomes as an industry's economic viability and an occupation's privileged status. Moreover, the gendered selves and relations entailed in airline pilot and stewardess subjectivity became the enduring (albeit unsettled), lived outcome of that discursive and material process.

❖ THE BIRTH OF AVIATION AND THE AVIATOR: EARLY VULNERABILITIES OF SIGNIFICANCE AND SAFETY

In the first few decades of the 20th century, public narratives of flight and fliers produced an array of social knowledge about pilots. Our purpose in this section is to briefly establish a collection of cultural meanings from which the airline pilot emerged. In keeping with the historical interest of our theoretical model, the account we offer here is less concerned with documenting key people or events and more interested in rendering a discursive map of continuities and shifts in pilot identity, as it emerged in exchange with the sociopolitical and economic realities of the time.

Turn-of-the-century depictions of aviation "pioneers" like the Wrights tapped a beloved U.S. icon: the "inventor-tinkerer" (Wecter, 1941). These initial images of fliers affirmed social faith in the progressive union of science with American adventure, risk, and practicality. Soon, the "intrepid birdman," a moniker in wide circulation by 1910, came to capture the flashy flier of air meets and shows (H. L. Smith, 1942). Trade magazines and the popular press celebrated this figure as a superman, unafraid of death and consummately athletic, his body and mind a perfect specimen: "an extraordinary combination of active energy, courage, decision of purpose, a quick eye, clearness of judgment, the utmost presence of mind, and great physical dexterity" (as cited in Corn, 1979, p. 558). Some even posited flight as the exclusive evolutionary capacity of those rare humans lucky enough to descend from birds (Corn, 1979). Alongside awe for his form and skill, many people esteemed birdmen as peculiar, unpredictable characters, entitled to eccentricity by the sheer feat of their artistry. In this sense, the birdman was comparable to a circus performer or rock star, cloaked in the "flamboyant and colorful quirks of character and dress common to show-business people" (Hopkins, 1998, p. 8). Aviation, by implication, was little more than entertaining sideshow, for the general public scarcely conceived of its military or commercial applications and, thus, did not imagine its profound and permanent impact. Indeed, many commentators characterized flight as a passing fad.

World War I (WWI) brought political significance to flight and a solemn face to the flier. It stirred public fervor for the fatalistic but gallant "ace," as he embodied "the ancient notions of bravery, camaraderie, and adventure, which so curiously merge in war" (Hopkins, 1998, p. 9). Despite their peripheral role in the outcome of the war, pilots like Eddie Rickenbacker and the infamous "Red Baron" became household names, heroes who effectively diverted public attention from the atrocities of battle on the ground. Not long after the war, many military pilots who wished to fly for a living became traveling salesmen of flight. Offering rides and lessons to locals, they generally improvised farm fields as airstrips. These so-called barnstormers came to epitomize the primitive, unregulated, dangerous days of flight. Most often, the barnstormer was (and is) rendered as a lone, rugged, risk-taking, hot-tempered daredevil.

In the years following the war, a host of civilian and military pilots achieved celebrity status, adding a layer of glamour to the swashbuckling image of aces and barnstormers. Featured prominently in Hollywood films, advertisements, and other popular texts, celebrity pilots often appeared as "hard-living, hard-drinking playboys" who magically merged physical perfection and (hetero)sexual potency with an eternal life of excess. For example, a 1936 issue of *Literary Digest* characterized fliers as technological marvels unto themselves:

> Sleek in mind and body as the streamlined machines they pilot through the skies, these modern day mercuries are sorted out of the common run of humanity by a selfless elimination process which tolerates no flaw of body, nerve, or character. ("Flying Supermen and Superwomen," 1936, p. 22)

And *Fortune* magazine later declared that

> something has kept these chaps young, and it isn't asceticism either. When they play poker they play all night. When they smoke they smoke too much. When they drink their glasses leak, and when they make love complaints are rare. (Lay, 1941, pp. 122–123)

By the late 1920s, airmail contracts and the start of passenger lines had bolstered public perception of commercial aviation's long-term import. And the prestigious profile of airmail aviators—the original airline pilots—had shaped the widespread perception of pilot as cultural idol (O. E. Allen, 1981; H. L. Smith, 1942). Renowned for his bravery, individualism, skill, and intolerance of bureaucratic nuisance, the airmail pilot enjoyed near-demigod status. "Popular magazines serialized his exploit, and he bore many of the hallmarks of hero worship which a later generation would transfer to astronauts"(Hopkins, 1998, p. 20). Not surprisingly, despite the risk and regular fatalities entailed in early postal aviation, young male applicants abounded.

In sum, the airplane appeared to symbolize "the perfect blending of idea and technology, and the man who sat at its controls personified untold centuries of human wonderment at the concept of flight" (Hopkins, 1998, p. 8). Available discourses of flight and flier wove distinctively masculine themes of physical and sexual prowess, individualism, debonair courage, and rugged adventure, peppered with a dash of science. Not surprisingly, however, these images at once summoned public fascination with *and* fear of flight. Due largely to belief in pilots' herculean capacities, few people perceived aviation as a safe and normal human activity. After all, awe for the daring flier does not easily translate into willingness to hop on his plane. As one commentator put it,

> The aviation industry has held up many alibis for the failure of its general public acceptance. . . . It has blamed you for being afraid to fly; but has muffed its job of selling you. It has told you flying is safe—but continued to hold great shows and circuses that prove to as many as 50,000 spectators at a time it can be hair-raising. . . . In the majority of such onlookers the superman myth is perpetuated; the frowzy old notion that flying requires extraordinary qualities which are not found in average people. (Courtney, 1935, p. 40)

For a faltering aviation industry, pervasive fear of flight posed an enormous problem. Consequently, new discourses of the pilot emerged around this time. Specifically, in the late 1920s and early 1930s, various constituents in the aviation industry launched public relations endeavors designed to boost confidence in aviation safety and thus to attract and sustain a passenger population. Below, we focus our attention on two of the most prominent discourses about pilots during this time period; rarely have these been overtly placed alongside one another in scholarly analysis or public consciousness. The first discourse emerged from the promotion and popularity of "lady-fliers" or "ladybirds"; the second materialized from concentrated efforts to construct the elite professional character of the commercial transport pilot. Although the former discourse signaled at least some opportunities for women in commercial aviation, our analysis demonstrates how, ultimately, both discourses played off of one another to naturalize the exclusion of things feminine from the airline cockpit. As should be clear, we do not mean to depict such discourses as "free-floating" notions that happened to surface conveniently at this time. Rather, in tune with Chapter 5's conception of subjectivity and agency, we reveal how institutions and individuals actively and, in many cases, strategically invoked gender as an organizing apparatus.

❖ SELLING *AVIATION* SAFETY, EMASCULATING THE PILOT: THE DISCOURSE OF THE LADY-FLIER

Almost from the advent of flight, gender registered on public consciousness about aviation. As one might expect, gender was overtly marked primarily when the issue of female fliers arose. Some early articles, for example, undertook the "scientific" exploration of physical and psychological sex differences that might determine women's aptitude as fliers (e.g., "Will Woman Drive Man Out of the Sky?" 1911). Remarkably, the gender coding of the pilot remained up for grabs, at least somewhat, during the first few decades of debate on the matter. At issue was more than the question of whether women could or should fly; some observers publicly entertained the possibility that women would prove to be superior pilots and that aviation would become women's work (e.g., M. Adams, 1931; Martyn, 1929; Quimby, 1912).

By the late 1920s, uncertainties about women and flight appeared to dissolve in favor of the perception that a particular breed of femininity (i.e., white, upper-middle class, and heterosexual) was thoroughly compatible with piloting planes. Specifically, public talk of gender and aviation converged around a rising star: the "lady-flier," "ladybird," or "lipstick pilot," as she was commonly called. As we illustrate below, the congruity of femininity and flight doubled as proof of aviation safety—a claim that simultaneously began to erode the pilot mystique. Our aim as we discuss the nuances of discourse in this and the remaining sections of the chapter is threefold: (a) to underscore the dialectical and material character of discursive struggle, as competing narratives of the pilot generated partial yet concrete opportunities, constraints, and loopholes; (b) to situate dialectical struggle in terms of the political economy of the time, as the aviation industry and its various constituents strove for survival and credibility; and (c) to reveal how discourse simultaneously articulates and gets articulated by particular subjects with vested interests (for example, pilots and airline managers), who invent and circulate discourses that privilege and/or marginalize themselves. In these ways, our analysis adds flesh to the feminist communicology principles proposed in Chapter 5.

Although aviation enjoyed a moderate mark of legitimacy by the late 1920s, it was still acclaimed as a novel source of entertainment and wonder. Often hailed as the "golden age of flight," the 1920s and 1930s were a time when air shows and races reached new heights of popularity, when flight records and feats made front-page news. And among the hottest aviation story subjects were a host of women pilots, like Amelia Earhart, Ruth Elder, Viola Gentry, Laura Ingalls, Opal Kunz, Ruth Nichols, Phoebe Omlie, Harriet Quimby, Elinor Smith, Louise Thaden, and Bobbi Trout, to name a few. These and other ladybirds figured prominently in a media blitz about female fliers that continued for roughly a decade.

Abundant newspaper articles confirmed that the lady-flier shared the "sheer resolve and determination," "grit," and "nerve" of her male counterpart. Beyond these basics, the lady-flier was portrayed as a distinctively captivating creature. Many reporters expressed what might now be viewed as thinly veiled surprise and patronizing accolades regarding women's flying accomplishments. More prominent across the newspaper coverage was the tendency to celebrate the harmony of femininity and flight. In 1929, for instance, an article in *The New York Times* explained that flying is by no means antithetical to womanhood, for it is "a graceful sport" and "there is nothing in it which can possibly rob her of what she has" (Martyn, 1929). And in 1932, a piece in *The Literary Digest* titled "Ladybirds Down With Powdered Noses and a Brand New Record" proclaimed, "Quite fit and fresh the Ladybirds looked when they landed. Five thousand loudly applausive spectators admired their freshly powdered noses and beautifully curled hair" ("Ladybirds Down," 1932).

As these excerpts reveal, the lady-flier's performance hinged on more than flying skill; it entailed careful management of the female body, in its physical appearance and communicative expressions. In fact, many lady-fliers took great pains to preserve a feminine persona by, for example, donning special flight apparel, "touching up" their make-up and hair prior to landing or in public after flight, attributing mechanical troubles to personal inadequacy, and posing as social butterflies (Corn, 1979). Consider the following quote from a 1932 article written by a female flier:

> The women pilots were very smartly dressed in the late fall styles and colors. . . . Amelia Earhart was lovely in blue with gray fur and gray hat. Mrs. Dorothy Lea, a vivid brunette, was dressed in garnet. . . . I have cited this in detail for the ones who are skeptical as to women pilots lacking in femininity. . . . They, to me, represented the true American Woman—women who could do things, the unusual, and yet be all womanly, many women fliers are mothers . . . who achieve a harmonious fusion of many interests. . . . Our modern women pilots of today meets [sic] any tension with a lipstick or vanity case, or possibly a cigarette. (Alexander, 1932)

As hinted by this quote, the "lipstick pilots" were thought to represent a new and improved strand of femininity. A wealth of commentators revered the lady-flier as the personification of modern, liberated womanhood. The bolded caption under the title of one 1929 article on air races stressed the lady-flier's social butterfly bent and nonchalant, modern attitude: "'Twasn't Flying Tired Us; It Was Banquets,' Slim, Gray-Eyed Winner Says, Puffing Cigaret, in Floral Horseshoe." The article went on to equate the lady-flier figure with a new and appealing generation of women:

> Young, small for the most part, and pretty, these women of our century wear goggles instead of knitted shawls. They burn up distance in a way which is ridiculous. Just imagine your dear old grandmother hopping in a plane, tossing away a cigaret butt, pulling goggles over her eyes, giving the ship the gun and heading from California to Ohio? "Is aviation a woman's game? " . . . Probably it is, for leather helmets and pretty faces go beautifully together, and there are some who believe that a Sam Browne belt looks well on a small trim shoulder. (Loveland, 1929)

Similarly, and around the same time, another commentator described how the props of aviation facilitated a fresh, alluring femininity:

> The pilot was a *girl!* She pulled off her helmet and goggles, smiled and emerged from her flying suit wearing an afternoon frock. . . . And a certain feminine character had fascinated me, eluding adjectives. She was debonair and gallant, self-assured and self-possessed, cool and candid yet intensely feminine, ardent, mystical at times. Here were women who were pilots; pilots who were women. (Munyan, circa 1929/1930, p. 80)

He also writes that, far from the "stern, horsey creatures" one might expect female pilots to resemble,

> Girl pilots, by some odd paradox, become not less feminine but more so. If they lose anything, it is the simpering and parasitical tricks which they can well do without. They are more feminine than women who devote themselves so piously to being only that. Indeed, there are any number of women who fly their ships, fall in love, marry, have children, hold their husbands and resume flying, all with less bother than a clinging vine experiences in inveigling a stray male into imagining he wants to marry her. The typical girl pilot is intensely fascinating to first rate men, not so much because of a glamour about her as because of her character and charm. (p. 121)

As progressive as the lady-flier might be, we learn, she remains faithful to the womanly impulse for love and family.

While the latter quotation pits the liberated ladybird against a scathing caricature of conventional femininity, other variations on the lady-flier narrative stress the happy marriage of flight with traditional womanhood. In this more conservative vision, aviation afforded another arena into which women's natural roles could extend. Commonly, lady-fliers were rendered (and depicted themselves) as "aerial housekeepers," purveyors of "safe and sane" flight, mothers of the next generation of aviators—in brief, figures of "aerial domesticity" (Corn, 1979, p. 564). Such domestic images held fast even in women pilots' early aspirations to military status. The Betsy Ross Corps, founded during this time period, was a "patriotic society" that sought to ready lady-fliers to support male combat pilots in war.[6] The August 1931 issue of their newsletter, *The Betsy Ross Corps News*, offered this description of the Corps:

> There were many fine qualities in the colonial lady that the modern girl would do well to remember. She did not cheapen herself in her dress, her appearance, or in her behavior. She had a quiet dignity and charm and the ability to run her household and to care for her children. There was a certain fragile dainty quality about the colonial girl which we would do well to try to preserve. There is no reason why we cannot do this and at the same time be first rate pilots. . . . We're not trying to bring forth a freakish lot of women, nor are we contemplating any theatrical, hysterical or sensational activities. Our work is the same humanitarian relief work which has always been done by women, only we are using the latest, most modern medium for our service. Most of our members are married and most of these have children. The requirements of the Corps will never interfere with a member's first duty—her children and her home.

Ample evidence suggests that women pilots themselves were divided over commitment to progressive versus traditional femininity; internal disputes among members of the Betsy Ross Corps provide just one example ("Women Fliers Prepared to Split on Regulations," 1931). However, to the extent that the conservative strand of lady-flier discourse served to ease the alarm provoked by the more popular "liberated woman" narrative, it can be seen as a complementary variation on the lady-flier theme. In other words, it explicitly assured what the liberated ladybird only implied: that women's advancements would leave existing gender arrangements intact. Put simply, the modern woman pilot was merely an upgrade, not a rejection, of her predecessor.

Across variations of lady-flier discourse, then, common themes emerged. Chief among these was the claim that femininity and flying were congruent performances. Importantly, the form of femininity at stake was far from generic or universal. As the preceding excerpts attest, it honored heterosexual and domestic obligations.[7] It also reflected an upper-middle class bias, as evidenced by the popular fixation on "society girls" who fly (e.g., Jones, 1929; Patterson, 1929); by mundane references to the lineage, financial means, "electrical appliances," and "competent servants" of the lady-flier (e.g., "Fair Play for Women Fliers," 1927); and by the class-conscious rhetoric of the Betsy Ross Corps, among other excerpts above. The "high-class," "first rate" femininity of the lady-flier was also undeniably white. Repeated references to blond hair aɪ.d fair skin imply the association; more obvious is the striking absence of Black female flier Bessie Coleman, who died in a crash in 1926, from ladybird activities and attendant publicity. A final theme underlying lady-flier discourse involved recognition that the lipstick pilot was exceptional in large part *because* she was a woman, a novelty in a man's arena. However great her achievements, she accepted that she would always come in second, or play a supporting role, to the male pilot. This assumption materialized, for example, in the maintenance of separate race and feat records for women, an institutional practice requested and endorsed by many ladybirds (Corn, 1979).

The surge of attention granted to lady-fliers did not simply surface out of nowhere—a point that is crucial to illustrating Chapter 5's conception of relations among discourse, political and material realities, and the active subject. The U.S. beauty and cigarette industries utilized the ladybird for advertising purposes (e.g., Courtney, 1935). And clearly, news and magazine agencies and authors became willing collaborators in her promotion. However, various members of the aviation industry commenced the trend; for example, airplane manufacturers and sales organizations, flight instruction schools, racing clubs, and so forth all had vested interests and exercised loud voices in publicizing the ladybird. For example, the first all-women's air race was held in 1929 at the invitation of the Cleveland Air Races, which had previously excluded women from its events. Officials orchestrated much publicity for the race, and they formally required the ladybirds to fly a craft "appropriate for women" (which, according to commentators at the time, meant "slower than the male racers' planes"). Over the years, lady-fliers' exploits were officially sponsored by a variety of aviation corporations. The ladybirds were featured prominently in a range of aviation advertisements, and they were frequently employed in private plane promotions and sales.

Why, one might reasonably ask, would the constituents of the male-dominated aviation industry adopt such intense interest in female fliers at this time? Put concisely, to sell the public on the safety of airplanes. In other words, the lady-flier was strategically deployed to make flight palatable to the public and thus to ensure the commercial viability of aviation (Corn, 1979). But why would women pilots be particularly useful for proving safety? That women could fly indicated the ease and minimal physical requirements of doing so; it also attested to the trustworthiness of the actual planes. To put the message bluntly, flying is effortless; better yet, these ships are so sturdy, they don't need a great pilot. As early as 1912, for instance, an author noted that

> Some of the inventors saw a chance for a new spectacle in the exhibition field, and the fact that a woman could handle a machine would seem to give confidence in the safety of flight, they reasoned. In view of these advantages woman mastered the situation. (Gregory, 1912, p. 316)

Some 20 years later, a *New York Times Magazine* author observed of ladybirds, "They will all tell you, with an almost identical twinkle in eyes that are gray, blue, brown, that they are valuable in promoting aviation because the public believes that 'if women can fly it must be easy and safe'" (M. Adams, 1931, p. 20). In effect, the lady-flier discourse became a pivotal means by which to shame the (male) public into purchasing planes, flight lessons, and passenger tickets.

As hinted in the preceding paragraph, many of the lady-fliers appeared to understand and exploit their utility to the aviation industry (e.g., "Ladybirds Down," 1932). However, many were also concerned that the obvious publicity drive would haunt any long-term quest for legitimacy (Kunz, 1929; "Wants Equal Rights in the Air," 1929). For reasons elaborated in the fourth section of our analysis, their fears were well-founded. For now, our point is that the lady-flier, whose effortless performance personified the safety of flight, occupied a central role in the aviation industry's publicity crusade. Women pilots of the time actively contributed to the lady-flier image, which at once enabled their right to fly and affirmed their feminine limitations. As industry members had hoped, the lady-flier captivated audiences and soothed the anxieties of would-be clients. And yet, while the industry thrived due to her presence, her identity was also threatening, for the lady-bird's rise to fame demystified, and even risked feminizing, the act of flying. The elusive manly ethos of earlier days perched perilously close to illusion.

The lady-flier embodied a palpable threat to pilot prestige, the logic of which unfolded as follows. First, the lady-flier raised the possibility that there are few, if any, sex differences in flight—that in the air, men and women can be equals. One author at the time mused, "It is a prospect that catches the breath, and sets up all kinds of questions in the mind. Is it merely a myth that women are weak creatures, subject to fear, liable to tears and fainting in the face of danger?" (Adams, 1931, p. 6). Another article avowed, "But it is the same for women as for men; neither sex has a monopoly of appreciation for the beauties of flying; neither has a greater feeling for the subtleties of flying, nor has one necessarily more skill than the other" (Martyn, 1929).

A second and related perception held that, if indeed there are few differences between men and women in aviation, this must be because flying is easy; that is, rather than cast suspicion on gender assumptions, the lack of difference warrants a second look at the worth of the activity itself. Many ladybirds seemed to relish this point, eagerly building the safety argument, often at their own expense. Noted lady-flier Harriet Quimby (1912) asserted that

> There is no sport that affords the same amount of excitement and enjoyment, and exacts in return so little muscular strength. It is easier than walking, driving, automobiling; easier than golf or tennis. I should say that it is an ideal pastime for the lazy sportsman. The men flyers have given out the impression that aeroplaning is very perilous work, something that an ordinary mortal should not dream of attempting; but when I saw how easily the men flyers manipulated their machines I said I could fly. (p. 315)

Another famous lady-flier, Opal Kunz, insisted that "Flying is no test of physical strength. I use three fingers on the stick" ("Wants Equal Rights," 1929). Some time later she added, "It requires no physical strength to fly an airplane. They are being made so perfectly today that they respond to the slightest touch" ("Aviation Urged as Career for Girls," 1929). Reporters began to reproduce the claim, repeating such insights as this: "The most striking proof that brawn is not essential is embodied in Miss Smith. A slender child, weighing not more than 115 pounds" (Adams, 1931, p. 20).

Third, descriptions of flight as a tacitly feminine pursuit—artistic, graceful, and sensitive—began to circulate. One commentator followed the question "Why do girls get into flying?" with the response that flying is an art, and that pilots as a rule tend to excel at other arts. He continued, "The observation deals a wallop to the idea that fliers are pretty tough birds. They are not: they are highly coordinated, sensitive types. Girl pilots very often have a singular delicacy, the long fingers and slender lines of physically sensitive people" (Munyan, circa 1929/1930, p. 120). Similarly, a popular lady-flier explained, "An airplane is rather like a musical instrument than a vehicle of transportation. It does not require physical strength to fly. The qualities necessary for success in this are mental and spiritual, rather than physical. An artist or musician often makes an exceptionally good pilot" (Kunz, 1930).

Together, these mounting perceptions lent support to the question: Why all the fuss over pilots? Challenging the awe inspired by ladybirds easily slipped into debating public reverence for flight and fliers. For example, *The New York Times* reported in 1929 that

> The woman flier has come to be looked upon as a romantic figure. Many writers have put her on a pedestal for no other reason, apparently, than that she is a woman. Where women are concerned there seems to be a strong temptation to dramatize their exploits. Flying itself becomes crowned with an aurora of higher adventure and thrills. Thrills there are of course; but they are not all the thrills of danger. . . . As in everything else, there is romance in flying, if one stops to search it out—an overwhelming appeal to the emotions and a resultant and seemingly inevitable sentimentation. . . . There are heroines among them, as there must be, but the young woman clad in a man's breeches and riding boots, with her open-necked shirt, goggles and helmet—even if a wrap of golden hair protrudes from under it—is no darling of the gods. . . . Flying an airplane need not, after all, be hard work. It has often been pointed out that it is more usual to move the controls a fractional part of an inch than three inches. There is no manual labor involved. (Martyn, 1929)

In this sense, the lady-flier became both boon and bane of aviators. But how, then, was the threat diffused, the pilot profession spared from emasculation? This question compels attention, for not only was this fate dodged, the opposite also occurred. Amid public fervor for female pilots, airline flying became deeply masculinized work, such that it appeared naturally, inevitably so. Astoundingly, the masculinization process was all but complete by the late 1930s, when the lady-flier was just beginning to fade from public view. The burning question is, what accounts for the dramatic shift from optimistic statements—like the 1935 pronouncement "Step by step the flying-jobs-for-women impasse seems headed for improvement" ("'Queen Helen of Air,'" 1935)—to the dismal 1938 proclamation that piloting work "has no room in it for any girl, however well qualified she may be . . . the result is, apparently, millions for publicity, but not one cent for salary" (Palmer, 1938)? The next two sections examine how this drastic transformation was made possible, much less persuasive, to a public enthralled with the beloved lady-flier. We begin with the concurrent overhaul of the commercial transport pilot's image, turning to the brief historical moment when a ladybird was hired to fly the line.

❖ SELLING *AVIATOR* SAFETY,
SECURING OCCUPATIONAL PRIVILEGE: THE
DISCOURSE OF THE PROFESSIONAL AIRLINE PILOT

Thus far, we have observed two broad discursive trends with respect to pilots. The first involved the heritage of early 20th century narratives, which crafted the aviator's supermanly mystique—his legendary physical and sexual capacities, his appetite for adventure, his brave self-sufficiency. As explained in the first section of our analysis, this confluence of images did little to legitimize aviation as a commercial enterprise, for it stimulated public awe and fear of flight by stressing its stunning fallibility. Faced with financial pressures to sell more private planes, flight lessons, and the like, many members of the aviation industry became sponsors and beneficiaries of the second discursive trend: the promotion of the lady-flier in the late 1920s and 1930s. For all her charms, however, the ladybird was no blessing to commercial transport.

The economic barrier created by public perceptions of danger, coupled with available discourses of pilots, presented a serious constellation of problems for the burgeoning commercial transport industry—problems only exacerbated by the lady-flier persona. Even with the considerable aid of federal airmail subsidies, U.S. commercial airlines were far from profitable in the late 1920s (*An Engineering Interpretation*, circa 1940). In the interest of long-term viability, they had to find a way to accomplish two related objectives—and soon: (a) ensuring the sale of passenger tickets and (b) doing so by cultivating a permanent audience. In other words, they had to persuade a skeptical public that flight was a reliable mode of modern transportation, not mere spectacle or private sport. From an airline management perspective, this imperative required "proving" the utility and dependability of an entire operation, from aircraft to scheduling to pilots. While the ladybird spurred faith in airplane technology, and seemed to dare many into sampling the thrills of flight, she did little to boost aviation as a regular means of travel and even less to inspire trust in the body that "manned" the cockpit.

The problems faced by airline pilots differed somewhat from those encountered by airline managers. The inherited masculine ethos of exceptional physicality and bold individuality distanced airline pilots from the conventional work cultures of white-collar professionals *and* organized labor, such that airline pilots lacked a strong collective identity with which to meet capricious—and, in some cases, malicious— management tactics. To make matters worse, the discourse of the lipstick flier subtly yet publicly mocked the pilot's importance, begging the question of whether his "work" was really labor at all.

Although a fair amount of friction typified management-pilot relations at the time (Baitsell, 1966; Hopkins, 1998; Northrup, 1947), there was cause for alliance. Airlines sought profit via passengers; pilots pursued profit by way of occupational status and protection from management. But for both parties, selling the enterprise of commercial transport meant selling a livelihood. Ironically, then, it was a partnership born (in the midst) of dialectical struggle. Airline managers and pilots colluded in a concerted effort to reconstruct pilots as authentic professionals. Yet this was no simple claim to stake. Consider the symbolic resources and vulnerabilities bestowed upon airline pilots by the legacy of manly mystique. "Suave superman" they could pull off, for instance, but surely not "reliable professional"? The early flier's aura "stemmed from sources which were distinctly nonprofessional. Self-taught inventors, daredevil birdmen, and hard-living celebrity fliers were in many respects the antithesis of the formally educated man with a college degree" (Hopkins, 1998, p. 15). However adored, the aviator appeared robust, untamed, even excessive—a far cry from the muted, stable bureaucratic body.

At the core of the ensuing public relations campaign stood the pilot's body. He underwent a meticulous makeover, literally redressed and supplied with props to facilitate professional performance. Specifically, several airlines designed the pilot's uniform to mimic that of a sea captain and, accordingly, to invoke a tradition of authority and rational decision making previously associated with officers. Crew members were assigned formal rank titles, such as "Captain" and "First Officer." Some airlines installed loudspeakers to enable air captains to communicate with passengers like their seafaring counterparts. *Aviation*, the dominant trade magazine, consistently praised these moves, arguing that customers would recoil if pilots dressed in "grease-stained or rough and tumble clothing" (Hopkins, 1998, p. 17). Crucial to professional dependability, the uniformed body was also white and male, with the "'clean-cut Anglo-American' type generally preferred" (Northrup, 1947, pp. 569–570). In fact, on the grounds that nonwhite members would soil the precarious professional image of pilots, the airline pilot's fledgling union—Air Line Pilot's Association (ALPA)—adhered to a formal whites-only clause until 1942, retaining a tacit prohibition against pilots of color for some time thereafter.

In addition to sculpting the pilot as an elite officer, commercial airlines began to stress the pilot's scientific knowledge and technical skills, carefully honed through rigorous training and testing. A compilation of reflections from airline executives, reported in a special issue of ALPA's magazine *The Air Line Pilot* on "fifty fabulous years of aviation," vividly reveals the shift in emphasis ("Men, Planes, and Faith," 1953). For instance, one airline president declared that, as a pilot himself, he could

> fully appreciate the skill and technical know-how that has been—and still is—demanded of airline pilots since the advent of powered flight. Most certainly it is an unending task of mastering the constantly improving techniques of one of man's most amazing conquests. (p. 16)

Other airline executives explained the emphasis on technical mastery as part of the pilot's evolution and as a sure sign of safety and modern progress. The following series of excerpts from "Men, Planes, and Faith" (1953), each from a different executive, illustrates the point:

> Many a chapter in that rapidly-unfolding history of commercial aviation in the West was written by the pilot in goggles and leather jacket. He set records now and then to make headlines and sell tickets. . . . Twenty-eight years later the man in the flight compartment of a four-engine Western Air Lines DC-6B depends no longer on luck or daring. He is a man of science and skill, commanding under trained eyes and hands the million-dollar product of the world's finest engineers and designers. (p. 15)

> Today we find them not only technically capable airmen but ambassadors of goodwill for the scheduled aircraft industry. Back in the early days of flying, pilots were regarded as reckless daredevils and stunt men. . . . The great pool of scientific knowledge which exists today in the aviation industry is due, in part, to contributions by thoughtful pilots. . . . All of these things have helped to popularize flying. (p. 10)

> Today the Captain of the modern, long-range airliner uses many new tools with which science has provided him but he must also be the master of a far more complex airplane. . . . The requirements of the pilot's profession are exacting. He must live up to rigid standards of personal qualification of conduct both on and off the job. (p. 23)

> In the pioneering era, they showed the daring of ancient explorers. In the barnstorming period, they flaunted a spectacular showmanship and an aerial skill that were uncanny. They licked the weather before navigation aides were set up. They developed new routes. As commercial aviation settled into a more established and substantial industry, they demonstrated a solid dependability. (p. 16)

It is worth noting the sharp contrast between these quotes and tales of the lady-flier, in which pilots needed scant knowledge and skill because planes practically flew themselves. Conversely, in the new discourse, the fate of the transport lines and their passengers rested in the capable hands of the airline pilot. One airline president captured him as a sort of renaissance man who heralded an optimistic future:

The true airline pilot, as I know him, is a conscientious, skilled and thorough-going gentleman who is interested in his job, his passengers, his company and his industry . . . with the pilot's adherence to the highest standards of his craft, we most certainly are going much further in the years ahead. ("Men, Planes, and Faith," 1953, p. 9)

Thus, the professional airline pilot, cream of the flying crop, was manufactured around a particular breed of white masculinity—commanding, civilized, rational, technical, and, as we illustrate in a moment, deeply heterosexual and paternal. We use the term *manufacture* to underscore the strategic production of this flying figure. One airline executive put it bluntly:

Not so often recognized, however, are the contributions pilots have made in the field of sales. The goal of the airline industry has been the creation of a "mass" market—a market which represents the acceptance of air transportation as a common mode of travel. In helping to build up this market, airline pilots have excelled. The assurances of safety and security which pilots have conveyed directly or indirectly to the traveling public is one of the chief reasons for the ever-expanding scope of air service. ("Men, Planes, and Faith," 1953, p. 9)

Others concurred that, "Their friendly dignity, their adherence to the highest professional standards, and the leadership exercised by aircraft commanders, have convinced the people of all lands that the U.S.-flag airlines are unsurpassed in safety, reliability, and friendly service" (p. 15).

Not only was the production of the professional airline pilot a calculated affair; it was a continuing process. For years to come, proponents of the airline pilot's elite professional identity would call for painstaking efforts at rehearsal and maintenance. Consider the following advice published in ALPA's *The Air Line Pilot* over 20 years after the first traces of pilot-as-professional discourse:

Communication with the unconscious anxiety-personalities of passengers has to be accomplished with the language of symbolism. . . . The captain is a symbol, a sort of "father image" in a situation where the passenger is incapable of controlling his own destiny and anxiety. This symbol-function of the captain is quite unrelated to the captain's own outer personality. The symbol function can be carried out successfully by a captain, no matter whether he is tall or short . . . handsome or drab . . . no matter whether he exudes charm or whether he feels uncomfortable while talking to strangers . . . no matter whether his voice is modulated or rasping . . . no matter whether the passengers ever see him or not. The captain's confidence must come through all of these. . . . At all times he must give the overall impression "I KNOW WHERE I AM. I KNOW WHAT I AM DOING. I KNOW WHAT IS UP AHEAD. I HAVE THINGS UNDER CONTROL. RELAX, AND LET ME BE CONCERNED WITH THE FLIGHT. I WILL KEEP YOU POSTED." (Kurtz, 1953, p. 6)

By reminding the pilot that his professional identity required disciplined performance, this passage tacitly denaturalized the discourse. At the same time, it offered the pilot a privileged subject position, which he was both entitled and coerced to occupy convincingly, despite corporeal limitations. To achieve persuasive performance, the article continued, each captain should recognize his strengths and frailties with respect to the desired identity and select communication channel(s) accordingly. Recommended channels include (a) talking over the plane's public address system, (b) instructing a crew member or stewardess to relay a message from the captain in his name, and (c) strolling through the cabin to speak face-to-face with passengers. The example attests to the strategic and precarious quality of the pilot-as-professional discourse. Simultaneously, it affirms the centrality of gendered performance to erasing these discursive features and stabilizing, even naturalizing, the identity.

The invention of the airline pilot's new professional image did more than pacify a flying public. It "elevated pilots to a profession unequaled by any class or craft in the confines of union jurisdiction, a position of public trust to be jealously guarded" (Kuhn, 1953, p. 7). Airline pilots themselves deployed the bodily—and, specifically, gender and race—bases of professionalism to seduce public and federal support, secure professional monopoly, and institutionalize high salaries. We do not retrace their steps here, for Hopkins's (1998) detailed account of the development and triumphs of ALPA chronicles the complicated path to these achievements. Our point is twofold. First, the gendered discourse of pilot professionalism anchored the airline pilot's prestigious social and political status and validated his claim to deserve substantial material reward. Second, several institutional bodies, including arms of the U.S. government, participated in the sedimentation of that discourse. In an early analysis of airline pilots' remarkable success at collective bargaining, Northrup (1947) explained that ALPA achieved its strength by masterfully wielding the pilot's image:

> Despite its limited numbers (and votes), it (ALPA) has won the aid of Congress to a degree which has been exceeded by few organizations. Taking full advantage of the "romantic allure" of the industry and jobs, pilots, lobbying in their smart uniforms, have impressed the legislators time and again. (p. 574)

Hopkins (1998) concurred, arguing that airline pilots soared to professional prestige by "manipulating the masculinity symbols which were so blatantly a part of aviation" (p. 2). Even ALPA's founder, David Behncke, recognized the material consequences of strategic symbolism. In an address at the 1934 ALPA convention, he observed,

> Before we organized there was no such thing as an air line pilot. . . . It has all been created by publicity. . . . What we have done, we have taken the air transport pilots that fly on the lines, we have given them their real names, we have given them their birth right, they are air line pilots. . . . Cartoons setting forth the air line pilot and . . . words blazing across the papers . . . have set you up separate and distinct with high qualifications and high in the economic set up of this country. That is worth plenty. (as cited in Hopkins, 1998, pp. 17–18)

For commercial airlines and pilots, it literally was "worth plenty." And in a kind of reverse or circular logic, transport lines and pilots began to cite the airline flier's high salary as a sure marker of professional credibility. One airline president mused, "I expressed the opinion that such a pilot never would be 'a dime a dozen' . . . if pilots ever get into that category, I don't want to fly with them" ("Men, Planes, and Faith," 1953, p. 9). Behncke was reputed to have summarized pithily, "The public would not have a cheap doctor and they don't want cheap pilots" (Kuhn, 1953, p. 6).

Of equal import to its political and economic effects, the discourse of pilot professionalism appeared to materialize in the everyday experience of flying the line. Many airline pilots began to internalize the privileged subjectivity that the discourse offered them, relishing in the dignified pleasures of membership in an elite, manly occupational club. One captain captured the visceral sensation this way: "Whenever I see the pilot of a modern airliner, handsome in a snappy uniform, competent and confident, I feel a surge of pride" (Lipsner, 1953, p. 18).

Pilot professionalism remained wedded to a particular form of white masculinity for decades and, as we argue in the fifth section of our analysis, the legacy of that union persists today. For at least 40 years, the claim that pilots are consummate professionals—the embodiment of technical, physical, and emotional mastery—was reproduced across domains of social activity, ranging from airline advertising campaigns and documentaries to (auto)biographies of airline captains to children's books.

In sum, commercial airlines and aviators effectively manufactured the airline pilot's professional prestige as a path to industry viability and occupational standing. They sold commercial flight and fliers, in large part, by fashioning a "new" professional body based on a parallel masculine model: the sea captain. Simultaneously, the larger aviation industry remained invested in the lady-flier. Did her popularity, as many believed at the time, signal declining sex discrimination and unprecedented access to flying jobs? Or would the effortless flying for which she was famous, not to mention her penchant for "aerial housekeeping," clash with the emerging figure of the commercial transport commander? Next, we examine what happened when the discourses of the lady-flier and professional pilot collided, as they did in the case of the first woman hired by a U.S. airline.

❖ CLOSING THE COCKPIT, OPENING THE CABIN: LADY-FLIER MEETS PROFESSIONAL PILOT (AND BECOMES A STEWARDESS)

In 1934, Helen Richey was a newly popular ladybird, propelled to fame by her recent achievement of a women's flight endurance record. That year, Central Airlines selected her from a pool of eight male candidates for a copilot post. Richey's appointment met with much enthusiasm in the media; after all, she had hurdled "the industry's last barrier to women job-seekers" ("'Queen Helen of Air,'" 1935). In the words of one commentator, "Newspapers heralded the announcement as meaning new recognition of the value of women fliers. . . . Helen Richey, commercial air pilot, was news" (Adams & Kimball, 1942, p. 190).

What record remains of Richey's brief tenure as an airline pilot indicates that her appointment, from its inception, was little more than a publicity stunt. Glen Kerfoot, the leading biographer of Helen Richey (see, e.g., G. Kerfoot, 1988), reported that Central Airlines' president James Condon planned to attract headlines "by doing something no other airline in history had done, he thought—hiring a woman to fly a commercial airliner" (G. Kerfoot, 1991a). Condon contacted the Department of Commerce to inform them of his intentions and to offer assurances that Richey would only fly for a few weeks before reassignment. "Since the officials were equally interested in promoting the fledgling aviation industry," they assented to the plan.

Over the next several months, a series of institutional moves converged to remove Richey from her job and, in the process, to sever the professional airline pilot from femininity. Among these moves, male airline pilots lobbied vociferously against their female colleague, reportedly even threatening to strike (G. Kerfoot, 1978). More specifically, their institutional voice, ALPA, rejected Richey's application for membership and began to pressure federal regulatory agencies. For example, ALPA sent a letter to the Department of Commerce, protesting Richey's copilot post:

> They said the idea was preposterous since you didn't see women operating locomotives or serving as ship captains. They insisted there was danger involved since women did not have the physical strength to handle a large airliner in bad weather. Finally, they pointed out, if the practice of hiring women to pilot airliners continued, where would that leave the men. (G. Kerfoot, 1991b)

As an aside, such logic implies the pilots' recognition that female colleagues could derail their campaign to come off as the (big) brothers of railroad engineers and sea captains. According to Kerfoot, the Department of Commerce assured ALPA that Richey's airline flying days were numbered. When she continued to fly, they questioned Condon, who claimed that the publicity for Richey was beyond his control and would have to subside before her removal from the cockpit. The Department of Commerce, "which was actively promoting safety in air travel," urged that Richey be assigned few trips and concluded that "it would not countenance Miss Richey's being sent out as copilot in bad weather" (Adams & Kimball, 1942, p. 190). Since the Department of Commerce had already considered a proposal to ground women fliers around the time of their menstrual cycle, the weather proclamation was not a huge argumentative leap (Corn, 1979). Girded by the institutional message that women were not reliable pilots under the grueling conditions of transport flight, Central Airlines began to restrict Richey's flying time (G. Kerfoot, 1978). Instead,

> she found herself being used largely for publicity photographs, talks to civic clubs and school groups, airport tours, and other public relations chores. In nine months of service she had flown only a dozen round trips between Washington and Detroit, and then only in good weather. (G. Kerfoot, 1983, p. 161)

Dissatisfied with work as a fair-weather flier, Richey resigned before the end of 1935—an action variously described as "friendly," "reluctant," "in disgust," and "in protest." Astonishingly, it would be 38 years before a U.S. airline hired another woman pilot.

Much controversy ensued. In November of 1935, the Washington, D.C. *Evening Star* reported Amelia Earhart's firm declaration that sex bias, particularly that of ALPA and the Department of Commerce, had forced Richey to resign. Given Earhart's wild popularity, her involvement in the story intensified its public traction. The article explained that

> Helen Richey . . . lost out as a commercial flyer because the pilots' union refused to accept her as a member, forcing her to resign from Central Airlines, according to Amelia Earhart, famed aviatrix. . . . Miss Earhart, the country's first lady of the air, brought Miss Richey's resignation to public attention in urging creation of a fund to "help woman to gain her proper place in aviation." ("Sex Held Reason for Pilot's Loss," 1935, p. A2)

The Department of Commerce expressed surprise at Richey's resignation, adding that "they had only suggested she be relieved of making runs in very rough weather because of the manual labor required to manage a big tri-motor ship" ("Sex Held Reason," 1935, p. A2). ALPA maintained that, although Richey was denied membership due to union by-laws, she was also invited to reapply at the union's next meeting, yet she had failed to do so. Meanwhile, Central Airlines claimed that Richey resigned voluntarily for personal reasons related to health and rest.

By the end of 1935, Richey was hired as an air-marking pilot by the Bureau of Air Commerce in Washington (Adams & Kimball, 1942) "to quiet things down" (G. Kerfoot, 1983, p. 161). Richey herself urged the silence, quipping to reporters, "Why all the fuss? Can't a person quit a job without everyone getting excited about it? I got all the experience I wanted and that's why I resigned" (G. Kerfoot, 1991b). Air-marking entailed the inscription of town names in large fluorescent letters on selected rooftops. Toward the development of a sort of sky map, air-marking pilots flew to identify optimum locations for marking. A 1937 article in the *San Francisco Chronicle,* devoted to the "four female flying aces" responsible for U.S. air-marking, gleefully exclaimed that

> There is one field in the aviation world where men are grounded while only women are up in the air. . . . Mrs. Thaden, the first woman to be employed when this strictly modern job for women was created two years ago, believes that women are the choice of the Bureau of Air Commerce because they attend to detail better than men do—and because town officials and WPA executives are more impressed when a woman suggests that a marker be placed on the corner bakery or motion picture house than they would be if men made the request. . . . The air-marker alights, powders her nose, and either gets herself announced to the mayor, or opens his door and walks into the office. . . . Air-marking, so the Bureau of Air Commerce has decided, is a woman's job! (Welshimer, 1937)

It seemed that the ladybird had found a more suitable set of wings, in a supporting work role with a necessarily dim future. The article noted Richey as "the only woman flyer who ever piloted a commercial air transport plane" and mentioned that "Miss Richey resigned her co-pilot's job after eight months and was appointed an air-marking pilot in December of 1935" (Welshimer, 1937). Later articles would also recall Richey's airline resignation as a matter of personal choice, or even as an upgrade. For example, "She quit after nine months for a government job flying around the country picking out sites for air markers" ("Woman Pilot Teaching Men," circa 1947). Although Richey flew for the British Air Transport Auxiliary (ATA) and, later, the U.S. Women's Air (Force) Service Pilots (WASPs) in WWII, she was unable to land substantial flying work afterward. Reportedly, she remarked to her sister in 1946 that "her flying days were over and life was a bore to her" (G. Kerfoot, 1978). Helen Richey committed suicide in January of 1947.

In a sense, the poignant story of Helen Richey symbolizes the fate of the lady-flier, even to the extent that she participated in facilitating her own demise. We argue that lady-flier discourse ironically supplied the raw materials for banishing women from the airline cockpit. Moreover, these are the resources upon which ALPA, the Department of Commerce, Central Airlines, various news agencies, and even some ladybirds drew in constructing a persuasive case for the requisite masculinity of the airline pilot.

At first glance, common themes in the lady-flier discourse (for instance, the seamless performance of femininity and flight, the ladybird as "proof" of airplane safety) permeated the coverage of Richey's hire. Most reports stressed her attractiveness and marveled at the effortlessness with which this "slight girl" with "tiny hands" could fly a large transport craft. "Yes, she's a girl," the caption of one article began. "She's young. She's pretty. She's a good flyer. But she's more than that. She's a force . . . at work transforming aviation from an interesting stunt into a major means of everyday transportation" (Courtney, 1935, p. 16). The article went on to assert that Richey's cockpit presence was appealing to passengers, who saw in her evidence of safety: "There are other vigilant observers of the affair Richey—the business diagnosticians who seek to learn why our brave and romantic compatriots stay away by the millions from airplane travel" (p. 16).

On closer inspection, the relationship between commercial transport flying and ladybird femininity exhibited signs of strain from the start of Richey's appointment. Despite studious attention to her beauty, for example, many articles portrayed flying for a living as an unfeminine pursuit: "Her work is hard. . . . No time for parties. She flies into Washington at three in the morning and sits at the lunch counter for a cup of coffee before she goes home . . . and she never uses cosmetics" (Courtney, 1935, p. 43). Most of the news coverage reflects a tension visible in one magazine article, which observed that Richey exhibited an "efficient air, but when she smiles you see a girl feminine as a lace and ivory fan. It sounds romantic. . . . But if you'll follow Helen Richey over one trip, you will see that the romance is all in the heart of the adventurer. Flying is hard work. . . . Flying is a tense occupation . . . she does not sleep or look idly at the scenery" (Davis, circa 1935, p. 28).

Later in the article, the conflict between femininity and airline flying became all the more palpable:

> Does she look haggard and blowsy after all this? On the contrary, she's unbelievably fresh and dewy. . . . Though she likes to play, to dance, go to theaters and parties, when she's on the job, she's just another pilot to herself and to her colleagues. She indulges no feminine mannerisms. . . . The French have the only word that describes Helen at work: A *bonne garconne;* a good boy, feminine gender. (p. 30)

Arguably, the discourse of the lady-flier activated the tension between femininity and commercial transport flying in the following ways. First, as argued above, the lipstick pilot was meant to prove the reliability of aircraft, not pilots; indeed, she testified to plane safety at the expense of pilots. The subtle difference between women as evidence of plane versus pilot safety surfaced immediately in press coverage of Richey's airline appointment. For example, just after invoking Richey to confirm the wonders of the modern transport craft, one article asked,

> Are passengers afraid to fly with a woman pilot? Officials of the airline say the only whimpers have come from other women. They are likely to forget that, as in any masculine calling, a woman has to be a great deal better than any man in the same job. When they note her excellence, they too say pridefully, "She flies like a man." (Davis, circa 1935, p. 30)

Note the underlying messages: While the ship itself is safe, it is reasonable to wonder whether one should take the added risk of climbing on it with a woman at the controls. In a fascinating move that deflects accountability for posing the question, such doubts are ascribed to other women.[8] Finally, the ultimate witness to Richey's credibility is the compliment that "she flies like a man," which served not only as the title of the article but also to affirm the masculinity of the airline pilot's professionalism.

Second, the shift from "ladybird as proof of safety" to "ladybird as unsafe to fly commercial transport" was not such a stretch, considering the kind of aircraft and flying with which the lady-flier was aligned. Chiefly, the ladybird flew smaller, private planes and flew for largely personal reasons. It was precisely because of this association with limited forms of aviation that the ladybird discourse could accept gender differences yet render these irrelevant to flight. Articles about the lady-flier commonly noted two exceptions to her seemingly boundless horizons but left these to future consideration. The first exception hinged on the difficulties of women's long-term employment in aviation. For example, some authors wondered how "these brides" could "fulfill their complex duties as wives and then mothers while retaining the pilot rating" (Munyan, circa 1929/1930). More typically, press coverage confirmed that women flew for sport and pleasure (e.g., Jones, 1929; Munyan, circa 1929/1930). One piece in *The New York Times* drew an analogy between flying and driving. Whereas women frequently drove cars, they rarely drove trucks or locomotives. The same would likely hold in aviation:

> Women seem much more likely to be the users of light planes for flying over short distances to pay calls and visit over week-ends and for purely sporting purposes than they ever are likely to be transport pilots driving the great air liners of the future. (Martyn, 1929)

The second exception revolved around physical strength and endurance. Several advocates of the lady-flier conceded that the development of increasingly large and technologically complex transport aircraft, especially when combined with nasty weather conditions, would necessarily limit the ladybird's flight (e.g., Adams, 1931; Martyn, 1929, 1930).

True to the larger social construction of women as private figures and men as public figures, the lady-flier was discursively aligned with domestic flight motives and practices, while the pilot-as-professional discourse depicted airline flying as a position of public trust. Several ladybirds contributed to the maintenance of the public-private separation and attendant division of flying labor, even in response to Richey's appointment and resignation. In an article celebrating Richey's airline hire, famous ladybird Ruth Nichols was quoted thus:

> That you or I or any woman of average physical equipment can in normal times fly a plane for pleasure or for business is my honest conviction. In fact I contend that women's entrance into aviation as a profession has proved that flying is really safe. . . . But, as a

matter of fact, it is through sport flying [non-commercial] that woman will find her place in aviation, for professionally she is subject to many handicaps. . . . But I don't see any more reason for women to act as transport-pilots than for them to act as sea-captains or truck-drivers. ("'Queen Helen of Air,'" 1935, brackets in original)

Likewise, when Amelia Earhart charged sex bias in the Richey resignation affair, lady-flier Ruth Haviland dissented on the grounds that

In private and race flying women need not give ground to men. . . . But I've flown big transport planes and it's hard physical work. It takes strength and sometimes a great deal of strength. A woman can't step in and fly at nights readily, either. ("Sex Held Reason," 1935, p. A2)

Ample evidence supports the claim that other ladybirds became public voices of their own doom, often while employed by various aviation institutions (e.g., Adams & Kimball, 1942). We make this point in an effort *not* to blame but to highlight the dialectical, hegemonic character of discursive struggle, wherein the object of a discourse is also its subject, who invokes gendered narrative ironically to open and close her own windows of opportunity. Put in terms of Chapter 5's communicology model, complicit ladybirds vividly illustrate a theory of subjectivity at once decentered and agentic.

The case of Helen Richey realized the worst fears of those lady-fliers who had questioned the superficial and paradoxical nature of ladybird publicity (e.g., O. Kunz, 1929; G. Palmer, 1938). In essence, the lady-flier was exploited to promote plane safety and was then promptly discarded as a viable commercial transport pilot.[9] Within the short span of roughly 2 years, the lady-flier's infinite possibilities had evaporated into a virtual lockout from the airline cockpit that would persist for nearly four decades. This palpable exclusion was enabled by the gender symbolism that bound together seemingly disparate publicity campaigns. Placed alongside one another, the airline professionalism and lady-flier crusades virtually ensured that "woman airline pilot" would appear to be an oxymoron. Consider the increasingly popular image of uniformed "captains" and "first officers," radiating scientific know-how and polished professionalism. Against this profile, the lady-flier ironically undermined her own right to fly. Her identity as frivolous and technically inept at once assured the public that anyone could fly and obliterated their trust in her capacity to do so in any reliable capacity.

With its emphasis on domesticating flight, the lady-flier image actually evoked the feminine figure that supplanted her. In fact, it was in the early 1930s that airlines began to employ attractive, amiable nurses in the service of passengers' in-flight comfort. The easy discursive slippage between the lady-flier and the stewardess surfaced early in Richey's fleeting airline career. For example, an article about her copilot post depicted her as the "Queen of the Court" of airline stewardesses ("'Queen Helen of Air,'" 1935). While it retained the cockpit-cabin hierarchy, this strange link across such disparate employee groups was sensible only through the lens of gender. Another article justified Richey's acceptability in the cockpit in terms of her place in the cabin:

Helen believes there is a definite place for girl co-pilots who are able to build up the necessary qualifications. On lines that have no provisions for stewardesses it is customary for the co-pilots to double. If you have ever had awkward country boys with big, hairy, freckled hands adjust your pillow, or rub away a headache and give you a crushed skull in its stead, or serve your meals aloft, you will agree with Helen that girls might do a more restful job. (Courtney, 1935, p. 43)

As Corn (1979) explained, "Stewardesses, in short, were professional nurturers, hired pursuant to the same business strategy of exploiting sex to make air travel seem safe and comfortable as were women pilots" (p. 571). The lady-flier "of the late 20s and 30s was the first to render the sky friendly and hospitable," yet ultimately, she unwittingly set the stage for her own replacement by the stewardess (p. 571).

In sum, the developing notion of the professional airline pilot played off of the larger aviation industry's image of the lady-flier, as well as the emerging identity of the airline stewardess, ultimately denying women's legitimate role in the professionalized cockpit. The discursive struggle that engendered this and other material outcomes unfolded at the lived nexus of a particular historical moment in gender relations, the political and economic imperatives of an industry, competing institutional interests and strategies, and the embodied pleasure and pain of real people.

Thus far, our analysis has traced the ways in which gendered communication organized the airline pilot's class identity. This is not to imply that airline pilots have occupied an entirely stable position. Even those who "touch the face of God" can fall from grace. Next, we briefly consider the contemporary legacy of these historical patterns.

❖ CRACKS IN THE COCKPIT DOOR? THE AIRLINE PILOT'S GENDERED DIALECTIC OF CLASS

By the late 1930s, the airline pilot's professionalism was wedded to masculinity, but that union was fraught with latent tension. For, despite his professional makeover, the airline pilot did not reject his heritage. He retained some of the character of his ancestors—namely, the individualistic, adventurous, antibureaucratic sensibility apparent in the following description:

> It is easy to define the air line pilot: a man with the look of a pioneer in his eye and bearing, intelligent, alert, courageous, modest and skillful. . . . All of us can remember the early days, when the pilot carried the future of air transportation and of the air line in his cockpit. It was often a lonesome business for the pilot was on his own, pitting his skill and knowledge against the great array of the unknowns. ("Men, Planes, and Faith," 1953, p. 8)

Crafted as a sort of professional cowboy, the airline pilot embraced *and* distanced himself from the masculine symbolism of white- *and* blue-collar labor cultures. For example, after much consideration and with some reluctance, the budding airline pilot's union opted in 1931 to officially affiliate with the American Federation of Labor (AFL) in an effort to borrow the institutional muscle of organized labor. Pilot leaders chose the AFL over the more prestigious Brotherhood of Locomotive Engineers because the former offered greater organizational autonomy (Hopkins, 1998). Even today, airline pilots walk the picket lines clad in officers' uniforms. As these observations suggest, pilots have long straddled conflicting class symbolism. More specifically, they embody an ongoing dialectic between what we self-consciously call the "civilized" masculinity of professionals and the "primitive" masculinity of organized labor (Ashcraft & Flores, in press). Alternately, and sometimes at the same time, airline aviators are businessmen with white collars, "outspoken rugged individualists," and "close-lipped advocates of union solidarity" (Hopkins, 1998, p. 2). In this sense, the airline pilot can be understood as a rare and precarious discursive construction.

The capacity to blend contradictory labor symbolism is a tremendous resource, if for no other reason than sheer flexibility; that is, it allows selective access to the arguments and advantages usually reserved for divergent labor groups. Yet such blends are also difficult to manage, for they require delicate acts of balance, and they risk the production of incoherent work identities. During labor negotiations, for example, the airline pilot's body can oddly mutate into that of a weary skilled laborer left to defend his assaulted interests. The image of uniformed officers on strike has been known to irk the public and incite depictions of greedy, "uppity" corporate aviators (Canyon, 1999a). Conversely, as Northrup (1947) remarked about the first airline pilot strike, "In the eyes of the public and the Congress, it reduced a group considered 'professional' to the regular employee level and stripped them of their glamour" (p. 575). Written over 50 years later, Canyon's (1999b) effort to defend striking pilots grapples with a similar class dialectic:

> How many government-mandated tests a year does your average brain surgeon take? Blue-collar workers? . . . Airline pilots are blue-collar labor: hourly workers who operate under a labor contract, just like coal miners or teamsters. Even though airline company managements tell us how grateful they are for our professionalism, at contract time they treat us like the hourly labor we really are. . . . Our goal is to return safely from every trip and with enough money to support the people we love. This is the same goal that the unionized coal miner, the farm worker and the teamster have—and probably the same goal that you have at your job. Pilots would always rather fly than fight, but we will fight if we feel threatened, endangered or cheated. (p. 60)

Canyon's account rests on a sort of "every working man" discourse of protector and provider, spiced up by the metaphor of an animal instinctually defending itself from undue provocation. Simultaneously, such claims can appear suspect when juxtaposed with a "captain's" rational, sophisticated "professionalism," not to mention his six-figure salary.

Likewise, the accounts of many contemporary airline pilots reflect class tensions. In interviews with Karen, they have overwhelmingly aligned their identification with an informal college of airline pilots, dissociating from airline management and unions. One recently retired captain explained that,

Back in the early 70s, if you became an 890 [similar to a line instructor], that meant you were on a track to go into management, because, you know, you're going into an office. I wanted to fly. Yeah, they told me, "Eventually, if you do this, we're gonna make you into a suit." That was always the joke, "Oh, now you'll be a suit." "Those suits." I just wanted to fly.

Similarly, most of the pilots interviewed shunned management aspirations, noting their passion for "flying the line"—for being "a doer, not someone who watches the other guys do." Lest this sentiment be read as antimanagement and prolabor, it is worth noting that participants did not take themselves for union enthusiasts either. One pilot abridged a common view: "I'm occasionally thankful to them (ALPA) because they do a function that I don't want to do, but I'm not the union type. I'm not a clubby, and I just like to not have a boss and do my own thing. . . . ALPA is just more administration." In similar shades, most interviewees painted unionization as an unfortunate necessity. A few even described twinges of shame triggered by reading union material:

A lot of times, honestly, the union mindset is pretty embarrassing to me. It's ridiculous, I mean, it's just not professional. You should see some of the materials they distribute, stuff that isn't spelled right all over it. It's just embarrassing, and several of us laugh about it a lot.

Airline pilots also characterize the nature of their work as "not quite" or "both" blue- and white-collar labor. When pressed to distinguish these categories and situate themselves accordingly, all participants echoed the pithy voice of one: "It kind of falls in between." One elaborated colorfully,

Well, there's a funny old saying: How do you know the difference between a mechanic and a technician? The mechanic washes his hands before he pisses, and a technician washes them afterward. So if you're talking white-collar and blue-collar work, I would almost consider my job as being both. Any white-collar job that deals with the diversity of people a captain has to deal with— airplane cleaners . . . to airport managers. . . . Or the kinds of problems I have to deal with in the air. You're the whole show when you're in the air, so I've had to crawl around in the belly of the plane on an overseas flight to figure out electrical problems. Blue-collar kind of work. You sort of do it all.

Although participants struggled to apply labor categories to their actual work, most concurred that the general public categorically perceives airline pilots as white-collar professionals. Respondents varied widely in attempts to justify their high occupational status, but most touched on one or more of the following rationales: (a) a high-risk environment requiring complex problem-solving under pressure; (b) responsibility for many lives; (c) responsibility for expensive equipment; (d) extensive training; and (e) high pay (note the similarity to what we called earlier the "reverse logic" of the initial airline professionalism campaign). That individual pilots internalize these rationales quite differently is evident in the range of occupations to which they compared their own: traveling salesman, truck driver, doctor or surgeon, lawyer, ship captain, artist or musician, and world leader, to name a few.

When pressed to support their rationales, most participants eventually granted that airline pilot status appeared to rest on somewhat arbitrary ground. Many turned to the pilot's traditionally glamorous public profile: "There's an image that may not fit the reality about the job . . . for men, it's the idea of freedom, the uniform, there's a certain amount of power and authority and respect associated with it." Most described such popular perceptions as half-truths, "probably partly true, but probably partly folklore." After one especially lively exchange on the relative economic status of pilots and mechanics, one respondent quipped with a satirical smile, "I don't know, really. But I'll tell you this . . . my feeling is, let's not change the game now that I'm playing it by these rules, you know what I'm saying?"

But the rules are changing, and many participants expressed keen awareness of that point. When asked to identify major trends shaping the airline pilot profession today, several respondents named the push to increase the number of female and minority pilots as the most significant shift under way. Not surprisingly, they disagreed on the consequences, which according to the respondents ranged from lowered standards and decreased safety (due to a dearth of qualified candidates) to diminished cockpit bonding to the addition of crucial new skills and perspectives. A few bared politically risky yet poignant feelings, as in this interview exchange:

A: You'd like to think of this job as something that's real, like you say, it kind of becomes something that takes a lot of skill. . . . And then you see this, some little slight gal, you know, flying away, flying this big airplane. . . . You kind of think, shit! . . . In fact, when I see one of these, sometimes when I see some of these gals. . . . I've thought, well, boy, you know, now if she can be a captain and do the job, hey, what do I, what's the big, what have I been sweating all this time, you know?

Q: And what do you mean, "Boy, if she's a captain, what have I been sweating?" What do you mean?

A: Well, it's just—There's the male-female thing for you. It's like, it's just like if you were going into combat, you know, and it's a big thing for you. You gotta well up the courage and determination to go fight that enemy, and you're thinking like that this could only be done by some hard, prepared guy. And then all of a sudden you see some woman walking out of the fray of the battle, holding a machine gun on her shoulder. And you realize, hey, how in the hell did you do that?

Q: And it hurts a little bit?

A: It does. Yeah. It does hurt just a tad. It pricks something.

This pilot (who had overcome physical obstacles to land his airline job and was now only a few years from retirement) proceeded to explain that the presence of women in the cockpit undermined the cherished feeling of manly accomplishment and social relevance he derived from flying. At the same time, he insisted that he flew with superb female pilots and firmly believed that women should be able to fly. Somehow, he said, this intellectual appreciation did not ease his sense of loss. With less frankness, other pilots confessed a vague sense of personal deflation at the sight of pilot diversity and, especially, of female pilots. For these fliers, a woman pilot appears to expose the potent officer as mere posturing, to shatter the myth of a necessarily closed cockpit—in short, to unravel over half a century of careful communicative labor. More than the unsteady, dialectical character of professional identity is revealed by such an analysis, for it also brings home the claim that the meeting of labor and class is a profoundly gendered and raced matter.

❖ CONCLUSION

In this chapter, we conducted a preliminary feminist communicology of the airline pilot profession. Our main goal was to demonstrate the application and potential of the theoretical model proposed in Chapter 5. In so doing, we aimed to further the study of gendered organization, first, by bringing within its scope forms of organizational communication that exceed the work*place* and, second, by illuminating the dialectical, historical, and material properties of discourse. Our analysis began with the claim that the discursive field available in the early days of aviation produced dilemmas concerning industry viability and occupational credibility. While the strategic propagation of "lady-flier" discourse eased public anxiety about the safety of smaller, private aircraft, it undermined the legitimacy of pilots, posing acute problems for the commercial transport industry and its fliers. "Pilot professionalism" discourse diffused those threats, at once attracting a steady stream of passengers and securing the occupational status of airline pilots, albeit at the expense of female fliers. For, as in the case of Helen Richey, when these two discursive formations converged, they functioned to naturalize men's seat in the cockpit and women's service in the cabin—thus calling for performances of gender relations that became institutionalized for decades to come. Our analysis demonstrated how these discursive transformations—far from mere "free-floating," ideational shifts—were communicated into existence by individuals and institutions with concrete interests situated within a specific political economy. Furthermore, these shifts engendered tangible effects, ranging from the rise of a passenger base that anchored a flailing industry to the privileged social and economic standing of a profession to the deeply personal experience of work.

At the heart of such discursive and material transformations lie fundamentally gendered characters and the consequential emotions they ignite—the dashing male specimen who arouses our fascination with flight, the whimsical girl whose guts shame us all into flying, the authoritative professional who soothes our worries with fatherly protection, the charming wife devoted to our every need in the air. While these figures were strategically invoked to alter public perceptions, our analysis indicated that the gendered nature of airline work is as important to pilots as to those who consume or evaluate their labor. For at least some airline pilots, masculinity (for example, belonging to an elite manly club or performing the role of protective father) is pivotal to the pleasure of commercial flying. Recall the captain who commented 50 years ago, "Whenever I see the pilot of a modern airliner, handsome in a snappy uniform, competent and confident, I feel a surge of pride" (Lipsner, 1953, p. 18). Consider also the contemporary airline pilots who confessed ambivalence about women in the cockpit. However one may read their reflections, their voices suggest a complex form of resistance to occupational diversification, wherein beneficiaries of professional privilege—however well intentioned—struggle with the intensely emotional experience of privilege under challenge or in decline.

Thus, by tracing the context, evolution, and materiality of gendered organizational discourse, a feminist communicology holds the potential to generate novel, practical questions and insights regarding social change. In the case of airline pilots, for example, (how) can more inclusive work identities yield alternate pleasures, ones not based on relations of dominance and subordination? Such a question becomes all the more pressing in light of another implication of feminist communicology: that the formation of work identities can engender material conditions. As sketched here, the contested meaning of a pilot's labor, body, and self is much more than a squabble over possible identities. It is a discursive struggle over the right for occupational control, claims to professionalism, and the political, economic, and social standing of a job. If so, diversifying pilot identity means more than revising the occupational identity and culture of airline pilots. Inclusiveness may literally prove costly, for it will likely cast suspicion on long-standing material systems of value and reward.

Chiefly, our analysis gave life to Chapter 5's claim that the communication of gender is pivotal to the organization of working subjectivities, *not* an incidental (or coincidental) player, process, or product. Since the inception of flight in the United States, the strategic communication of particular gender discourses has proven crucial to the social construction of fliers and, eventually, to the success of a world-changing industry and a much-romanticized profession.

Moreover, the study of gendered labor is about more than present organizational identities, roles, and cultures. Gendered symbolism is intimately bound up with material arrangements, such as the economic status and bodily practices of airline pilots. And the dialectical relation between discursive and material worlds reflects a complex history of political pressure and struggle, as in the strategic efforts of airlines and pilot associations to remake the pilot image and restrict access to the cockpit.

We suggest, then, that the feminist communicology approach modeled in this chapter affords a promising way to conduct analysis across micro- and macro-level processes and historical and contemporary contexts. By expanding the usual scope of feminist organization studies, it can yield more holistic, textured, even practicable communication theories of gender and work. As we draw our efforts to a close in the next chapter, we link our analysis of U.S. airline pilot identity to specific feminist communicology principles and address key issues, tensions, and future considerations sparked along the way.

7

Conclusion

Reworking Gender in
Critical Organization Studies

❖ ❖ ❖

We began this project by entering the conversation about gender, power, and organizing and, specifically, by rethinking the relationship between feminist and critical organization scholarship. We proposed the validity of two renditions of that relationship: One is that gender and feminist research can be seen as a specialized branch of radical organization studies. The other is that feminist organization scholarship can simultaneously be understood as independent of and central to radical theories of organization. For example, feminism has uncovered the gendered foundations of organizational theory, including critical versions. In addition, the "revolutionary pragmatism" of feminism, manifest in its ambivalence toward high theory and dedication to grass roots social change, has generated a rich history of real-life experiments with alternative forms of organization.

And so, without denying the ways in which feminist organization scholarship borrows critical insights to illuminate gender relations, we set out to establish and elaborate the merit of a different read—namely, that feminism provides a model or guide for radical organization scholars. Among the many contributions one might stress, we chose to emphasize how feminism has long embodied the sorts of struggles that currently occupy radical organization scholars, who increasingly grapple with the alleged incommensurability of critical modernist and postmodernist perspectives. Consequently, their struggles entail tensions between, for example, epistemological and political impulses, symbolic and material realities, deconstructive and reconstructive motives, fixed and fragmented accounts of identity, and visions of power as negative and top-down or productive and self-enforced. It is our contention that, with its rich history of working through conceptual and practical irony, feminism represents a means of productively navigating through such tensions.

We went about developing this argument in several steps. Chapter 1 identified a substantial, relatively coherent body of literature dedicated to the study of gender and organization in the wake of the discursive turn. We articulated four common ways in which scholars "frame" the complex links among discourse, gender, and organization. We then suggested that key metatheoretical tensions concerning identity, power, discourse, and micro-macro relations cut across the prevailing frames, but that because these tensions and ways of managing them remained latent in the literature, the claim that feminism represents a way to maneuver metatheoretical dilemmas—especially those stemming from conflicts between modernism and postmodernism—was thus far underdeveloped.

This assertion defined the task we shouldered in the next few chapters: to explicate the subtle tensions and alliances among modernism, postmodernism, and feminism. Our purpose was to situate the "feminism-as-guide" claim in the context of the main metatheoretical debates that have informed critical and feminist organization studies over the past few decades. We argued that feminist scholars have engaged modernism and postmodernism in a multifaceted, often contradictory manner that draws upon and discards aspects of both logics. For example, some feminists have appropriated "lessons" from modernist thought regarding the stability of social structures, the reality of material consequences, and the possibility of a normative grounding for critique. They have concurrently rejected modernist propensities for correspondence theories of truth, value-neutral epistemologies, and objectivist ontologies. Feminist scholars have also criticized postmodern tendencies toward political quietism and epistemological and ethical relativism. Simultaneously, many have embraced the shifting, fragmented, local, and performative character of identity and social relations. Taken together, feminist interventions in metatheoretical debate suggest that an adequate account of organizational communication would grant its ironic, ambiguous character and acknowledge that it at once constitutes agentic possibilities and reifies sedimented, institutional power relations.

Thus, the conceptual context offered in Chapters 2 through 4 sets the stage for the organizational communication model articulated in Chapter 5. There, we proposed a feminist communicology premised on the communicative constitution of subjectivity; the dialectics of power-resistance, discourse-materiality, and masculinity-femininity; the historical specificity of gendered organizational formations; and an ethical, political commitment to the exploration of lived consequences and possibilities for praxis. Chapter 6 applied this framework to the empirical case of professional identity formation among U.S. commercial airline pilots. In closing, we wish to comb that analysis more carefully in light of specific feminist communicology premises. Based on our review of the case, we alter slightly the original order of those premises and expand upon their initial statement in Chapter 5. Our aim is a heuristic one: to unearth and examine key insights, dilemmas, and future considerations aroused by a feminist communicology and its empirical applications.

❖   A FEMINIST COMMUNICOLOGY OF ORGANIZATION: ELABORATING THE PREMISES

Premise 1: Communication Constitutes Subjectivity But Does Not Work Alone

Applying a postmodern feminist view of subjectivity, Chapter 6 began by destabilizing the notion that the airline pilot is a fixed or self-evident category of worker whose labor is naturally conducive to professional esteem and simply happens to be performed by white men. Rather, as revealed by the contrast between the early visions of fliers and the later professionalism campaign, airline pilots' identity can be aligned with multiple, even opposed, gender and class meanings. Which meanings come to hold sway is a consequential matter, since discourse and materiality are mutually constitutive, as we elaborate in a moment. Hence, the identity of the airline pilot is a site of discursive and political contest; that is, institutions and individuals perceiving tangible stakes in the outcome vie to define the pilot.

While it has become something of a truism among many contemporary theorists to concede the unstable, fragmented, and political character of subjectivity, the following two questions are often left with, at best, vague answers: (1) By what means or mechanisms do we go about the struggle over subjectivity, tweaking larger discourses to suit local circumstances? and (2) Why do some of these efforts take root more than others? Frames 2 and 4, as discussed in Chapter 1, best encapsulate how feminist organization scholars have invoked various threads of postmodernism to address the first question. In frame 2, the struggle is located in routine microperformances or situated interactions, which are inevitably partial and ongoing (e.g., Butler, 1990; Weedon, 1987; West & Fenstermaker, 1995); in frame 4, the answer is representational systems, such as those that comprise popular culture, scholarship, and even routine interaction (e.g., Carlone & Taylor, 1998; Du Gay, Hall, Janes, Mackay, & Negus, 1997). Our work in Chapters 5 and 6 integrated and sharpened these answers in several ways.

To begin with, mundane, public, and scholarly performances/ representations are part of an essential social process we know as communication. Chapter 5 identified communication as the basic mechanism of discursive struggle—as the dynamic, situated, embodied, and contested process of creating systems of gendered meanings and identities by invoking, articulating, and/or transforming available discourses. As this definition suggests, we understand communication as a web of (dis)organizing practices that, while "contained" in seemingly discrete incidents and contexts, are interwoven with other episodes and settings in a play that never ends. It is reasonable to ask, then, why we prefer the term *communication* over the term *practice* or similar alternatives. It is less our fixation on disciplinary terms and more our concern to stress the ways in which (dis)organizing practices are fundamentally symbol-based and interactive in character. They trade in messages that require "speakers" (individual or collective), "audiences" (imagined, anticipated, or real), situational applications and parameters, "real-time" participation and exchange, and so on. With this characterization, we do not mean to summon tired models, for example, of the intentionality and linearity of communication. As should be clear by now, our theory of subjectivity as both agentic and decentered foregrounds the matter of how messages ironically speak their speaker into being, while the dialectical texture of our model denies any neat progression to the communication process.

Thus far, however, we have made our own vague references to "various communication practices" and "webs" thereof. Our analysis in Chapter 6 began to refine the claim that communication is the central means of discursive struggle by specifying an array of relevant practices, which could be usefully categorized in many ways. Our purpose here is not to advance a superior schema but to expand current notions of what qualifies as organizational communication, beyond the boundaries usually associated with "internal" and "external" messages. Chapter 6 revealed the organizing capacity of, at minimum, the following communication practices: forming, disseminating, consuming, and responding to organized "PR" campaigns; defining, reporting, and consuming "news"; depicting and consuming representations of work/ers in popular culture (e.g., advertisements, film, children's literature), museums, and other educational forums (ranging from informal career socialization in families to published occupational guides to formal training programs); building interinstitutional networks and alliances, as well as managing related conflicts (e.g., among airlines, labor unions, and federal agencies); articulating a collective voice within and circulating organizational newsletters; performing routine work roles in tandem with coworkers and clients; and reflecting on personal experience with "outsiders" (e.g., in research interviews and published autobiographies). Crucially, these are dynamic practices (thus, the present participle) that often play off of one another and meet, at least temporarily, in unpredictable ways, all the while supporting, challenging, and/or altering the available discursive field.

If indeed organizational communication can assume so many shapes and sizes, talk of the "micro" and "macro" becomes problematic but, we think, usefully so. It might be tempting, for example, to read the above list of practices as if ordered from macro to micro—or, more specifically, as if it steps down a ladder of abstraction from mass/public, to interinstitutional, to organization/site-specific, to individual/interpersonal communication practices. And yet, this interpretation misses the personal intensity of engagements with public communication (e.g., the young man inspired to a career in flight by the film *Top Gun*), as well as how once-private reflections (e.g., the personal memoirs of an airline pilot) become part of public consciousness through translation to film or literature. When the practices identified above are considered at varied levels through varied lenses, it becomes apparent that extant accounts of macro and micro, structure and agency, and their interrelation provide, at best, a broad template in need of careful, contextual explication.

It follows that expanding what counts as organizational communication sparks theoretical and methodological dilemmas for organization scholars. Currently, for instance, we lack adequate conceptions of relevant differences among specific communication practices, as well as how such differences limit the possible claims one might make based on studying a particular practice. Moreover, organization scholars often receive little training in pertinent forms of textual and/or historical analysis, especially as applied to mass-mediated texts—a point that becomes more salient in our discussion of historical context.

As it centers, specifies, and complicates the constitutive force of communication, the organizational communication theory developed in Chapters 5 and 6 also dislocates organization. Extending the recent scholarship reviewed in Chapter 1 (see our discussion of frame 4), communicology encourages a shift in focus from particular physical sites of work to diverse and loosely entangled "sites" of communication practice where organizing—of work identities, systems, relationships, and so forth—occurs. Certainly, the organization of many professions attracts less public interest than that of pilots, suggesting that relevant communication practices will vary accordingly. Chiefly, we are proposing a broader scope for the study of gender and organization—one that would elucidate the complex intersections among public discourse and the cultures of industries, occupations, and particular organizations. Chapter 6 stressed the organization of professional identity across these arenas, but scholars can (and already have begun to) investigate the larger societal organization of various work phenomena, from the alleged disintegration of the bureaucratic form (Du Gay, 2000) to prevailing discourses of legitimate labor (Clair, 1996) and business behavior (Cheney, 2000b). Such projects are guided *not* by indifference to specific organizations but, rather, by a complementary interest in how work gets organized beyond their conventional boundaries.

Here, we have considered how the communicology model develops current answers to the question of mechanism. But the second question—why some discursive efforts seem to "stick" more than others—remains open. Sure, one can assert generically that communication constitutes, but it is clear that all acts of communicating are not equally constitutive, certainly not in any kind of enduring way. It is here that the material dimensions of our model become crucial.

Premise 2: The Dialectic of Discourse-Materiality Lends Communication Its Constitutive Force

From the outset of the book, we established our interest in realities beyond text. Although discourse renders the world meaningful and mediates our experience of it, that is hardly the end of the story. In an effort to avoid the so-called text positivism of some postmodern approaches while retaining the feminist commitment to praxis, we endeavored to account for the ways in which the privileging of certain discourses translates into lived consequences for people and communities, as well as the ways in which the "real world" impinges on the communication of discourse. Thus, in Chapter 5, we proposed the dialectical relation between discourse and materiality as a guiding concern of feminist communicology.

Chapter 6 brought into focus at least three dimensions of the dialectic. First, the material world serves up impetus for communication. In other words, communication arises in response to (perceived) material conditions, as in the case of a financially faltering airline industry, or of pilots who marshal their symbolic resources to resist managerial control and preserve high salaries. In this sense, communication is inevitably embedded in a tangled history of competing interests. However, as we explain in the next section, the material context of discursive formations often seems to fade from view as they become more entrenched in mundane communication.

Second, communication takes the material world as its material. In particular, discursive formations are inscribed on the body and performed in concrete interactions and mediated representations (Conquergood, 1991, 1994). As such, communication generates ways of being, seeing, feeling, and acting in the world. The physical overhaul of the airline pilot provides a compelling example of the productive capacity of discourse across institutions and individuals. Prominently displayed in an officer's uniform by airline management, the pilot's body exuded technical competence, professional confidence, and emotional mastery. This embodied discipline generated feelings of safety among (potential) passengers, boosting consumer confidence and ticket sales. In addition, airline pilots themselves began to mobilize the pilot's body as a symbolic resource in the quest for tangible professional privileges.

These examples suggest a third, and less often recognized, material quality of communication; namely, communication generates material conditions beyond embodied subjectivities. Here, we are saying more than that communication practices give meaning to an already existing material world. We are claiming that communication can literally invent, not only reproduce, material conditions. Chapter 6 illustrated how the communicative manipulation of professional symbolism enabled airline pilots to consistently negotiate an enviable labor position. Similarly, the discourses of the "lady-flier" and the "professional pilot" allowed a financially shaky industry to achieve economic viability by situating itself persuasively within public consciousness. The cumulative impact of the aviation industry's success is difficult to underestimate, for it has dramatically altered the way societies and individuals experience time and distance, as well as communication with and connectedness to the larger world.

In sum, communication is deeply entangled with the emotional lives and concrete circumstances of real people, who come to experience in their own bodies the "authenticity" of particular discourses with a power to which most of us can attest. Beyond its embodied character, discursive struggle occurs within the parameters of material environments, which grant to certain messages the tangible backing of institutions, the weight of economic imperatives, and so forth. Hence, it is in its inevitable liaison with materiality—its chronic susceptibility, responsiveness, and original contribution to the "real world"—that communication finds its constitutive force. And it is by attending to the discourse-materiality dialectic that we can begin to produce compelling accounts of why and how some communication efforts exhibit more "purchase" than others.

Premise 3: The Historical Context—and, Especially, Political Economy—of Communication Is Crucial to Understanding the Discourse-Materiality Dialectic

Chapter 6 indicated the importance of examining discursive formations in light of history and political economy. In the absence of such context, the white male face and fiscal portfolio of today's airline pilots may be taken as "naturally" warranted, as coincidence, as a lingering sign of the social prejudices of times gone by, or perhaps—by observers with unusual critical savvy—as the legacy of stereotypes about public and private labor, which "leaked" into various occupations. Not one of these readings quite grasps the case. Our analysis in Chapter 6 suggested that in historical communication of and about pilots, the neat reproduction of larger societal discourses about gender was by no means predetermined; simultaneously, the appearance of these familiar discourses was no accident. Ultimately, individual and institutional messages resisted, preserved, and creatively appropriated societal discourses in ways that opened up short-term opportunities *and* sealed off long-term opportunities for women who wished to fly. In our later discussion of the power-resistance dialectic, we pursue the simultaneous presence of subversion and reproduction in communication. For now, we develop a different angle, amplifying the above claim that communication is susceptible to material conditions.

In particular, communication responds to political and economic exigencies. For the aviation industry of the early 20th century, the public's fear of flight and subsequent refusal to buy passenger tickets posed one such pressure. Public relations crusades designed to comfort and seduce the public—one with lady-fliers and another with airline pilot professionals—demonstrate the varied yet overlapping discourses that emerge to answer a single exigency. In this case, seemingly contradictory constructions of the pilot (i.e., "if a woman can fly, anyone can" vs. "only qualified technical experts can fly") worked in concert to entrust white, (upper) middle-class men with control of the airline cockpit and white, middle-class women with the work of in-flight domesticity. Although pilot identity retained its manliness, the specific character of that masculinity altered dramatically. Airline pilot organizers also grasped the potency of masculine professionalism and brandished this image to obtain unparalleled occupational status and economic reward. Particularly notable is the way in which airline pilot professionalism, now taken for granted, was virtually invented out of thin air. Using the borrowed tools of officer symbolism, the flier's daring, fast-living, and antibureaucratic body was remodeled into that of a refined, reliable professional.

Such historical context is vital, not only because it marks the political and economic demands that prompt communicative maneuvers but also because it denaturalizes present labor arrangements. It unearths the heritage of material motivations and strategic discursive work on which contemporary labor identities and relations rest. Complex histories of competing interests appear to get erased, or to increasingly lurk "behind the scenes," as the identity effects of communication—for example, the patent professional authority of airline pilots—become taken for granted. Put plainly, we forget that pilots achieving the look of elite labor was (and is) in itself labor.

And yet, as we noted earlier, commitment to historically informed analyses induces methodological dilemmas for most organization scholars. Appropriate boundaries provide one quandary: How does one know where to look and when to stop in the search for "relevant" historical context? Furthermore, the archival/textual character of most historical research raises questions of comparability, temporality, and training, such as, What sorts of historical texts matter? How should we conceive of meaningful differences among text genres (e.g., airline promotional materials, children's books, formal histories of commercial aviation)? To what extent does the actual historical consumption of texts make a difference? and How do these distinctions affect the claims we can feasibly make? In addition, since historical texts are relatively static, at least in that they cannot be questioned as an interview participant can, in what sense can they be analyzed alongside contemporary ethnographic data? Indeed, ethnographic methodology cultivates sensitivity to context-specific cues and to the interpretations of cultural members, yet these features are usually inaccessible in historical research. To complicate matters, organization scholars are rarely trained in historical methods—reason for considerable caution about the hasty application of generic qualitative analytic skills to archival data.

We believe these are dilemmas worth engaging, for in addition to the theoretical gains identified above, historical context can expose ongoing struggles that underlie seemingly stable work identities and relations, as well as help to explain how abiding tensions become embedded in a given discourse. As we have shown, the airline pilot professional did not entirely dismiss his ancestry. Instead, his brand of professionalism retained a manly passion for autonomous adventure and thus resisted the development of bureaucratic sensibilities, even as it also shied away from affiliation with working-class culture. Chapter 6 pointed to this class contradiction as a pivotal dialectic of airline pilot subjectivity—a persistent tension that requires ongoing negotiation and offers simultaneous advantages and susceptibilities, possibilities for control and resistance.

Premise 4: The Power-Resistance Dialectic Marks Communication as Ironic, But the Discourse-Materiality Dialectic Marks the Limits of Irony

Part of our purpose has been to build a more dialectical understanding of the relationship between power and resistance. As we explained earlier, radical organization research is strikingly bifurcated in its approach to this issue. Most scholars emphasize the (re)production of power and domination; where resistance appears, it seems ultimately complicit in reproducing the status quo. Recently, scholars have begun to stress tactics of resistance that signify discursive space(s) for the articulation of alternate realities, yet what counts as resistance seems to rely as much on the interpretive powers of the researcher as on the particular relations and conditions examined. For example, Bell and Forbes's (1994) case for secretaries' "office graffiti" as a form of resistance could just as easily be read as stereotypically gendered behavior that serves to reinscribe the marginality of female administrative workers. Given the general tendency toward bifurcation, communication is rarely understood as inherently ambiguous, ironic, and conflicted, open simultaneously to resistant and reproductive possibilities. Even within our own field of communication studies, an entrenched disciplinary preference for clear and open communication has meant that arguments for the ambiguity of communication, however persuasive, often struggle to find a foothold (e.g., Eisenberg, 1984, 1998).

Feminist communicology redresses bifurcation by demonstrating how communication generates a complicated array of potential and constraint, subversive meanings, and discursive closure. It is our contention that communication is inherently ambiguous and ironic, though not limitlessly so. With this claim, we recognize the "limits of polysemy" (Condit, 1989), since the relationship among communication, power, and resistance plays out amid already established cultural and economic circumstances. Thus, reading the political implications of communication does not entail an interpretive carte blanche in an effort to either reveal latent agency or bare the velvet fist of the status quo. Rather, it requires turning an eye to the larger contextual features of specific communication practices.

In other words, interpretive limits come into sharper focus in light of the material and discursive conditions noted above. Imagine, for example, a micro-level analysis of ladybird discourse that parallels Bell and Forbes's (1994) argument about the subversive functions of secretarial folklore. From this view, the communicative performances of female fliers could look like the playful manipulation of discursive and material resources made available by the aviation industry and complicit media outlets. Their theatrical, public application of makeup post-flight could be seen both as accommodation to industry discourse *and* as an effort to "burlesque" that gendered discourse in order to undermine it. But such irony cannot be read apart from the larger discourses of masculinity, femininity, and professionalism that circulated at the time or from the material limits of ironic performance as a tactic of resistance. Put bluntly, one cannot ignore the fact that the lady-flier persona ultimately served to remove women from the cockpit and relocate them in the cabin. Analyses of communicative irony would therefore do well to attend not only to the ways in which social actors strategically exploit contradictions but also to the links among their efforts, larger material and discursive resources, and institutions, which themselves act as macro agents (Cooren & Taylor, 1997).

Given their relative comfort with contradiction and tension, feminist scholars are well situated to study organizational communication as an ironic process. To date, however, most of this work has yielded micro-level analyses that tend to downplay limitations to irony and the endless deferral of meaning (e.g., Bell & Forbes, 1994; Hatch, 1997; Trethewey, 1997, 1999b). In response, our dialectical approach to power and resistance foregrounds the interplay between communication (understood as an ongoing, localized process) and larger material and discursive formations (understood as a crystallized yet provisional macro process). Ultimately, the point is to explore how ambiguous, conflicted messages and meanings become directed toward various, sometimes competing ends, *not* to establish certain communication practices as inherently enabling or disabling.

As this suggests, one of the most significant implications of adopting a dialectical view of power and resistance is foregoing congruency in favor of contradiction. That is, a dialectical lens surrenders any incipient "correspondence theory" of power and resistance (i.e., this act is an exercise of power, this of resistance), preferring contingency and ambiguity instead. The trick, then, is not to align particular communication efforts with oppression or resistance but, rather, to trace the complicated ways in which discourses get appropriated, adapted, invented, enacted, and so forth toward coherent and conflicted effects. How does one discourse get articulated with another at a given historical moment, and perhaps with a third discourse at some other moment, to produce certain subjectivities? How do these identities open and close possibilities for agency? How do such formations entail concurrent processes of subjectification and objectification (Foucault, 1982)? For example, the emergence of the lady-flier as cultural icon can be read both as the creation of a new space to exercise some degree of agency and as the appropriation of familiar cultural images to instantiate extant gender, class, and race relations in a new organizational arena. In this case, the aviation industry strategically fashioned a discourse out of political and economic expediency, but it then had to cope with the contradictions of that discourse. Thanks to the complicity of many female fliers, ladybird discourse served its intended function, yet it also took on a life of its own in public consciousness, as it became manifest and acted upon in mundane communication. An unintended consequence of such discourse was its threat to the carefully crafted masculine ethos of the professional airline pilot. At the same time, lady-flier discourse ironically supplied tools with which to curb its own threat. Pitted against the professional pilot, the ladybird laid a discursive foundation for her progeny, the cabin stewardess. In this way, masculine and feminine subjectivities were organized alongside one another.

Premise 5: Discourses of (Gender) Difference Emerge (and Are Best Understood) in Relation to One Another

Clearly, our project has attempted to move beyond a "separate spheres" approach to the study of gender. As we indicated in Chapter 5 and at other points in the book, the field of organization studies no longer equates gender research exclusively with the study of women, recognizing that men are gendered too. Indeed, the development of a significant body of literature on the organization of masculinity is an important theoretical and empirical advance in critical organization studies. However, we stress that the analysis of masculine and feminine identities requires a focus on the dialectics of gender relations and the co-construction of masculinities and femininities—a task that has yet to be taken on in a significant way in critical organization studies.

It should be clear from our analysis that it is impossible to adequately understand the social construction of the professional airline pilot without closely examining its gendered character. Furthermore, this construction process only makes sense by exploring how discourses by and about men (pilots) are articulated in relation to discourses by and about women (pilots). We have also shown how *multiple* discourses of masculinity play off of multiple discourses of femininity. Hence, the rugged individualism and rampant heterosexuality of the postwar celebrity pilot provided both an interpretive frame for, and a barrier to, the later construction of the pilot as cool professional and technical expert in command of a different sexuality, embodied in the paternalistic persona of the captain. Simultaneously, the discourse of the lady-flier both supported and challenged the emergent identity of airline pilots as consummate professionals. In one sense, the glamorous, upper middle-class, white ladybird complemented the professional pilot by affirming the allure of flight and the elite status of fliers. Conversely, the lady-flier exposed the apparent ease of flight, questioning the need for technical expertise and manly brawn. The rearticulation of ladybird as cabin stewardess was therefore necessary, at least in part, to ensure the hegemony of the masculine professional pilot. Our analysis demonstrated how this transformation preserved features of the old discourse in a new setting: Gone was the notion that anyone could fly a plane; maintained were gendered, raced, and classed images of women's service as sexy airborne caregivers who assured passengers of aviation safety. It is worth noting how this new discourse of stewardess as mother and sexual object articulates closely with the discourse of pilot as a dashing, potent father figure.

But our interests move beyond exclusive concern with the coconstruction of gendered identities. From the outset of the book, we situated our project within a growing body of scholarship that examines intersecting discourses of gender, race, class, and sexuality and that brings long overdue complexity to the study of difference (e.g., Allen, in press; Crenshaw, 1991; Frankenberg, 1993; Hegde, 1998; Hossfeld, 1993; Kondo, 1990; Parker, 2003). While we have emphasized questions of gender, we have also been at pains to stress the partial, political character of gender identities as they collide with, and are constructed through, other discourses of difference. Chapter 6, for example, described how specific forms of white, upper middle-class, heterosexual femininity and masculinity found footing at the expense of other potential identities. Consequently, ladybird popularity and airline pilot privilege—however the two may have clashed—shared not only articulations of gender but also those of race, class, and sexuality. Put simply, only some women and men stood to gain from these discursive formations.

Beyond affirming the inevitable partiality of gender discourses, our analysis began to demonstrate the strategic invocation of race and sexuality as means to organize professional identity. We suggested that discourses of race and sexuality get juxtaposed with those of gender in complementary, conflicted, and precarious ways. What remain consistent are ongoing efforts to stabilize identity in a discursive field characterized by constant slippage and elusive closure. For airline pilots (and managers), the primary pragmatic concern entailed securing elite professional status (to assuage passenger fears). Accomplishing this involved a number of thorny discursive moves. One such move involved the dissociation of pilots from "dark" bodies through rhetorical appeals to symbols of whiteness, including "cultured" affluence, glamorous and well-to-do white women, and a blend of rationality, science, and civilization. This simultaneous dissociation and affiliation was achieved through such tactics as job advertisements summoning the "'clean-cut Anglo-American' type" (Northrup, 1947, pp. 569–570), a whites-only clause in the ALPA constitution, advertising campaigns featuring wealthy white passengers, and publicity links to distinguished lady-fliers. Pilots' pursuit of elite labor status also entailed their dissociation from "grease monkeys" through appeals to a white, "high-class" heterosexuality. This was accomplished through pilots' wearing officer uniforms and through advertising that stressed the scientific and technical education of pilots and evoked the imagery of a debonair and dependable father who invariably knows best. In addition, pilot professionalism depended on dissociation from "women's work," which was achieved by simultaneously affiliating with and trivializing white women, by sexualizing them as objects of desire contrasted against sexually potent officers, and by evoking familiar familial relations in the air (i.e., protective dad and comforting mom)— in short, by appealing to heterosexual symbolism.

In each discursive strand, we see strong yet potentially vulnerable petitions to whiteness, heterosexuality, and a kind of upper-class sensibility. Yet the relations among these discourses are far from stable. In fact, the reproduction of a seemingly fixed, "natural" airline pilot identity requires constant policing of the discursive field. For, if only the masculinity of flight is emphasized, men of color and working-class men could venture into the cockpit. Thus, the concurrent visibility of discourses of whiteness and class elitism become necessary to maintain exclusion. On the other hand, overemphasis of whiteness and class elitism could open a discursive door to some women and feminized men; therefore, discourses of heterosexual masculinity become crucial to preserving exclusion. In this sense, intersectionality can be understood as more than a fundamental feature of social identity; it can serve as a strategic device for coordinating privilege and exclusion. In other words, the discursive struggle for control of the cockpit entails a delicate dance, the success of which depends on constant, shifting deferrals to parallel discourses of gender, race, class, sexuality, and so forth. As Chapter 6 suggested, it is neither faceless institutional forces nor broad monolithic discourses that enact this dance; rather, it is performed by individuals and collectives engaged in strategic, pragmatic efforts to fashion remarkably flexible identities in the face of irony and ambiguity.

Gender, then, cannot work alone as a form of control or as a mechanism for organizing exclusion. Thus, while it is important to shift from studying masculinities *or* femininities to examining their co-construction, it is equally vital that we expand our scope to include multiple discourses of difference. We encourage analyses that shift our focus on gender to highlight how race, sexuality, ability, class, age, and so on are invoked to organize work identity, while mindful that these are inevitably gendered discourses. In sum, "effectively" achieving exclusion appears to rely on savvy alliances among discourses of difference. Should we not then consider whether creating inclusion involves the same?

Premise 6: Feminist Communicology Pursues Provisional Praxis by Taking an Ethical Stand on Admittedly Shifting Ground

In Chapter 5, we suggested that a feminist communicological ethic rejects the foundationalism of some feminist perspectives on the one hand and a "let difference be" approach on the other. While the former invokes a form of moral absolutism, the latter provides no grounds for making normative judgments about desirable or undesirable modes of being. In contrast, our position involves both the critical examination of the relationships among gender, power, and organizing and a normative, ethical move that addresses the consequences of various configurations of power for human identity and meaning formation. Framed in a Foucauldian manner, we are interested in how prevailing "regimes of truth" are produced and maintained, and with what consequences for various interest groups. From an ethical perspective, we are concerned in part with destabilizing fixed and taken-for-granted systems of meaning, and hence engaging in "the subversion of closure" (Willmott, 1998, p. 93). Thus the first move in our feminist communicological ethic is deconstructive. Derrida (1996) highlights the connection between deconstruction and ethics when he states,

> All that a deconstructive move tries to show, is that since convention, institutions and consensus are stabilization (sometimes stabilization of great duration, sometimes micro-stabilization), this

means that they are stabilization of something essentially unstable and chaotic. . . . If there were continual stability, there would be no need for politics, and it is to the extent that stability is not natural, essential or substantial, that politics exists and ethics is possible. (as cited in Willmott, 1998, p. 92)

From a feminist communicological perspective, we are concerned with dereifying and critiquing the discursive and material mechanisms that create stable structures and hierarchies of value—men over women, white over black, reason over emotion, and so forth—that become sedimented over time. Thus, the primary normative purpose of Chapter 6 was to illustrate the consequences for different groups of certain discursive articulations and fixing of meaning formations. The discourse and decision-making that emerged around the construction of airline pilot identity systematically and strategically excluded voices that might legitimately stake a claim to inclusion in that profession. Furthermore, such discourse not only engaged in processes of exclusion but also actively constructed complementary identities of "the other" that institutionalized that exclusion. Women were constructed as nonrational, "flighty(!)," lacking in adequate physical strength, and subject to the vagaries of their bodies; nonwhites were positioned as uncivilized, ill-disciplined, and lacking in technical skill. Thus, the effort to construct a stable, rational, and coherent discourse of flight as a safe activity was rooted in the suppression and demonizing of that which the dominant group feared.

From an ethical standpoint, however, our goal here is not to render a definitive judgment about the morality of such discourses. Such a position is inconsistent with our theoretical framework and its emphasis on irony, ambiguity, and contradiction rather than congruence and correspondence. Instead, we are more interested in how such discourses become contested in various and often contradictory ways to create different forms of communication community. For example, one might argue that the lady-fliers' appropriation of the strategically managed discourse of femininity to which they were subject was a form of "strategic essentializing" that both reproduced the gendered discourse of flight and attempted to expand—through irony—extant notions of "flying community." Indeed, they themselves were complicit in embracing elements of privilege, often conspiring with dominant institutions to reproduce a discourse that marginalized other groups (black women fliers, for example, who were systematically excluded from official promotion of the lady-flier image). Thus, the lady-flier discourse—both official and unofficial—enabled inclusion and exclusion. Lady-fliers both participated in that dominant discourse and exercised agency against it (however ineffectually); in other words, they made ethical choices (though not necessarily conscious and deliberate) about who enjoyed the fruits of an expanded notion of community. The ethical framework that we work with, then, does not invoke some a priori notion of emancipation. Instead, it asks that we examine how subordinate groups utilize both the ironies and the contradictions in dominant discourses as means of social transformation, and how such groups may be complicit in the reproduction of dominant discourses. In this sense, studies of intersectionality involve examination of (a) the ways that gendered, raced, and classed discourses are articulated to produce exclusion and closure; and (b) the means by which subordinate groups similarly appropriate principles of intersectionality—perhaps in contradictory and ironic ways—to create more inclusive forms of community.

If, as we suggested in Chapter 5, ethical communication involves engagement with the other and the willingness to give up one's fixed sense of subjectivity, then one can examine a particular set of discourses and the communication community that they (implicitly or explicitly) invoke in terms of the degree to which they foment or foreclose dialogue among different interests and voices. Again, note that this is not a variation on the "let difference be" perspective but, instead, suggests that difference is merely the starting point for the examination of discursive processes of inclusion and exclusion. Do discourses strategically construct and marginalize "the other," or do they radically and dialectically engage with other voices and possibilities? Seyla Benhabib (1992) captures this notion in her articulation of a "postmetaphysical" feminist ethics:

> My goal is to situate reason and the moral self more decisively in contexts of gender and community, while insisting upon the discursive power of individuals to challenge such situatedness in the name of universalistic principles, future identities and as yet undiscovered communities. (p. 8)

If the arbitrariness of stability suggests the possibility of politics and ethics, then Benhabib's position suggests how we might realize that politics and ethics through praxis. That is, ethical community is possible, but it is always provisional and situated within specific discursive contexts that are open to change and transformation. In this sense, all forms of praxis are provisional in that they appeal to inter-subjectively shared (this is what Benhahbib means by "universal") possibilities for action that challenge stable discourses but are themselves open to interrogation.

As a way to more adequately situate this notion of praxis, we begin with a key implication of feminist communicology: *dislocating organization*. We use this term to make concrete our attempt to articulate a feminist communicological perspective between modernism and post-modernism, in that it appeals to simultaneous notions of decentering/destabilization and enduring organizational and/or community arrangements. Thus, we wish to invoke forms of praxis that both dislocate and decenter extant understandings of organizing *and* invoke alternative—perhaps provisional, subversive, and ironic—forms of collective action. The former is more deconstructive, while the latter is more reconstructive.

First, then, dislocating organization calls attention to multiple sites and practices of organizing that extend well beyond the conventional sites of work. For example, the classroom can be viewed as a site where the organizing of work and professional identity takes center stage. In our own teaching, we see courses in organizational communication as sites for developing critical conceptions of "career socialization." As critical scholars, we take seriously the need to "dislocate" students' extant conceptions of work and their relationship to the corporate organization. By engaging students dialogically and challenging them not only to be critical consumers of corporate discourse but also to engage alternative organizing sites, we expand their understanding of possibilities for community. This form of engagement works at two levels of praxis. At the first level, it politicizes the classroom in enabling students to gain insight into the relations among discourse, knowledge, organizing, and power. At the second level of praxis, it plants potential seeds of change and transformation as students enter corporate environments with a more critical sensibility. Similarly, popular discourse about work becomes another potential site of intervention (Hassard & Holliday, 1998). Here, dislocating organization involves exploring and critiquing the representations of work and professional identity that characterize popular media. How do popular discourses organize professional identities? In what ways are these organizing processes articulated through particular raced, classed, and gendered discourses?

How might organization scholars intervene in these popular discourses to suggest other forms of organizational identity, connected, for example, to nonprofit organizations and different social movements? In this sense, praxis means engaging in scholarly work that challenges and shifts common sense understandings of organizational and corporate life.

Second, dislocating organization entails the pursuit and development of alternative organizational forms and practices. From our feminist communicological perspective, we are interested in communication practices that create new organizational forms and discourse communities that resist conventional modes of organizing. In this sense, communicology emphasizes the process of organizing discourse rather than focusing on particular structures. Feminist praxis between modernism and postmodernism requires that we retain a notion of resistance and change that goes beyond local, micro-level forms of emancipation (e.g., Bell & Forbes, 1994) and makes claims for the possibility of collective action and macro-level forms of social change. However, such collective behavior does not have to be framed in terms of grand, revolutionary oppositional strategies but, rather, can be seen as shifting, ironic, partial, and subversive. Ashcraft's (1998a, 2000, 2001) research on a feminist hybrid organization (discussed in earlier chapters) seeks this kind of organizational form, suggesting how the use of ironic communication practices can mediate the relationship between feminist praxis and bureaucratic structure. As Alvesson and Willmott (1992a) state, emancipation involves

> an emphasis on partial, temporary movements that break away from diverse forms of oppression, rather than successive moves toward a predetermined state of liberation. . . . The critical project is thus formulated as a precarious, endless enterprise; its believers fight continuously in order to create more space for critical reflection and to counter the effects of traditions. (p. 447)

However, Alvesson and Willmott's (1992a) conception of praxis remains rather firmly rooted in conventional organizational forms. Furthermore, their reframing of emancipation involves "listening to people," "new styles of writing," and "looking for emancipatory elements in texts" (pp. 454–460)—moves that, we argue, do little to "dislocate organization" and invoke alternative organizing forms and communication practices. Such organizational forms may even exist in the interstices of mainstream social and organizational life. For example, while not explicitly feminist, Duneier's (1999) ethnography of homeless African American men who sell books and magazines on the streets of New York City highlights such interstitial, collective organizing. Duneier illustrates the connections between a gendered and raced politics of marginality and an ethic of care that the men practice toward each other. The men construct the sidewalk as a material and discursive system of informal social control that functions redemptively; drug users who cared little for themselves or others develop a renewed sense of self-worth and responsibility toward fellow street vendors. Thus, the study simultaneously explores a "dislocated" organization and dislocates mainstream notions of what collective, transformational forms of organizing might look like. The men construct an ethical communication community that is constantly subject to the vagaries of police attitudes toward the unhoused, city ordinances, and the hostility of local business owners.

At the same time, Duneier's focus on the intersection of discourses of race, class, and gender enables him to paint this particular community not as some pristine space of resistance against a hostile world but, rather, as one that is provisional and shot through with contradiction. For example, according to Duneier (1999), some of the men use their visibility on the streets to deliberately ensnare women in unwanted conversations, engaging in "interactional vandalism" (p. 199). Duneier writes that

Though Mudrick [a homeless black man] is in a lower social-class position, he uses his status as a man to create entanglements with women on a public sidewalk whereby he can achieve a limited measure of power. . . . In effect, he can use the privileged position men enjoy in the public sphere to influence what will happen on the street. (p. 200)

Duneier therefore shows that even ostensibly neutral public spaces can be appropriated and organized in ways that position men and women in complex, raced, classed, and gendered power dynamics. Thus, while the men's discourse community might be described as a "subaltern counterpublic" (Fraser, 1990/1991; Maguire & Mohtar, 1994) that provides opportunities for voice that might not otherwise exist, Duneier's analysis raises important questions about how this community both enables and constrains certain gendered and raced identities.

In sum, our feminist communicology addresses the ethics of organizing in its concern to examine the regimes of truth that form sedimented discourses and to suggest possibilities for provisional forms of praxis. The notion of "dislocating organization" enables us to position ourselves in a way that recognizes both the fragility and the durability of organizational forms. We would argue, then, that any ethical model must embody a deconstructive moment that acknowledges the need for politics and a (provisionally, contingently, ironically) utopian moment that recognizes the possibility of community that arises out of praxis.

❖ REWORKING THE CONVERSATION

As we meant to imply with the title of the book, our project has aimed to rework gender in multiple senses. Among them, we set out to underscore the working dimensions of gender. Perhaps most obviously, we claimed that "work"—spanning occupational choice and culture, labor identity and professional formations, organizational form, the actual performance of tasks, and material systems of value and reward—is a thoroughly gendered endeavor. We also claimed that gender "works," or performs an organizing function, in that it serves as a central mechanism by which to produce and maintain labor identities and arrangements. In another sense, gender itself—not to mention the process of gendering organization—is work-in-progress. Put differently, "doing gender" entails ongoing, interactive effort; in particular, performances of gendered work identity are never complete and thus are themselves forms of labor. It is in this sense that we depicted gender, work, and their variable intersection(s) as fundamentally communicative in character; hence, our project also reworks the role of communication in gender and organization studies. It seems that, in keeping with the spirit of the book, we could fruitfully continue this play on the relation between "gender" and "work," and we invite others to join us in that effort well beyond these pages.

For now, we want to emphasize another sense in which we sought to rework gender. Here, *reworking* assumes the more literal meaning of revising or amending. First, we aimed to challenge the common view of gender as a specialized, peripheral interest in organization studies, instead positioning gender as integral to organizing and, as such, necessarily central to organization theory. Relatedly, we articulated an alternative to the prevailing understanding of feminist organization studies as an offshoot of critical organization scholarship; namely, we situated feminism as a potential role model for navigating the many tensions that have come to define the contemporary landscape of organization scholarship and practice. In this way, we also sought to revise typical accounts of metatheoretical disputes, shifting from an incommensurability lens to one premised on productive tension.

By proposing a feminist communicology, we meant not only to develop the potential of feminism-as-guide but also to provide a useful starting point from which to "rework gender" in all of these senses—to center gender in the organizing process by revealing the extent to which gender literally organizes, to expose the rich legacy of discursive and material labor that underlies contemporary organizational arrangements, to enable the imagination of future alternatives, and to engage theory and practice accordingly. Mainly, we hoped to evoke a powerful range of possibilities for reworking gender in our public and private lives.

Notes

1. This concern is shared among many scholars of whiteness, for whom the parallel fear of reinscribing white dominance exists in tension with the desire to render it visible (e.g., Flores & Moon, 2002; Projansky & Ono, 1999).

2. In this usage, "the erotic" is loosened from strictly sexual connotations and redefined broadly as joy, playfulness, sensuality, and embodied feeling and pleasure.

3. Such neglect is especially evident in feminist critiques of traditional organizational forms. The research on feminist organization, for example, offers notable exceptions (e.g., Morgen, 1988; Scott, 1998; West, 1990).

4. While the term *post-positivism* is sometimes used to describe a social constructionist perspective, we use it here to designate the efforts of mainstream social science to move beyond correspondence theories of truth and to recognize the contingent, perspectival character of all research.

5. See Ashcraft and Mumby (in press) for an earlier version of this analysis.

6. Arguably, this organization initiated the discursive basis for the formation of the Women's Air (Force) Service Pilots (WASPs), Women's Auxiliary Ferrying Squadron (WAFS), and similar efforts of WWII.

7. Pancho Barnes, a popular woman flier around this time, represents an important exception to this ideal. Yet even she ended up honoring heterosexual obligations, albeit in an unconventional way, by operating a brothel for male pilots.

8. We do not mean to imply that women of the time did not experience or express doubt; our point is simply that the attribution serves a useful rhetorical function.

9. A parallel pattern occurred again with the WASP fliers and other "Rosie-the-Riveter" figures of WWII. Calás & Smircich (1993) argue that the feminization of clerical work and the recent fervor for "feminine" managers reflect a similar pattern—namely, the temporary promotion of women in nontraditional work roles, based on fleeting, instrumental logics.

References

Aaltio-Marjosola, I., & Lehtinen, J. (1998). Male managers as fathers? Contrasting management, fatherhood, and masculinity. *Human Relations, 51*, 121–136.

Abrams, P. (1982). *Historical sociology*. Somerset, UK: Open Books.

Acker, J. (1990). Hierarchies, jobs, bodies: A theory of gendered organizations. *Gender & Society, 4*, 139–158.

Acker, J. (1992). Gendering organizational theory. In A. J. Mills & P. Tancred (Eds.), *Gendering organizational analysis* (pp. 248–260). Newbury Park, CA: Sage.

Acker, J., & Van Houten, D. R. (1974). Differential recruitment and control: The sex structuring of organizations. *Administrative Science Quarterly, 19*, 152–163.

Adams, J., & Kimball, M. (1942). *Heroines of the sky*. New York: Doubleday, Doran.

Adams, M. (1931, June 7). Woman makes good her claim for a place in the skies. *New York Times Magazine*. 99s Museum of Women Pilots, Oklahoma City, OK, Helen Richey file.

Adkins, L. (1992). Sexual work and the employment of women in the service industries. In M. Savage & A. Witz (Eds.), *Gender and bureaucracy* (pp. 207–229). Oxford, UK: Basil Blackwell.

Ahrens, L. (1980). Battered women's refuges: Feminist cooperatives vs. social service institutions. *Radical America, 14*, 41–47.

Albrecht, T. L., & Bach, B. W. (1997). *Communication in complex organizations: A relational approach*. Fort Worth, TX: Harcourt Brace.

Alexander, M. (1932, June 26). The first meeting of the "ninety-niners." *Allentown Morning Call*. 99s Museum of Women Pilots, Oklahoma City, OK, Helen Richey file.

Allen, B. J. (1995). "Diversity" in organizations. *Journal of Applied Communication Research, 23*, 143–155.

Allen, B. J. (1996). Feminist standpoint theory: A black woman's (re)view of organizational socialization. *Communication Studies, 47*, 257–271.

Allen, B. J. (1998). Black womanhood and feminist standpoints. *Management Communication Quarterly, 11*, 575–586.

Allen, B. J. (in press). *Difference matters: Communicating social identity in organizations*. Prospect Heights, IL: Waveland.

Allen, O. E. (1981). *The epic of flight: The airline builders.* Alexandria, VA: Time-Life Books.

Althusser, L. (1971). *Lenin and philosophy.* New York: Monthly Review.

Alvesson, M. (1985). A critical framework for organizational analysis. *Organization Studies, 6,* 117–138.

Alvesson, M. (1995). The meaning and meaningless of postmodernism: Some ironic remarks. *Organization Studies, 16,* 1047–1075.

Alvesson, M. (1998). Gender relations and identity at work: A case study of masculinities and femininities in an advertising agency. *Human Relations, 51,* 969–1005.

Alvesson, M., & Billing, Y. D. (1992). Gender and organization: Toward a differentiated understanding. *Organization Studies, 13,* 73–102.

Alvesson, M., & Billing, Y. D. (1997). *Understanding gender and organizations.* London: Sage.

Alvesson, M., & Deetz, S. (1996). Critical theory and postmodernism approaches to organizational studies. In S. Clegg, C. Hardy, & W. Nord (Eds.), *The handbook of organization studies* (pp. 191–217). Thousand Oaks, CA: Sage.

Alvesson, M., & Karreman, D. (2000a). Taking the linguistic turn in organizational research: Challenges, responses, consequences. *The Journal of Applied Behavioral Science, 36,* 136–158.

Alvesson, M., & Karreman, D. (2000b). Varieties of discourse: On the study of organizations through discourse analysis. *Human Relations, 53,* 1125–1149.

Alvesson, M., & Willmott, H. (1992a). On the idea of emancipation in management and organization studies. *Academy of Management Review, 17,* 432–464.

Alvesson, M., & Willmott, H. (Eds.). (1992b). *Critical management studies.* Newbury Park, CA: Sage.

Ashcraft, K. L. (1998a). *Assessing alternative(s): Contradiction and invention in a feminist organization.* Unpublished doctoral dissertation, Department of Communication, University of Colorado, Boulder.

Ashcraft, K. L. (1998b). "I wouldn't say I'm a feminist, but . . . ": Organizational micropractice and gender identity. *Management Communication Quarterly, 11,* 587–597.

Ashcraft, K. L. (1999). Managing maternity leave: A qualitative analysis of temporary executive succession. *Administrative Science Quarterly, 44,* 240–280.

Ashcraft, K. L. (2000). Empowering "professional" relationships: Organizational communication meets feminist practice. *Management Communication Quarterly, 13,* 347–392.

Ashcraft, K. L. (2001). Organized dissonance: Feminist bureaucracy as hybrid form. *Academy of Management Journal, 44,* 1301–1322.

Ashcraft, K. L. (in press). Gender, discourse, and organizations: Framing a shifting relationship. In D. Grant, C. Hardy, C. Oswick, N. Phillips, & L. L. Putnam (Eds.), *Handbook of organizational discourse.* London: Sage.

Ashcraft, K. L., & Allen, B. J. (2003). The racial foundation of organizational communication. *Communication Theory, 13*, 5–38.

Ashcraft, K. L., & Flores, L. A. (in press). "Slaves with white collars": Persistent performances of masculinity in crisis. *Text and Performance Quarterly.*

Ashcraft, K. L., & Mumby, D. K. (in press). Organizing a critical communicology of gender and work. *International Journal of the Sociology of Language.*

Ashcraft, K. L., & Pacanowsky, M. E. (1996). "A woman's worst enemy": Reflections on a narrative of organizational life and female identity. *Journal of Applied Communication Research, 24*, 217–239.

Aviation urged as career for girls. (1929, August 7). *New York Journal.* 99s Museum of Women Pilots, Oklahoma City, OK, Helen Richey file.

Axley, S. (1984). Managerial and organizational communication in terms of the conduit metaphor. *Academy of Management Review, 9*, 428–437.

Ayer, A. J. (1960). *Language, truth, and logic.* London: Gollancz.

Baitsell, J. M. (1966). *Airline industrial relations: Pilots and flight engineers.* Boston: Harvard University Press.

Baker, A. J. (1982). The problem of authority in radical movement groups: A case study of a lesbian-feminist organization. *Journal of Applied Behavioral Science, 18*, 323–341.

Balsamo, A. (1987). Un-wrapping the postmodern: A feminist glance. *Journal of Communication Inquiry, 11*, 64–72.

Banks, A., & Banks, S. P. (Eds.). (1998). *Fiction and social research: By ice or fire.* Walnut Creek, CA: AltaMira.

Banta, M. (1993). *Taylored lives: Narrative production in the age of Taylor, Veblen, and Ford.* Chicago: University of Chicago Press.

Bantz, C. R. (1993). *Understanding organizations: Interpreting organizational communication cultures.* Columbia: University of South Carolina Press.

Barker, J. R. (1993). Tightening the iron cage: Concertive control in self-managing teams. *Administrative Science Quarterly, 38*, 408–437.

Barker, J. R. (1999). *The discipline of teamwork: Participation and concertive control.* Thousand Oaks, CA: Sage.

Barker, J. R., & Cheney, G. (1994). The concept and practices of discipline in contemporary organizational life. *Communication Monographs, 61*, 19–43.

Barley, S., & Tolbert, P. S. (1997). Institutionalization and structuration: Studying the links between action and institution. *Organization Studies, 18*, 93–117.

Barrett, M. (1988). *Women's oppression today: The marxist/feminist encounter* (2nd ed.). London: Verso.

Bass, B. M., & Avolio, B. (1994). Shatter the glass ceiling: Women make better managers. *Human Resource Management, 33*, 549–560.

Bate, B. (1988). *Communication and the sexes.* New York: Harper & Row.

Bate, B., & Taylor, A. (Eds.). (1988). *Women communicating: Studies of women's talk.* Norwood, NJ: Ablex.

Beauvoir, S. de (1973). *The second sex* (E. M. Parshley, Trans.). New York: Random House.

Bederman, G. (1995). *Manliness and civilization: A cultural history of gender and race in the United States, 1880–1917.* Chicago: University of Chicago Press.

Belenky, M. F., Clinchy, B. M., Goldberger, N. R., & Tarule, J. M. (1986). *Women's ways of knowing: The development of self, voice, and mind.* New York: Basic Books.

Bell, E. L., & Forbes, L. C. (1994). Office folklore in the academic paperwork empire: The interstitial space of gendered (con)texts. *Text and Performance Quarterly, 14,* 181–196.

Belsky, J., & Eggebeen, D. (1991). Early and extensive maternal employment and young children's socioemotional development: Children of the National Longitudinal Survey of Youth. *Journal of Marriage and the Family, 53,* 1083–1110.

Benhabib, S. (1990). Epistemologies of postmodernism: A rejoinder to Jean-Francois Lyotard. In L. Nicholson (Ed.), *Feminism/postmodernism.* New York: Routledge.

Benhabib, S. (1991). Feminism and postmodernism: An uneasy alliance. *Praxis International, 11,* 137–150.

Benhabib, S. (1992). *Situating the self: Gender, community and postmodernism in contemporary ethics.* New York: Routledge.

Benson, J. K. (1977). Organizations: A dialectical view. *Administrative Science Quarterly, 22,* 1–21.

Benson, S. (1992). "The clerking sisterhood": Rationalization and the work culture of saleswomen in American department stores, 1890–1960. In A. J. Mills & P. Tancred (Eds.), *Gendering organizational analysis* (pp. 167–184). Newbury Park, CA: Sage.

Bergquist, W. (1992). *The postmodern organization: Mastering the art of irreversible change.* San Francisco: Jossey-Bass.

Bernstein, R. (1992). *The new constellation: The ethical-political horizons of modernity/postmodernity.* Cambridge: MIT Press.

Best, S., & Kellner, D. (1991). *Postmodern theory: Critical interrogations.* New York: Guilford.

Best, S., & Kellner, D. (1997). *The postmodern turn.* New York: Guilford.

Betsy Ross Corps News. (1931, August). 99s Museum of Women Pilots, Oklahoma City, OK, Helen Richey file.

Billing, Y. D., & Alvesson, M. (1998). *Gender, managers, and organizations.* New York: Walter de Gruyter.

Bingham, S. G. (Ed.). (1994). *Conceptualizing sexual harassment as discursive practice.* Westport, CT: Praeger.

Boje, D. M. (1991). The storytelling organization: A study of story performance in an office-supply firm. *Administrative Science Quarterly, 36,* 106–126.

Boje, D. M. (1995). Stories of the storytelling organization: A postmodern analysis of Disney as "Tamara-Land." *Academy of Management Journal, 38,* 997–1035.

Boje, D. M., Luhman, J. T., & Baack, D. E. (1999). Hegemonic stories and encounters between storytelling organizations. *Journal of Management Inquiry, 8,* 340–360.

Bordo, S. (1990). Feminism, postmodernism and gender-scepticism. In L. J. Nicholson (Ed.), *Feminism/postmodernism* (pp. 133–156). New York: Routledge.

Bordo, S. (1992). Postmodern subjects, postmodern bodies. *Feminist Studies, 18,* 159–175.

Bordo, S. (1993). *Unbearable weight: Feminism, Western culture, and the body.* Berkeley: University of California Press.

Bordo, S. (1999). *The male body: A new look at men in public and private.* New York: Farrar, Straus & Giroux.

Braverman, H. (1974). *Labor and monopoly capital: The degradation of work in the twentieth century.* New York: Monthly Review.

Brenner, O. C., Tomkiewicz, J., & Schein, V. E. (1989). The relationship between gender role stereotypes and requisite management characteristics revisited. *Academy of Management Journal, 32,* 662–669.

Brewis, J. (1998). Who do you think you are? Feminism, work, ethics, and Foucault. In M. Parker (Ed.), *Ethics and organizations* (pp. 53–75). London: Sage.

Brewis, J., & Grey, C. (1994). Re-eroticizing the organization: An exegesis and critique. *Gender, Work and Organization, 1,* 67–82.

Brewis, J., Hampton, M. P., & Linstead, S. (1997). Unpacking Priscilla: Subjectivity and identity in the organization of gendered appearance. *Human Relations, 50,* 1275–1304.

Brittan, A. (1989). *Masculinity and power.* Cambridge, MA: Basil Blackwell.

Britton, D. M. (1997). Gendered organizational logic: Policy and practice in men's and women's prisons. *Gender & Society, 11,* 796–818.

Britton, D. M. (2000). The epistemology of the gendered organization. *Gender & Society, 14,* 418–434.

Brod, H., & Kaufman, M. (1994). *Theorizing masculinities.* Thousand Oaks, CA: Sage.

Brodribb, S. (1992). *Nothing mat[t]ers: A feminist critique of postmodernism.* Melbourne, Australia: Spinifex.

Brown, A. D. (1998). Narrative, politics and legitimacy in an IT implementation. *Journal of Management Studies, 35,* 35–58.

Brown, M. H. (1990). Defining stories in organizations: Characteristics and functions. In J. A. Anderson (Ed.), *Communication yearbook 13* (pp. 162–190). Newbury Park, CA: Sage.

Bullis, C. (1993). At least it is a start. In S. A. Deetz (Ed.), *Communication yearbook 16* (pp. 144–154). Newbury Park, CA: Sage.

Bullis, C. A., & Tompkins, P. K. (1989). The forest ranger revisited: A study of control practices and identification. *Communication Monographs, 56,* 287–306.

Burawoy, M. (1979). *Manufacturing consent: Changes in the labor process under monopoly capitalism.* Chicago: University of Chicago Press.

Burawoy, M. (1985). *The politics of production: Factory regimes under capitalism and socialism.* London: Verso.

Burke, R. J., & McKeen, C. A. (1992). Women in management. In C. L. Cooper & I. T. Robertson (Eds.), *International review of industrial and organizational psychology* (Vol. 7, pp. 245–283). New York: John Wiley.

Burr, V. (1995). *An introduction to social constructionism.* New York: Routledge.

Burrell, G. (1988). Modernism, postmodernism and organizational analysis 2: The contribution of Michel Foucault. *Organization Studies, 9,* 221–235.

Burrell, G. (1992). The organization of pleasure. In M. Alvesson & H. Willmott (Eds.), *Critical management studies* (pp. 66–89). Newbury Park, CA: Sage.

Burrell, G., & Morgan, G. (1979). *Sociological paradigms and organisational analysis.* London: Heinemann.

Burris, B. H. (1996). Technocracy, patriarchy, and management. In D. Collinson & J. Hearn (Eds.), *Men as managers, managers as men: Critical perspectives on men, masculinities and managements* (pp. 61–77). Thousand Oaks, CA: Sage.

Butler, J. (1990). *Gender trouble: Feminism and the subversion of identity.* New York: Routledge.

Butler, J. (1991). Contingent foundations: Feminism and the question of "postmodernism." *Praxis International, 11,* 150–165.

Butterfield, D. A., & Grinnell, J. P. (1999). "Re-viewing" gender, leadership, and managerial behavior: Do three decades of research tell us anything? In G. N. Powell (Ed.), *Handbook of gender and work* (pp. 223–238). Thousand Oaks, CA: Sage.

Buzzanell, P. M. (1994). Gaining a voice: Feminist organizational communication theorizing. *Management Communication Quarterly, 7,* 339–383.

Buzzanell, P. M. (1995). Reframing the glass ceiling as a socially constructed process: Implications for understanding and change. *Communication Monographs, 62,* 327–354.

Buzzanell, P. M. (Ed.). (2000). *Rethinking organizational and managerial communication from feminist perspectives.* Thousand Oaks, CA: Sage.

Buzzanell, P. M., Ellingson, L., Silvio, C., Pasch, V., Dale, B., Mauro, G., Smith, E., Weir, N., & Martin, C. (1997). Leadership processes in alternative organizations: Invitational and dramaturgical leadership. *Communication Studies, 48,* 285–310.

Byers, T. B. (1995). Terminating the postmodern: Masculinity and pomophobia. *Modern Fiction Studies, 41,* 5–33.

Calás, M. B. (1992). An/other silent voice? Representing "Hispanic woman" in organizational texts. In A. J. Mills & P. Tancred (Eds.), *Gendering organizational analysis* (pp. 201–221). Newbury Park, CA: Sage.

Calás, M. B. (1993). Deconstructing charismatic leadership: Re-reading Weber from the darker side. *Leadership Quarterly, 4,* 305–328.

Calás, M. B., & Smircich, L. (1988). Reading leadership as a form of cultural analysis. In J. G. Hunt, R. D. Baliga, H. P. Dachler, & C. A. Schriesheim (Eds.), *Emerging leadership vistas* (pp. 201–226). Lexington, MA: Lexington.

Calás, M. B., & Smircich, L. (1991). Voicing seduction to silence leadership. *Organization Studies, 12,* 567–602.

Calás, M. B., & Smircich, L. (1992a). Re-writing gender into organizational theorizing: Directions from feminist perspectives. In M. Reed & M. Hughes (Eds.), *Rethinking organization: New directions in organization theory and analysis* (pp. 227–253). Newbury Park, CA: Sage.

Calás, M. B., & Smircich, L. (1992b). Using the "F" word: "Feminist theories and the social consequences of organizational research. In A. J. Mills & P. Tancred (Eds.), *Gendering organizational analysis* (pp. 222–234). Newbury Park, CA: Sage.

Calás, M. B., & Smircich, L. (1993). Dangerous liaisons: The "feminine-in-management" meets "globalization." *Business Horizons, 36,* 71–81.

Calás, M. B., & Smircich, L. (1996). From "the woman's point of view": Feminist approches to organization studies. In S. R. Clegg, C. Hardy & W. R. Nord (Eds.), *Handbook of organization studies* (pp. 218–257). Thousand Oaks, CA: Sage.

Callinicos, A. (1990). *Against postmodernism.* New York: St. Martin's.

Campbell, K. K. (1988). What really distinguishes and/or ought to distinguish feminist scholarship in communication studies? *Women's Studies in Communication, 11,* 4–5.

Campbell, K. K. (1989). *Man cannot speak for her: A critical study of early feminist speakers.* Westport, CT: Greenwood.

Canary, D. K., & Hause, K. S. (1993). Is there any reason to study sex differences in communication? *Communication Quarterly, 41,* 129–144.

Canyon, S. B. (1999a). Airline pilot 101. *Upside, 11,* 40.

Canyon, S. B. (1999b). When good pilots turn bad. *Upside, 11,* 60.

Carless, S. A. (1998). Gender differences in transformational leadership: An examination of superior, leader, and subordinate perspectives. *Sex Roles, 39,* 887–902.

Carlone, D., & Taylor, B. (1998). Organizational communication and cultural studies. *Communication Theory, 8,* 337–367.

Carter, K., & Spitzack, C. (Eds.). (1989). *Doing research on women's communication: Perspectives on theory and method.* Norwood, NJ: Ablex.

Certeau, M. de (1984). *The practice of everyday life* (S. Rendall, Trans.). Berkeley: University of California Press.

Cheney, G. (1983). On the various and changing meanings of organizational membership: A field study of organizational identification. *Communication Monographs, 50,* 342–362.

Cheney, G. (1991). *Rhetoric in an organizational society: Managing multiple identities.* Columbia: University of South Carolina Press.

Cheney, G. (1999). *Values at work: Employee participation meets market pressure at Mondragon.* Ithaca, NY: Cornell University Press.

Cheney, G. (2000a). Interpreting interpretive research: Toward perspectivism without relativism. In S. R. Corman & M. S. Poole (Eds.), *Perspectives on organizational communication: Finding common ground* (pp. 17–45). New York: Guilford.

Cheney, G. (2000b). Thinking differently about organizational communication: Why, how, and where? *Management Communication Quarterly, 14,* 132–141.

Cheng, C. (Ed.). (1996). *Masculinities in organizations.* Thousand Oaks, CA: Sage.

Chia, R. (2000). Discourse analysis as organizational analysis. *Organization, 7,* 513–518.

Child, J. (1995). Follett: Constructive conflict. In P. Graham (Ed.), *Mary Parker Follett—prophet of management: A celebration of writings from the 1920s* (pp. 87–96). Boston, MA: Harvard Business School Press.

Clair, R. P. (1993a). The bureaucratization, commodification, and privatization of sexual harassment through institutional discourse. *Management Communication Quarterly, 7,* 123–157.

Clair, R. P. (1993b). The use of framing devices to sequester organizational narratives: Hegemony and harassment. *Communication Monographs, 60,* 113–136.

Clair, R. P. (1994). Resistance and oppression as a self-contained opposite: An organizational communication analysis of one man's story of sexual harassment. *Western Journal of Communication, 58,* 235–262.

Clair, R. P. (1996). The political nature of the colloquialism, "A real job": Implications for organizational socialization. *Communication Monographs, 63,* 249–267.

Clair, R. P. (1998). *Organizing silence: A world of possibilities.* Albany: State University of New York Press.

Clegg, S. (1975). *Power, rule, and domination.* New York: Routledge & Kegan Paul.

Clegg, S. (1989). *Frameworks of power.* Newbury Park, CA: Sage.

Clegg, S. (1990). *Modern organizations: Organizations in a postmodern world.* Newbury Park, CA: Sage.

Clifford, J. (1988). *The predicament of culture.* Cambridge, MA: Harvard University Press.

Clifford, J., & Marcus, G. (Eds.). (1986). *Writing culture: The poetics and politics of ethnography.* Berkeley: University of California Press.

Cloud, D. (2001). Laboring under the sign of the new: Cultural studies, organizational communication, and the fallacy of the new economy. *Management Communication Quarterly, 15,* 268–278.

Cockburn, C. (1984). *Brothers.* London: Verso.

Collins, P. H., Maldonado, L. A., Takagi, D. Y., Thorne, B., Weber, L., & Winant, H. (1995). Symposium: On West & Fenstermaker's "Doing Difference." *Gender & Society, 9*, 491–513.

Collinson, D. (1988). "Engineering humor": Masculinity, joking and conflict in shop-floor relations. *Organization Studies, 9*, 181–199.

Collinson, D. (1992). *Managing the shop floor: Subjectivity, masculinity, and workplace culture*. New York: Walter de Gruyter.

Collinson, D., & Collinson, M. (1989). Sexuality in the workplace: The domination of men's sexuality. In J. Hearn, D. Sheppard, P. Tancred-Sheriff, & G. Burrell (Eds.), *The sexuality of organization* (pp. 91–109). Newbury Park, CA: Sage.

Collinson, D., & Hearn, J. (1994). Naming men as men: Implications for work, organization and management. *Gender, Work and Organization, 1*, 2–22.

Collinson, D., & Hearn, J. (1996a). "Men" at "work": Multiple masculinities/ multiple workplaces. In M. Mac an Ghaill (Ed.), *Understanding masculinities: Social relations and cultural arenas* (pp. 61–76). Buckingham, UK: Open University Press.

Collinson, D., & Hearn, J. (Eds.). (1996b). *Men as managers, managers as men: Critical perspectives on men, masculinities and managements*. London: Sage.

Communication Studies 298. (1997). Fragments of self at the postmodern bar. *Journal of Contemporary Ethnography, 26*, 251–292.

Comte, A. (1970). *Introduction to positive philosophy* (F. Ferre, Trans.). Indianapolis, IN: Bobbs-Merrill. (Original work published 1830–1842)

Condit, C. M. (1989). The rhetorical limits of polysemy. *Critical Studies in Mass Communication, 6*, 103–122.

Connell, R. W. (1987). *Gender and power: Society, the person and sexual politics*. Stanford, CA: Stanford University Press.

Connell, R. W. (1993). The big picture: Masculinities in recent world history. *Theory and Society, 22*, 597–623.

Connell, R. W. (1995). *Masculinities*. Berkeley: University of California Press.

Conquergood, D. (1991). Rethinking ethnography: Toward a critical cultural politics. *Communication Monographs, 58*, 179–194.

Conquergood, D. (1994). Homeboys and hoods: Gang communication and cultural space. In L. Frey (Ed.), *Group communication in context* (pp. 23–56). Hillsdale, NJ: Lawrence Erlbaum.

Conrad, C. (1991). Communication in conflict: Style-strategy relationships. *Communication Monographs, 58*, 135–151.

Conrad, C. (Ed.). (1993). *Ethical nexus*. Norwood, NJ: Ablex.

Cooper, R. (1989). Modernism, postmodernism and organizational analysis 3: The contribution of Jacques Derrida. *Organization Studies, 10*, 479–502.

Cooper, R., & Burrell, G. (1988). Modernism, postmodernism and organizational analysis: An introduction. *Organization Studies, 9*, 91–112.

Cooper, V. W. (1997). Homophily or the Queen Bee syndrome: Female evaluation of female leadership. *Small Group Leadership, 28*, 483–499.

Cooren, F. (2000). *The organizing property of communication*. Amsterdam: John Benjamins.

Cooren, F., & Taylor, J. R. (1997). Organization as an effect of mediation: Redefining the link between organization and communication. *Communication Theory, 7*, 219–260.

Corey, F. C. (2000). Masculine drag. *Critical Studies in Media Communication, 17*, 108–110.

Corman, S. R., & Poole, M. S. (Eds.). (2000). *Perspectives on organizational communication: Finding common ground*. New York: Guilford.

Corn, J. J. (1979). Making flying "unthinkable": Women pilots and the selling of aviation, 1927–1940. *American Quarterly, 31*, 556–571.

Courtney, W. B. (1935, March 30). Ladybird. *Collier's*, 15, 16, 40, 43.

Crawford, L. (1996). Personal ethnography. *Communication Monographs, 63*, 158–170.

Crenshaw, C. (1997). Women in the Gulf War: Toward an intersectional feminist rhetorical criticism. *Howard Journal of Communications, 8*, 219–235.

Crenshaw, K. (1991). Mapping the margins: Intersectionality, identity politics, and violence against women of color. *Stanford Law Review, 43*, 1241–1299.

Czarniawska-Joerges, B., & Monthoux, P. G. (1994). *Good novels, better management: Reading organizational realities in fiction*. New York: Gordon & Breach.

Dace, K. L. (1998). "Had Judas been a black man . . .": Politics, race, and gender in African America. In J. M. Sloop & J. P. McDaniel (Eds.), *Judgment calls: Rhetoric, politics, and indeterminacy* (pp. 163–181). Boulder, CO: Westview.

Dale, K. (2001). *Anatomising embodiment and organisation theory*. Basingstoke, UK: Palgrave.

Daly, M. (1978). *Gyn/ecology: The metaethics of radical feminism*. Boston: Beacon.

Daudi, P. (1986). *Power in the organisation*. Oxford, UK: Basil Blackwell.

Davis, M. (circa 1935). She flies like a man. 99s Museum of Women Pilots, Oklahoma City, OK, Helen Richey file.

Deetz, S. (1973a). An understanding of science and a hermeneutic science of understanding. *Journal of Communication, 23*, 139–159.

Deetz, S. (1973b). Words without things: Toward a social phenomenology of language. *The Quarterly Journal of Speech, 59*, 40–51.

Deetz, S. (1978). Conceptualizing human understanding: Gadamer's hermeneutics and American communication research. *Communication Quarterly, 26*, 12–23.

Deetz, S. (1982). Critical interpretive research in organizational communication. *The Western Journal of Speech Communication, 46*, 131–149.

Deetz, S. (1985). Critical-cultural research: New sensibilities and old realities. *Journal of Management, 11*(2), 121–136.

Deetz, S. (1992a). *Democracy in an age of corporate colonization: Developments in communication and the politics of everyday life*. Albany: State University of New York Press.

Deetz, S. (1992b). Disciplinary power in the modern corporation. In M. Alvesson & H. Willmott (Eds.), *Critical management studies* (pp. 21–45). Newbury Park, CA: Sage.

Deetz, S. (1994). Future of the discipline: The challenges, the research, and the social contribution. In S. Deetz (Ed.), *Communication yearbook 17* (pp. 565–600). Thousand Oaks, CA: Sage.

Deetz, S. (1995). *Transforming communication, transforming business: Building responsive and responsible workplaces.* Cresskill, NJ: Hampton.

Deetz, S. (1996). Describing differences in approaches to organization science: Rethinking Burrell and Morgan and their legacy. *Organization Science, 7,* 191–207.

Deetz, S., & Kersten, A. (1983). Critical models of interpretive research. In L. L. Putnam & M. Pacanowsky (Eds.), *Communication and organizations: An interpretive approach* (pp. 147–171). Beverly Hills, CA: Sage.

Deetz, S., & Mumby, D. K. (1990). Power, discourse, and the workplace: Reclaiming the critical tradition. In J. Anderson (Ed.), *Communication yearbook 13* (pp. 18–47). Newbury Park, CA: Sage.

Dellinger, K., & Williams, C. L. (1997). Makeup at work: Negotiating appearance rules in the workplace. *Gender & Society, 11,* 151–177.

Derrida, J. (1976). *Of grammatology* (G. Spivak, Trans.). Baltimore: Johns Hopkins University Press.

Dervin, B. (1987). The potential contribution of feminist scholarship to the field of communication. *Journal of Communication, 37,* 107–120.

Diamond, I., & Quinby, L. (Eds.). (1988). *Feminism and Foucault.* Boston: Northeastern University Press.

DiMaggio, P. J. (1995). Comments on "what theory is not." *Administrative Science Quarterly, 40,* 391–397.

Dines, G. (1998). *King Kong and the white woman: Hustler magazine and the demonization of Black masculinity.* Retrieved from http://ehostvgw3.epnet.com/ehost1.asp

Donaldson, L. (1985). *In defence of organization theory: A reply to the critics.* Cambridge, UK: Cambridge University Press.

Donaldson, L. (1988). In successful defence of organization theory: A routing of the critics. *Organization Studies, 9,* 28–32.

Donaldson, L. (1994). The liberal revolution and organization theory. In J. Hassard & M. Parker (Eds.), *Towards a new theory of organizations* (pp. 190–208). London: Routledge.

Donaldson, L. (1995). *American anti-management theories of organization: A critique of paradigm proliferation.* Cambridge, UK: Cambridge University Press.

Donaldson, M. (1993). What is hegemonic masculinity? *Theory and Society, 22,* 643–657.

Du Gay, P. (2000). *In praise of bureaucracy: Weber, organization, ethics.* Thousand Oaks, CA: Sage.

Du Gay, P., Hall, S., Janes, L., Mackay, H., & Negus, K. (1997). *Doing cultural studies: The story of the Sony Walkman*. London: Sage/Open University Press.

Duneier, M. (1999). *Sidewalk*. New York: Farrar, Straus & Giroux.

Eagleton, T. (1995). Where do postmodernists come from? *Monthly Review, 47*(3), 59–70.

Eagly, A. H., & Johannesen-Schmidt, M. C. (2001). The leadership styles of women and men. *Journal of Social Issues, 57*, 781–797.

Eagly, A. H., & Johnson, B. (1990). Gender and leadership style: A meta-analysis. *Psychological Bulletin, 108*, 233–256.

Eagly, A. H., Makhijani, M. G., & Klonsky, B. G. (1992). Gender and the evaluation of leaders: A meta-analysis. *Psychological Bulletin, 111*, 3–22.

Eagly, A. H., Makhijani, M. G., & Otto, S. (1991). Are women evaluated more favorably than men? *Psychology of Women Quarterly, 15*, 203–216.

Ebert, T. L. (1996). *Ludic feminism and after: Postmodernism, desire, and labor in late capitalism*. Ann Arbor: The University of Michigan Press.

Edley, P. P. (2000). Discursive essentializing in a woman-owned business: Gendered stereotypes and strategic subordination. *Management Communication Quarterly, 14*, 271–306.

Egendorf, K. L. (Ed.). (2000). *Male/female roles: Opposing viewpoints*. San Diego, CA: Greenhaven.

Ehrenhaus, P. (1993). Cultural narratives and the therapeutic motif: The political containment of Vietnam veterans. In D. K. Mumby (Ed.), *Narrative and social control* (pp. 77–96). Newbury Park, CA: Sage.

Eisenberg, E. (1984). Ambiguity as strategy in organizational communication. *Communication Monographs, 51*, 227–242.

Eisenberg, E. (1998). Flirting with meaning. *Journal of Language and Social Psychology, 17*, 97–108.

Eisenberg, E., & Goodall, B. (1997). *Organizational communication: Balancing creativity and constraint* (2nd. ed.). New York: St. Martin's.

Eng, D. L. (2001). *Racial castration: Managing masculinity in Asian America*. Durham, NC: Duke University Press.

An engineering interpretation of the economic and financial aspects of American industry: Volume 1. The aviation industry. (circa 1940). New York: George S. Armstrong.

Epstein, C. F. (1981). *Women in law*. New York: Basic Books.

Fagenson, E. A. (Ed.). (1993). *Women in management: Trends, issues, and challenges in managerial diversity*. Newbury Park, CA: Sage.

Fair play for women fliers. (1927, November 22). *New York Times*. 99s Museum of Women Pilots, Oklahoma City, OK, Helen Richey file.

Fairhurst, G. (1993). The leader-member exchange patterns of women leaders in industry: A discourse analysis. *Communication Monographs, 60*, 321–351.

Faludi, S. (1998). *Stiffed: The betrayal of the American man*. New York: William Morrow.

Featherstone, M. (1988). In pursuit of the postmodern. *Theory, Culture & Society,* 5, 195–215.

Fenstermaker, S., & West, C. (Eds.). (2002). *Doing gender, doing difference: Inequality, power and institutional change.* New York: Routledge.

Ferdman, B. M. (1999). The color and culture of gender in organizations: Attending to race and ethnicity. In G. N. Powell (Ed.), *Handbook of gender and work* (pp. 17–34). Thousand Oaks, CA: Sage.

Ferguson, A. A. (1991). Managing without managers: Crisis and revolution in a collective bakery. In M. Burawoy, A. Burton, A. A. Ferguson, H. J. Fox, J. Gamson, N. Gartrell, L. Hurst, C. Hurzman, L. Salzinger, J. Schiffman, & S. Ui (Eds.), *Ethnography unbound: Power and resistance in the modern metropolis* (pp. 108–132). Berkeley: University of California Press.

Ferguson, K. (1984). *The feminist case against bureaucracy.* Philadelphia: Temple University Press.

Ferguson, K. (1993). *The man question: Visions of subjectivity in feminist theory.* Berkeley: University of California Press.

Ferguson, K. (1994). On bringing more theory, more voices and more politics to the study of organization. *Organization, 1,* 81–99.

Ferguson, K. (1997). Postmodernism, feminism, and organizational ethics: Letting difference be. In A. Larson & R. E. Freeman (Eds.), *Women's studies and business ethics: Toward a new conversation* (pp. 80–91). Oxford, UK: Oxford University Press.

Ferree, M. M., & Martin, P. (Eds.). (1995). *Feminist organizations: Harvest of the new women's movement.* Philadelphia: Temple University Press.

Fine, M. (1988). What makes it feminist? *Women's Studies in Communication, 11,* 18–19.

Fine, M. (1993). New voices in organizational communication: A feminist commentary and critique. In S. Bowen & N. Wyatt (Eds.), *Transforming visions: Feminist critiques in communication studies* (pp. 125–166). Cresskill, NJ: Hampton.

Fine, M. (2000). Walking the high wire: Leadership theorizing, daily acts, and tensions. In P. M. Buzzanell (Ed.), *Rethinking organizational and managerial communication from feminist perspectives* (pp. 128–156). Thousand Oaks, CA: Sage.

Fine, M., Weis, L., Addelston, J., & Marusza, J. (1997). (In)secure times: Constructing white working class masculinities in the late 20th century. *Gender & Society, 11,* 568.

Fitzpatrick, M. A. (1983). Effective interpersonal communication for women of the corporation: Think like a man, talk like a lady. In J. Pilotta (Ed.), *Women in organizations: Barriers and breakthroughs* (pp. 73–84). Prospect Heights, IL: Waveland.

Flax, J. (1990). *Thinking fragments: Psychoanalysis, feminism, and postmodernism in the contemporary West.* Berkeley: University of California Press.

Flax, J. (1992). The end of innocence. In J. Butler & J. Scott (Eds.), *Feminists theorize the political* (pp. 445–463). New York: Routledge.

Fletcher, J. (1994). Castrating the female advantage: Feminist standpoint research and management science. *Journal of Management Inquiry, 3*, 74–82.

Fletcher, J. (1998). Relational practice: A feminist reconstruction of work. *Journal of Management Inquiry, 7*, 163–186.

Fletcher, J. (1999). *Disappearing acts: Gender, power, and relational practice at work.* Cambridge: MIT Press.

Flores, L. A., & Moon, D. G. (2002). Rethinking race, revealing dilemmas: Imagining a new racial subject in Race Traitor. *Western Journal of Communication, 66*, 181–207.

Flying supermen and superwomen. (1936, November 14). *Literary Digest, 122*, 22.

Fondas, N. (1997). Feminization unveiled: Management qualities in contemporary writings. *Academy of Management Review, 22*, 257–282.

Forester, J. (1992). Fieldwork in a Habermasian way. In M. Alvesson & H. Willmott (Eds.), *Critical management studies* (pp. 46–65). Newbury Park, CA: Sage.

Forester, J. (1993). *Critical theory, public policy and planning practice.* Albany: State University of New York Press.

Foss, K. A., & Rogers, R. A. (1994). Particularities and possibilities: Reconceptualizing knowledge and power in sexual harassment research. In S. G. Bingham (Ed.), *Conceptualizing sexual harassment as discursive practice* (pp. 159–172). Westport, CT: Praeger.

Foucault, M. (1973). *The order of things: An archaeology of the human sciences.* New York: Random House.

Foucault, M. (1977). *Language, counter-memory, practice: Selected essays and interviews* (D. Bouchard & S. Simon, Trans.). Ithaca, NY: Cornell University Press.

Foucault, M. (1979). *Discipline and punish: The birth of the prison* (A. Sheridan, Trans.). New York: Random House.

Foucault, M. (1980a). *The history of sexuality: An introduction* (Vol. 1, R. Hurley, Trans.). New York: Random House.

Foucault, M. (1980b). *Power/knowledge: Selected interviews and other writings 1972–1977* (L. M. C. Gordon, J. Mepham, & K. Soper, Trans.). New York: Pantheon.

Foucault, M. (1982). The subject and power. In H. F. Dreyfus & P. Rabinow (Eds.), *Michel Foucault: Beyond structuralism and hermeneutics* (pp. 202–226). Brighton, UK: Harvester.

Foucault, M. (1986). *The use of pleasure* (R. Hurley, Trans.). New York: Random House.

Foucault, M. (1988a). The ethic of care for the self as a practice of freedom. In J. Bernauer & D. Rasmussen (Eds.), *The final Foucault* (J. D. Gauthier, Trans.; pp. 1–20). Cambridge: MIT Press.

Foucault, M. (1988b). *Politics, philosophy, culture: Interviews and other writings, 1977–1984* (A. Sheridan, Trans.). New York: Routledge.

Frankenberg, R. (1993). *White women, race matters: The social construction of whiteness*. Minneapolis: University of Minnesota Press.

Fraser, N. (1989). *Unruly practices: Power, discourse and gender in contemporary social theory*. Minneapolis: University of Minnesota Press.

Fraser, N. (1990/91). Rethinking the public sphere: A contribution to the critique of actually existing democracy. *Social Text, 25/26*, 56–80.

Fraser, N., & Nicholson, L. (1990). Social criticism without philosophy: An encounter between feminism and postmodernism. In L. Nicholson (Ed.), *Feminism/postmodernism* (pp. 19–38). New York: Routledge.

Gadamer, H.-G. (1989). *Truth and method* (2nd ed., J. W. D. G. Marshall, Trans.). New York: Continuum.

Geertz, C. (1983). *Local knowledge: Further essays in interpretive anthropology*. New York: Basic Books.

Gergen, K. (1992). Organization theory in the postmodern era. In M. Reed & M. Hughes (Eds.), *Rethinking organization: Rethinking organization theory and analysis* (pp. 207–226). Newbury Park, CA: Sage.

Gherardi, S. (1994). The gender we think, the gender we do in our everyday organizational lives. *Human Relations, 47*, 591–610.

Gherardi, S. (1995). *Gender, symbolism and organizational cultures*. London: Sage.

Gherardi, S. (1996). Gendered organizational cultures: Narratives of women travellers in a male world. *Gender, Work and Organization, 3*, 187–201.

Gibson, M. K., & Papa, M. J. (2000). The mud, the blood, and the beer guys: Organizational osmosis in blue-collar work groups. *Journal of Applied Communication Research, 28*, 68–88.

Gibson, M. K., & Schullery, N. M. (2000). Shifting meanings in a blue-collar worker philanthropy program: Emergent tensions in traditional and feminist organizing. *Management Communication Quarterly, 14*, 189–236.

Giddens, A. (1979). *Central problems in social theory: Action, structure and contradiction in social analysis*. Berkeley: University of California Press.

Giddens, A. (1984). *The constitution of society: Outline of the theory of structuration*. Berkeley: University of California Press.

Gilligan, C. (1982). *In a different voice: Psychological theory and women's development*. Cambridge, MA: Harvard University Press.

Gingrich-Philbrook, C. (1998). Disciplinary violation as gender violation: The stigmatized masculine voice of performance studies. *Communication Theory, 8*, 203–220.

Goffman, E. (1959). *The presentation of self in everyday life*. New York: Doubleday.

Goffman, E. (1976). Gender display. *Studies in the Anthropology of Visual Communication, 3*, 69–77.

Goffman, E. (1977). The arrangement between the sexes. *Theory & Society, 4*, 301–331.

Gottfried, H. (1994). Learning the score: The duality of control and everyday resistance in the temporary-help service industry. In J. M. Jermier,

D. Knights, & W. R. Nord (Eds.), *Resistance and power in organizations* (pp. 102–127). London: Routledge.

Gottfried, H., & Graham, L. (1993). Constructing difference: The making of gendered subcultures in a Japanese automobile assembly plant. *Sociology, 27*, 611–628.

Gottfried, H., & Hayashi-Kato, N. (1998). Gendering work: Deconstructing the narrative of the Japanese economic miracle. *Work, Employment & Society, 12*, 25–46.

Gottfried, H., & Weiss, P. (1994). A compound feminist organization: Purdue University's Council on the Status of Women. *Women and Politics, 14*(2), 23–44.

Graham, L. (1993). Inside a Japanese transplant: A critical perspective. *Work and Occupations, 20*, 147–173.

Gramsci, A. (1971). *Selections from the prison notebooks* (Q. Hoare & G. N. Smith, Trans.). New York: International Publishers.

Grant, D., Keenoy, T., & Oswick, C. (Eds.). (1998). *Discourse and organization.* London: Sage.

Grant, J., & Tancred, P. (1992). A feminist perspective on state bureaucracy. In A. J. Mills & P. Tancred-Sheriff (Eds.), *Gendering organizational analysis* (pp. 112–128). Newbury Park, CA: Sage.

Greenhaus, J. H., & Parasuraman, S. (1999). Research on work, family, and gender: Current status and future directions. In G. N. Powell (Ed.), *Handbook of gender and work* (pp. 391–412). Thousand Oaks, CA: Sage.

Gregg, N. (1993). Politics of identity/politics of location: Women workers organizing in a postmodern world. *Women's Studies in Communication, 16*(1), 1–33.

Gregory, E. H. (1912, September). Women's record in aviation. *Good Housekeeping, 55*, 316–319.

Grimes, D. S. (2001). Putting our own house in order: Whiteness, change and organization studies. *Journal of Organizational Change Management, 14*, 132–149.

Grimes, D. S. (2002). Challenging the status quo? Whiteness in the diversity management literature. *Management Communication Quarterly, 15*, 381–409.

Haas, T., & Deetz, S. (2000). Between the generalized and the concrete other: Approaching organizational ethics from feminist perspectives. In P. M. Buzzanell (Ed.), *Rethinking organizational and managerial communication from feminist perspectives* (pp. 24–46). Thousand Oaks, CA: Sage.

Habermas, J. (1971). *Knowledge and human interests* (J. Shapiro, Trans.). Boston: Beacon.

Habermas, J. (1979). *Communication and the evolution of society* (T. McCarthy, Trans.). Boston: Beacon.

Habermas, J. (1984). *The theory of communicative action: Reason and the rationalization of society* (Vol. 1, T. McCarthy, Trans.). Boston: Beacon.

Habermas, J. (1987). *The philosophical discourse of modernity: Twelve lectures* (F. Lawrence, Trans.). Cambridge: MIT Press.

Hall, S. (1985). Signification, representation, ideology: Althusser and the post-structuralist debates. *Critical Studies in Mass Communication, 2*, 91–114.

Hall, S. (1991). Brave new world. *Socialist Review, 21*(1), 57–64.

Hall, S. (1997). The work of representation. In S. Hall (Ed.), *Representation: Cultural representations and signifying practices* (pp. 13–64). London: Sage/Open University Press.

Hamada, T. (1996). Unwrapping Euro-American masculinity in a Japanese multinational corporation. In C. Cheng (Ed.), *Masculinities in organizations* (pp. 160–176). Thousand Oaks, CA: Sage.

Hancock, P., & Tyler, M. (2001a). Managing subjectivity and the dialectic of self-consciousness: Hegel and organization theory. *Organization, 8*, 565–585.

Hancock, P., & Tyler, M. (2001b). *Work, postmodernism and organization: A critical introduction*. London: Sage.

Hanson, R. L. (1996). A comparison of leadership practices used by male and female communication department chairpersons. *Journal of the Association for Communication Administration, 1*, 40–55.

Harding, S. (1997). Comment on Hekman's "Truth and method: Feminist standpoint theory revisited": Whose standpoint needs the regimes of truth and reality? *Signs: Journal of Women in Culture and Society, 22*, 382–391.

Hardy, C., & Phillips, N. (1999). No joking matter: Discursive struggle in the Canadian refugee system. *Organization Studies, 20*, 1–24.

Hartmann, H. I. (1979). The unhappy marriage of marxism and feminism: Towards a more progressive union. *Capital & Class, 8*, 1–33.

Hartsock, N. C. (1996). Theoretical bases for coalition building: An assessment of postmodernism. In H. Gottfried (Ed.), *Feminism and social change: Bridging theory and practice* (pp. 256–274). Urbana: University of Illinois Press.

Hartsock, N. C. (1997). Comment on Hekman's "Truth and method: Feminist standpoint theory revisited": Truth or justice? *Signs: Journal of Women in Culture and Society, 22*, 367–374.

Hartsock, N. C. (1998). *The feminist standpoint revisited and other essays*. Boulder, CO: Westview.

Harvey, D. (1989). *The condition of postmodernity: An enquiry into the origins of cultural change*. Oxford, UK: Basil Blackwell.

Haslett, B., Geis, F. L., & Carter, M. R. (1992). *The organizational woman: Power and paradox*. Norwood, NJ: Ablex.

Hassard, J. (1993a). Postmodernism and organizational analysis: An overview. In J. Hassard & M. Parker (Eds.), *Postmodernism and organizations* (pp. 1–24). Newbury Park, CA: Sage.

Hassard, J. (1993b). *Sociology and organization theory: Positivism, paradigms and postmodernity*. Cambridge, UK: Cambridge University Press.

Hassard, J., & Holliday, R. (Eds.). (1998). *Organization representation: Work and organizations in popular culture*. London: Sage.

Hassard, J., Holliday, R., & Willmott, H. (Eds.). (2000). *Body and organization*. London: Sage.

Hatch, M. J. (1997). Irony and the social construction of contradiction in the humor of a management team. *Organization Science, 8*, 275–288.

Hawes, L. (1977). Toward a hermeneutic phenomenology of communication. *Communication Quarterly, 25*(3), 30–41.

Hawkins, K. (1989). Exposing masculine science: An alternative feminist approach to the study of women's communication. In K. Carter & C. Spitzack (Eds.), *Doing research on women's communication: Perspectives on theory and method* (pp. 40–64). Norwood, NJ: Ablex.

Hearn, J. (1994). The organization(s) of violence: Men, gender relations, organizations, and violences. *Human Relations, 47*, 731–754.

Hearn, J. (1996). Deconstructing the dominant: Making the one(s) the other(s). *Organization, 3*, 611–626.

Hearn, J., & Collinson, D. L. (1994). Theorizing unities and differences between men and between masculinities. In H. Brod & M. Kaufman (Eds.), *Theorizing masculinities* (pp. 97–118). Thousand Oaks, CA: Sage.

Hearn, J., & Morgan, D. (Eds.). (1990). *Men, masculinities, and social theory*. London: Unwin Hyman.

Hearn, J., & Parkin, W. (1983). Gender and organizations: A selective review and critique of a neglected area. *Organization Studies, 4*, 219–242.

Hearn, J., Sheppard, D., Tancred-Sheriff, P., & Burrell, G. (Eds.). (1989). *The sexuality of organization*. London: Sage.

Hegde, R. S. (1998). A view from elsewhere: Locating difference and the politics of representation from a transnational feminist perspective. *Communication Theory, 8*, 271–297.

Heidegger, M. (1977). *Basic writings*. New York: Harper & Row.

Heilman, M. E., Block, C. J., Martell, R. E., & Simon, M. C. (1989). Has anything changed? Current characterizations of men, women, and managers. *Journal of Applied Psychology, 59*, 935–942.

Hekman, S. (1990). *Gender and knowledge: Elements of a postmodern feminism*. Boston: Northeastern University Press.

Hekman, S. (1997). Truth and method: Feminist standpoint theory revisited. *Signs: Journal of Women in Culture and Society, 22*, 341–365.

Helgesen, S. (1990). *The female advantage: Women's ways of leadership*. New York: Doubleday.

Helmer, J. (1993). Storytelling in the creation and maintenance of organizational tension and stratification. *The Southern Communication Journal, 59*, 34–44.

Higginbotham, E., & Romero, M. (Eds.). (1997). *Women and work: Exploring race, ethnicity, and class*. Thousand Oaks, CA: Sage.

Hill Collins, P. (1991). *Black feminist thought: Knowledge, consciousness and the politics of empowerment*. New York: Routledge.

Hill Collins, P. (1997). Comment on Hekman's "Truth and method: Feminist standpoint theory revisited": Where's the power? *Signs: Journal of Women in Culture and Society, 22*, 375–381.

Hochschild, A. (1983). *The managed heart: Commercialization of human feeling*. Berkeley: University of California Press.

Holmer Nadesan, M. (1996). Organizational identity and space of action. *Organization Studies, 17*, 49–81.

Holmer Nadesan, M. (1997). Constructing paper dolls: The discourse of personality testing in organizational practice. *Communication Theory, 7*, 189–218.

Holmer Nadesan, M. (1999). The discourses of corporate spiritualism and evangelical capitalism. *Management Communication Quarterly, 13*, 3–42.

Holmer Nadesan, M. (2001). Post-Fordism, political economy, and critical organizational communication studies. *Management Communication Quarterly, 15*, 259–267.

Holmer Nadesan, M., & Trethewey, A. (2000). Performing the enterprising subject: Gendered strategies for success (?). *Text and Peformance Quarterly, 20*, 223–250.

Holvino, E. (1997). Reading organizational development from the margins: Outsider within. *Organization, 3*, 520–533.

hooks, b. (1981). *Ain't I a woman: Black women and feminism*. Boston: South End.

hooks, b. (1984). *Feminist theory: From margin to center*. Boston: South End.

hooks, b. (1992). *Black looks: Race and representation*. Boston: South End.

Hopkins, G. E. (1998). *The airline pilots: A study in elite unionization*. Cambridge, MA: Harvard University Press.

Horgan, D. (1990, November-December). Why women sometimes talk themselves out of success and how managers can help. *Performance & Instruction*, 20–22.

Horkheimer, M., & Adorno, T. (1988). *Dialectic of enlightenment* (J. Cumming, Trans.). New York: Continuum.

Hossfeld, K. J. (1993). "Their logic against them": Contradictions in sex, race, and class in Silicon Valley. In P. S. Rothenberg (Ed.), *Feminist frameworks: Alternative theoretical accounts of the relations between women and men* (pp. 346–358). New York: McGraw-Hill.

Howard, L. A., & Geist, P. (1995). Ideological positioning in organizational change: The dialectic of control in a merging organization. *Communication Monographs, 62*, 110–131.

Huspek, M., & Kendall, K. (1991). On withholding political voice: An analysis of the political vocabulary of a "nonpolitical" speech community. *The Quarterly Journal of Speech, 77*, 1–19.

Iannello, K. P. (1992). *Decisions without hierarchy: Feminist interventions in organizational theory and practice*. London: Routledge.

Irigaray, L. (1985). *This sex which is not one.* Ithaca, NY: Cornell University Press.

Ivy, D. K., & Backlund, P. (2000). *Exploring genderspeak: Personal effectiveness in gender communication* (2nd ed.). Boston: McGraw-Hill.

Jackson, M. (1989). *Paths toward a clearing: Radical empiricism and ethnographic inquiry.* Bloomington: Indiana University Press.

Jacques, R. (1992). Critique and theory building: Producing knowledge "from the kitchen." *Academy of Management Review, 17,* 582–606.

Jacques, R. (1996). *Manufacturing the employee: Management knowledge from the 19th to 21st centuries.* London: Sage.

Jaggar, A. M. (1991). Feminist ethics: Projects, problems, prospects. In C. Card (Ed.), *Feminist ethics* (pp. 78–104). Lawrence: University of Kansas Press.

Jameson, F. (1984). Foreword to J-F Lyotard. In *The postmodern condition* (pp. vii–xi). Minneapolis: University of Minnesota Press.

Jamieson, K. H. (1995). *Beyond the double bind: Women and leadership.* New York: Oxford University Press.

Jermier, J. M. (1998). Introduction: Critical perspectives on organizational control. *Administrative Science Quarterly, 43,* 235–256.

Jermier, J. M., Knights, D., & Nord, W. R. (Eds.). (1994). *Resistance and power in organizations.* London: Routledge.

Johnson, F. L. (1989). Women's culture and communication: An analytic perspective. In C. M. Lont & S. A. Friedley (Eds.), *Beyond boundaries: Sex and gender diversity in communication* (pp. 301–316). Fairfax, VA: George Mason University Press.

Jones, C. S. (1929). Sky-riding in skirts. *The Texaco Star,* pp. 29–31. 99s Museum of Women Pilots, Oklahoma City, OK, Helen Richey file.

Jorgenson, J. (2002). Engineering selves: Negotiating gender and identity in technical work. *Management Communication Quarterly, 15,* 350–380.

Kahn, A., & Yoder, J. (1989). The psychology of women and conservatism. *Psychology of Women Quarterly, 13,* 417–432.

Kanter, R. M. (1975). Women and the structure of organizations: Explorations in theory and behavior. In M. Millman & R. M. Kanter (Eds.), *Another voice: Feminist perspectives on social life and social science* (pp. 34–74). New York: Doubleday.

Kanter, R. M. (1977). *Men and women of the corporation.* New York: Basic Books.

Kanter, R. M., & Zurcher, L. A. (1973). Concluding statement: Evaluating alternatives and alternative valuing. *Journal of Applied Behavioral Science, 9,* 381–397.

Kauffman, B. J. (1991). Feminist facts: Interview strategies and political subjects in ethnography. *Communication Theory, 2,* 187–206.

Keenoy, T., Marchak, R. J., Oswick, C., & Grant, D. (2000). The discourses of organizing. *The Journal of Applied Behavioral Science, 36,* 133–135.

Keenoy, T., Oswick, C., & Grant, D. (1997). Organizational discourses: Text and context. *Organization, 4,* 147–159.

Kerfoot, D., & Knights, D. (1993). Management, masculinity and manipulation: From paternalism to corporate strategy in financial services in Britain. *Journal of Management Studies, 30,* 659–677.

Kerfoot, G. (1978). Helen Richey: First lady of the airlines. *The Ninety-Nine News,* 17–18, 34. 99s Museum of Women Pilots, Oklahoma City, OK, Helen Richey file.

Kerfoot, G. (1983). Does anybody out there remember Helen Richey? *The Almost Journal, 54*(5), 160–166.

Kerfoot, G. (1988). Propeller Annie: The story of Helen Richey: The Kentucky Aviation History Roundtable.

Kerfoot, G. (1991a, March). *The story of Helen Richey—The real first lady of the airlines.* Newsletter of the International Society of Women Airline Pilots.

Kerfoot, G. (1991b, October). *The story of Helen Richey—the real first lady of the airlines (continued).* Newsletter of International Society of Women Airline Pilots.

Kilduff, M. (1993). Deconstructing organizations. *Academy of Management Review, 18,* 13–31.

Kilduff, M., & Mehra, A. (1997). Postmodernism and organizational research. *Academy of Management Review, 22,* 453–481.

Kimmel, M. (1996). *Manhood in America: A cultural history.* New York: Free Press.

Kleinman, S. (1996). *Opposing ambitions: Gender identity in an alternative organization.* Chicago: University of Chicago Press.

Knights, D. (1990). Subjectivity, power and the labor process. In D. Knights & H. Willmott (Eds.), *Labour process theory* (pp. 297–335). London: MacMillan.

Knights, D. (1997). Organization theory in the age of deconstruction: Dualism, gender and postmodernism revisited. *Organization Studies, 18,* 1–19.

Knights, D., & McCabe, D. (2001). "A different world": Shifting masculinities in the transition to call centres. *Organization, 8,* 619–646.

Knights, D., & Morgan, G. (1991). Strategic discourse and subjectivity: Towards a critical analysis of corporate strategy in organizations. *Organization Studies, 12,* 251–274.

Knights, D., & Vurdubakis, T. (1994). Foucault, power, resistance and all that. In J. M. Jermier, D. Knights, & W. R. Nord (Eds.), *Resistance and power in organizations* (pp. 167–198). London: Routledge.

Kondo, D. K. (1990). *Crafting selves: Power, gender, and discourses of identity in a Japanese workplace.* Chicago: University of Chicago Press.

Kramarae, C. (1981). *Women and men speaking: Frameworks for analysis.* Rowley, MA: Newbury House.

Kramarae, C. (1992). Harassment in everyday life. In L. F. Rakow (Ed.), *Women making meaning: New feminist directions in communication* (pp. 100–120). New York: Routledge, Chapman, & Hall.

Kristeva, J. (1981). Women can never be defined. In E. Marks (Ed.), *New French feminisms.* New York: Schocken.

Krizek, B. (1992). Goodbye old friend: A son's farewell to Comiskey Park. *Omega, 25*(2), 87–93.

Kuhn, D. B. (1953, May). Secure in our memory. *The Air Line Pilot, 22*, 6–7.

Kunda, G. (1992). *Engineering culture: Control and commitment in a high-tech corporation.* Philadelphia: Temple University Press.

Kunz, O. (1929). Personal letter inviting "Miss Brown" to join the 99s. 99s Museum of Women Pilots, Oklahoma City, OK, Helen Richey file.

Kunz, O. (1930). Girls are learning to fly. *The Guidon: A Political Review, 1.* 99s Museum of Women Pilots, Oklahoma City, OK, Helen Richey file.

Kurtz, H. G. (1953). The common man up in the air. *The Air Line Pilot, 22*, 18–21.

Laclau, E., & Mouffe, C. (1985). *Hegemony and socialist strategy: Towards a radical democratic politics.* London: Verso.

Ladybirds down with powdered noses and a brand-new record. (1932, September 3). *Literary Digest.* 99s Museum of Women Pilots, Oklahoma City, OK, Helen Richey file.

Lay, B. J. (1941). Airman. *Fortune, 23*, 122–123.

Leonard, P. (2002). Organizing gender? Looking at metaphors as frames of meaning in gender/organizational texts. *Gender, Work and Organization, 9*, 60–80.

Linstead, S. (1997). Abjection and organization: Men, violence, and management. *Human Relations, 50*, 1115–1145.

Lipsner, B. P. (1953, December). The air line pilots heritage. *The Airline Pilot, 22*, 18–21.

Loden, M. (1985). *Feminine leadership, or how to succeed in business without being one of the boys.* New York: Times Books.

Loseke, D. (1992). *The battered woman and shelters: The social construction of wife abuse.* Albany: State University of New York Press.

Loveland, R. (1929). Throngs at air races cheer as Mrs. Thaden leads women pilots in. *Cleveland Plain Dealer.* 99s Museum of Women Pilots, Oklahoma City, OK, Helen Richey file.

Lovibond, S. (1989). Feminism and postmodernism. *New Left Review, 178*, 5–28.

Lukács, G. (1971). *History and class consciousness: Studies in marxist dialectics* (R. Livingstone, Trans.). Cambridge: MIT Press.

Luthar, H. K. (1996). Gender differences in evaluation of performance and leadership ability: Autocratic vs. democratic managers. *Sex Roles, 35*, 337–361.

Lynch, E. M. (1973). *The executive suite—feminine style.* New York: AMACOM.

Lyotard, J.-F. (1984). *The postmodern condition: A report on knowledge* (G. Bennington & B. Massumi, Trans.). Minneapolis: University of Minnesota Press.

Madden, T. R. (1987). *Women vs. women: The uncivil business war.* New York: AMACOM.

Maguire, M., & Mohtar, L. F. (1994). Performance and the celebration of a subaltern counterpublic. *Text and Performance Quarterly, 14*, 238–252.

Maier, M. (1999). On the gendered substructure of organization: Dimensions and dilemmas of corporate masculinity. In G. N. Powell (Ed.), *Handbook of gender and work* (pp. 69–94). Thousand Oaks, CA: Sage.

Maltz, D., & Borker, R. (1982). A cultural approach to male-female miscommunication. In J. J. Gumperz (Ed.), *Language and social identity* (pp. 196–216). Cambridge, UK: Cambridge University Press.

Mansbridge, J. J. (1973). Time, emotion, and inequality: Three problems of participatory groups. *Journal of Applied Behavioral Science, 9*, 351–367.

Markham, A. (1996). Designing discourse: A critical analysis of strategic ambiguity and workplace control. *Management Communication Quarterly, 9*, 389–421.

Marshall, J. (1989). Re-visioning career concepts: A feminist invitation. In M. B. Arthur, D. Hall, & B. Lawrence (Eds.), *Handbook of career theory* (pp. 275–291). Cambridge, UK: Cambridge University Press.

Marshall, J. (1993). Viewing organizational communication from a feminist perspective: A critique and some offerings. In S. A. Deetz (Ed.), *Communication yearbook 16* (pp. 122–141). Newbury Park, CA: Sage.

Martin, B. (1982). Feminism, criticism and Foucault. *New German Critique, 27*, 3–30.

Martin, J. (1990). Deconstructing organizational taboos: The suppression of gender conflict in organizations. *Organization Science, 1*, 339–359.

Martin, J. (1992). *Culture in organizations: Three perspectives.* New York: Oxford University Press.

Martin, J. (1994). The organization of exclusion: Institutionalization of sex inequality, gendered faculty jobs and gendered knowledge in organizational theory and research. *Organization, 1*, 401–432.

Martin, J. (2000). Hidden gendered assumptions in mainstream organizational theory and research. *Journal of Management Inquiry, 9*, 207–216.

Martin, J., Knopoff, K., & Beckman, C. (1998). An alternative to bureaucratic impersonality and emotional labor: Bounded emotionality at The Body Shop. *Administrative Science Quarterly, 43*, 429–469.

Martin, P. Y. (1990). Rethinking feminist organizations. *Gender & Society, 4*, 182–206.

Martin, P. Y. (1993). Feminist practice in organizations: Implications for management. In E. A. Fagenson (Ed.), *Women in management: Trends, issues, and challenges in managerial diversity* (pp. 274–296). Newbury Park, CA: Sage.

Martin, P. Y. (2001). "Mobilizing masculinities": Women's experience of men at work. *Organization, 8*, 587–618.

Martin, P. Y., & Collinson, D. (2002). "Over the pond and across the water": Developing the field of "gendered organizations". *Gender, Work and Organization, 9*, 244–265.

Martyn, T. J. C. (1929, August 27). Women find a place among the fliers. *New York Times.* 99s Museum of Women Pilots, Oklahoma City, OK, Helen Richey file.

Martyn, T. J. C. (1930, August 10). Women fliers of the uncharted skies. *New York Times.*

May, S. K. (1997, November). *Silencing the feminine in managerial discourse*. Paper presented at the annual meeting of the National Communication Association, Chicago.

Mayer, A. M. (1995, May). *Feminism-in-practice: Implications for feminist theory.* Paper presented at the annual conference of the International Communication Association, Chicago.

McGee, M. C. (1990). Text, context, and the fragmentation of contemporary culture. *Western Journal of Speech Communication, 54,* 274–289.

McKinlay, A., & Starkey, K. (Eds.). (1998). *Foucault, management, and organization theory: From panopticon to technologies of self.* London: Sage.

McMillan, J. J., & Cheney, G. (1996). The student as consumer: The implications and limitations of a metaphor. *Communication Education, 45,* 1–15.

McNay, L. (1992). *Foucault and feminism.* Boston: Northeastern University Press.

McRobbie, A. (1981). Settling accounts with subcultures: A feminist critique. In T. Bennett, G. Martin, C. Mercer, & J. Woolacott (Eds.), *Culture, ideology, and social process* (pp. 111–124). London: Open University Press.

Mechling, E. W., & Mechling, J. (1994). The Jung and the restless: The mythopoetic men's movement. *Southern Communication Journal, 59,* 97–111.

Men, planes, and faith. (1953, December). *The Air Line Pilot, 22,* 8–17, 22–23.

Merleau-Ponty, M. (1960). *Phenomenology of perception* (C. Smith, Trans.). London: Routledge & Kegan Paul.

Mies, M. (1983). Towards a methodology for feminist research. In G. Bowles & R. D. Klein (Eds.), *Theories of women's studies* (pp. 117–139). London: Routledge & Kegan Paul.

Mies, M. (1991). Women's research or feminist research? The debate surrounding feminist science and methodology. In M. M. Fonow & J. A. Cook (Eds.), *Beyond methodology: Feminist scholarship as lived research* (pp. 60–82). Bloomington: Indiana University Press.

Milkie, M. A., & Pelotal, P. (1999). Playing all the roles: Gender and the work-family balancing act. *Journal of Marriage and the Family, 61,* 476–490.

Miller, K. I. (2000). Common ground from the post-positivist perspective: From "straw person" argument to collaborative co-existence. In S. R. Corman & M. S. Poole (Eds.), *Perspectives on organizational communication: Finding common ground* (pp. 46–67). New York: Guilford.

Mills, A. J. (1988). Organization, gender and culture. *Organization Studies, 9,* 351–369.

Mills, A. J. (1995). Man/aging subjectivity, silencing diversity: Organizational imagery in the airline industry—the case of British Airways. *Organization, 2,* 243–270.

Mills, A. J. (2002). Studying the gendering of organizational culture over time: Concerns, issues and strategies. *Gender, Work and Organization, 9,* 286–307.

Mills, A. J., & Chiaramonte, P. (1991). Organization as gendered communication act. *Canadian Journal of Communication, 16,* 381–398.

Mills, A. J., & Tancred, P. (Eds.). (1992). *Gendering organizational analysis.* Newbury Park, CA: Sage.

Mitchell, B. (1963a, January-February). Pancho Barnes: A legend in our lifetime. *Antelope Valley Spectator, 2,* 7–9, 30–31.

Mitchell, B. (1963b, July-August). Pancho Barnes: A legend in our lifetime. *Hi-Desert Spectator, 2,* 14–24.

Monge, P. R., & Contractor, N. S. (2001). Emergence of communication networks. In L. L. Putnam & M. Pacanowsky (Eds.), *The new handbook of organizational communication: Advances in theory, research, and methods* (pp. 440–502). Thousand Oaks, CA: Sage.

Monroe, C., DiSalvo, V., Lewis, J. J., & Borzi, M. G. (1990). Conflict behaviors of difficult subordinates: Interactive effects of gender. *Southern Communication Journal, 56,* 12–23.

Morgan, D. (1996). The gender of bureaucracy. In D. Collinson & J. Hearn (Eds.), *Men as managers, managers as men: Critical perspectives on men, masculinities and managements* (pp. 61–77). Thousand Oaks, CA: Sage.

Morgen, S. (1988). The dream of diversity, the dilemma of difference: Race and class contradictions in a feminist health clinic. In J. Sole (Ed.), *Anthropology for the nineties* (pp. 370–380). New York: Free Press.

Morgen, S. (1990). Contradictions in feminist practice: Individualism and collectivism in a feminist health center. In C. Calhoun (Ed.), *Comparative social research supplement 1* (pp. 9–59). Greenwich, CT: JAI.

Morgen, S. (1994). Personalizing personnel decisions in feminist organizational theory and practice. *Human Relations, 47,* 665–684.

Morris, M. (1988). *The pirate's fiancee: Feminism, reading, postmodernism.* London: Verso.

Mouffe, C. (1979). Hegemony and ideology in Gramsci. In C. Mouffe (Ed.), *Gramsci and Marxist theory* (pp. 168–204). London: Routledge & Kegan Paul.

Mouffe, C. (1995). Feminism, citizenship, and radical democratic politics. In L. J. Nicholson & S. Seidman (Eds.), *Social postmodernism* (pp. 315–331). Cambridge, UK: Cambridge University Press.

Mulac, A., Tiyaamornwong, V., & Seibold, D. R. (1999, May). *Constructive criticisms of co-workers by male and female managers and professionals: Strategies and outcomes.* Paper presented at the annual conference of the International Communication Association, San Francisco.

Mumby, D. K. (1987). The political function of narrative in organizations. *Communication Monographs, 54,* 113–127.

Mumby, D. K. (1988). *Communication and power in organizations: Discourse, ideology, and domination.* Norwood, NJ: Ablex.

Mumby, D. K. (1993). Feminism and the critique of organizational communication studies. In S. Deetz (Ed.), *Communication yearbook 16* (pp. 155–166). Newbury Park, CA: Sage.

Mumby, D. K. (1996). Feminism, postmodernism, and organizational communication: A critical reading. *Management Communication Quarterly, 9,* 259–295.

Mumby, D. K. (1997a). Modernism, postmodernism, and communication studies: A rereading of an ongoing debate. *Communication Theory, 7,* 1–28.

Mumby, D. K. (1997b). The problem of hegemony: Rereading Gramsci for organizational communication studies. *Western Journal of Communication, 61,* 343–375.

Mumby, D. K. (1998). Organizing men: Power, discourse, and the social construction of masculinity(s) in the workplace. *Communication Theory, 8,* 164–183.

Mumby, D. K., & Clair, R. P. (1997). Organizational discourse. In T. A. van Dijk (Ed.), *Discourse as structure and process* (Vol. 2, pp. 181–205). London: Sage.

Mumby, D. K., & Putnam, L. L. (1992). The politics of emotion: A feminist reading of bounded rationality. *Academy of Management Review, 17,* 465–486.

Mumby, D. K., & Stohl, C. (1992). Power and discourse in organization studies: Absence and the dialectic of control. *Discourse & Society, 2,* 313–332.

Mumby, D. K., & Stohl, C. (1996). Disciplining organizational communication studies. *Management Communication Quarterly, 10,* 50–72.

Munyan, A. T. (circa 1929/1930). *The ninety-nines.* 99s Museum of Women Pilots, Oklahoma City, OK, Helen Richey file.

Murphy, A. G. (1998). Hidden transcripts of flight attendant resistance. *Management Communication Quarterly, 11,* 499–535.

Murphy, B. O., & Zorn, T. (1996). Gendered interaction in professional relationships. In J. T. Wood (Ed.), *Gendered relationships* (pp. 213–232). Mountain View, CA: Mayfield.

Murray, S. B. (1988). The unhappy marriage of theory and practice: An analysis of a battered women's shelter. *NWSA Journal, 1,* 75–92.

Nakayama, T. (2000). The significance of "race" and masculinities. *Critical Studies in Media Communication, 17,* 111–113.

Natalle, E. J. (1996). Gendered issues in the workplace. In J. T. Wood (Ed.), *Gendered relationships* (pp. 253–274). Mountain View, CA: Mayfield.

Nelson, M. W. (1988). Women's ways: Interactive patterns in predominantly female research teams. In B. Bate & A. Taylor (Eds.), *Women communicating: Studies of women's talk* (pp. 199–232). Norwood, NJ: Ablex.

Newman, K. (1980). Incipient bureaucracy: The development of hierarchies in egalitarian organizations. In G. M. Britan & R. Cohen (Eds.), *Hierarchy and society* (pp. 143–163). Philadelphia: Institute for the Study of Human Issues.

Newton, T. (1998). Theorizing subjectivity in organizations: The failure of Foucauldian studies? *Organization Studies, 19,* 415–447.

Nicholson, L. (Ed.). (1990). *Feminism/postmodernism.* New York: Routledge.

Nicholson, L. (1994a). Feminism and the politics of postmodernism. In M. Ferguson & J. Wicke (Eds.), *Feminism and postmodernism* (pp. 69–85). Durham, NC: Duke University Press.

Nicholson, L. (1994b). Interpreting gender. *Signs: Journal of Women in Culture and Society, 20*, 79–105.

Nkomo, S. (1992). The emperor has no clothes: Rewriting "race in organizations." *Academy of Management Review, 17*, 487–513.

Norris, C. (1993). *The truth about postmodernism*. Oxford, UK: Basil Blackwell.

Northrup, H. R. (1947). Collective bargaining by airline pilots. *Quarterly Journal of Economics, 61*, 533–576.

O'Connor, E. (1997). Discourse at our disposal: Stories in and around the garbage can. *Management Communication Quarterly, 10*, 395–432.

O'Connor, E. (1999). The politics of management thought: A case study of the Harvard Business School and the human relations school. *Academy of Management Review, 24*, 117–131.

Orbe, M. P. (1998). Constructions of reality on MTV's "The Real World": An analysis of the restrictive coding of black masculinity. *Southern Communication Journal, 64*, 32–47.

Oswick, C., Keenoy, T., & Grant, D. (2000). Discourse, organizations and organizing: Concepts, objects and subjects. *Human Relations, 53*, 1115–1123.

Pacanowsky, M. (1988). Slouching towards Chicago. *Quarterly Journal of Speech, 74*, 453–467.

Pacanowsky, M., & O'Donnell-Trujillo, N. (1982). Communication and organizational cultures. *The Western Journal of Speech Communication, 46*, 115–130.

Pahl, J. (1985). Refuges for battered women: Ideology and action. *Feminist Review, 19*, 25–43.

Palmer, G. (1938, October). Crusading wings. 99s Museum of Women Pilots, Oklahoma City, OK, Helen Richey file.

Palmer, R. (1969). *Hermeneutics*. Evanston, IL: Northwestern University Press.

Papa, M. J., Auwal, M. A., & Singhal, A. (1995). Dialectic of control and emancipation in organizing for social change: A multitheoretic study of the Grameen Bank in Bangladesh. *Communication Theory, 5*, 189–223.

Parker, M. (1995). Critique in the name of what? Postmodernism and critical approaches to organization. *Organization Studies, 16*, 553–564.

Parker, M. (Ed.). (1998). *Ethics and organizations*. London: Sage.

Parker, M. (1999). Capitalism, subjectivity and ethics: Debating labour process analysis. *Organization Studies, 20*, 25–45.

Parker, M. (2000). "The less important sideshow": The limits of epistemology in organizational analysis. *Organization, 7*, 519–523.

Parker, P. S. (2002). African American women's executive leadership communication within dominant-culture organizations: (Re)conceptualizing notions of collaboration and instrumentality. *Management Communication Quarterly, 15*, 42–82.

Parker, P. S. (2003). Control, resistance, and empowerment in raced, gendered, and classed work contexts: The case of African-American women. In

P. Kalbfleisch (Ed.), *Communication yearbook 27* (pp. 257–291). Thousand Oaks, CA: Sage.

Patterson, A. (1929, September 7). I want to be a transport. *Liberty*, 18–20, 22, 24.

Pearson, J. C., Turner, L. H., & Todd-Mancillas, W. R. (1991). *Gender and communication* (2nd. ed.). Dubuque, IA: Wm. C. Brown.

Penley, C., & Willis, S. (Eds.). (1993). *Male trouble*. Minneapolis: University of Minnesota Press.

Perrow, C. (1986). *Complex organizations* (3rd ed.). New York: Random House.

Peters, T. J., & Waterman, R. M. (1982). *In search of excellence*. New York: Harper & Row.

Pfeffer, J. (1993). Barriers to the advance of organizational science: Paradigm development as a dependent variable. *Academy of Management Review, 18*, 599–620.

Pfeffer, J. (1995). Mortality, reproducibility, and the persistence of styles of theory. *Organization Science, 6*, 681–686.

Phillips, D. C. (1990). Postpositivistic science: Myths and realities. In E. G. Guba (Ed.), *The paradigm dialog* (pp. 31–45). Newbury Park, CA: Sage.

Pierce, J. L. (1995). *Gender trials: Emotional lives in contemporary law firms*. Berkeley: University of California Press.

Pollitt, K. (1992, December 28). Marooned on Gilligans' Island: Are women morally superior to men? *The Nation*, pp. 799–807.

Poole, M. S., & Lynch, O. H. (2000). Reflections on finding common ground. In S. R. Corman & M. S. Poole (Eds.), *Perspectives on organizational communication: Finding common ground* (pp. 211–223). New York: Guilford.

Poole, M. S., Putnam, L. L., & Seibold, D. R. (1997). Organizational communication in the 21st century. *Management Communication Quarterly, 11*, 127–138.

Powell, G. N. (1993). *Women and men in management*. Newbury Park, CA: Sage.

Powell, G. N. (1999). Reflections on the glass ceiling: Recent trends and future prospects. In G. N. Powell (Ed.), *Handbook of gender and work* (pp. 325–346). Thousand Oaks, CA: Sage.

Pringle, R. (1989). *Secretaries talk: Sexuality, power and work*. London: Verso.

Projansky, S., & Ono, K. A. (1999). Strategic whiteness as cinematic racial politics. In T. Nakayama & J. N. Martin (Eds.), *Whiteness: The communication of social identity* (pp. 149–174). Thousand Oaks, CA: Sage.

Putnam, L. L. (1983). The interpretive perspective: An alternative to functionalism. In L. L. Putnam & M. Pacanowsky (Eds.), *Communication and organizations: An interpretive approach* (pp. 31–54). Beverly Hills, CA: Sage.

Putnam, L. L., & Mumby, D. K. (1993). Organizations, emotion, and the myth of rationality. In S. Fineman (Ed.), *Emotion in organizations* (pp. 36–57). London: Sage.

Putnam, L. L., & Pacanowsky, M. (Eds.). (1983). *Communication and organizations: An interpretive approach*. Beverly Hills, CA: Sage.

'Queen Helen of air.' (1935, October 26). *The Literary Digest*. 99s Museum of Women Pilots, Oklahoma City, OK, Helen Richey file.

Quimby, H. (1912, September). American bird women. *Good Housekeeping, 55*, 315–316.

Rajchman, J. (1991). *Philosophical events: Essays of the '80s*. New York: Columbia University Press.

Ramsay, K., & Parker, M. (1992). Gender, bureaucracy and organizational culture. In M. Savage & A. Witz (Eds.), *Gender and bureaucracy* (Vol. 39, pp. 253–276). Oxford, UK: Basil Blackwell/The Sociological Review.

Rasmussen, C. (1992, April 20). L.A. scene: Then and now. *Los Angeles Times*, p. B3.

Ray, S. (1999). Hunks, history, and homophobia: Masculinity politics in Braveheart and Edward II. *Film & History, 29*, 22–31.

Reardon, K. K. (1997). Dysfunctional communication patterns in the workplace: Closing the gap between men and women. In D. Dunn (Ed.), *Workplace/women's place: An anthology* (pp. 165–180). Los Angeles: Roxbury.

Redding, W. C. (1996). Ethics and the study of organizational communication: When will we wake up? In J. A. Jaksa & M. S. Pritchard (Eds.), *Responsible communication: Ethical issues in business, industry, and the professions* (pp. 17–40). Cresskill, NJ: Hampton.

Redding, W. C., & Tompkins, P. K. (1988). Organizational communication: Past and present tenses. In G. Goldhaber & G. Barnett (Eds.), *Handbook of organizational communication* (pp. 5–33). Norwood, NJ: Ablex.

Reed, M. I. (1988). The problem of human agency in organizational analysis. *Organization Studies, 9*, 33–46.

Reed, M. I. (2000). The limits of discourse analysis in organizational analysis. *Organization, 7*, 524–530.

Reinelt, C. (1994). Fostering empowerment, building community: The challenge for state-funded feminist organizations. *Human Relations, 47*, 685–705.

Reinharz, S. (1992). *Feminist methods in social research*. New York: Oxford University Press.

Reuther, C., & Fairhurst, G. (2000). Chaos theory and the glass ceiling. In P. M. Buzzanell (Ed.), *Rethinking organizational and managerial communication from feminist perspectives* (pp. 236–253). Thousand Oaks, CA: Sage.

Ricoeur, P. (1970). *Freud and philosophy: An essay on interpretation* (D. Savage, Trans.). New Haven, CT: Yale University Press.

Riger, S. (1994). Challenges of success: Stages of growth in feminist organizations. *Feminist Studies, 20*, 275–300.

Ristock, J. L. (1990). Canadian feminist social service collectives: Caring and contradictions. In L. Albrecht & R. M. Brewer (Eds.), *Bridges of power: Women's multicultural alliances* (pp. 172–181). Philadelphia: New Society.

Robinson, S. (2000). *Marked men: White masculinity in crisis*. New York: Columbia University Press.

Rodriguez, N. M. (1988). Transcending bureaucracy: Feminist politics at a shelter for battered women. *Gender & Society, 2,* 214–227.

Roper, M. (1996). "Seduction and succession": Circuits of homosocial desire in management. In D. Collinson & J. Hearn (Eds.), *Men as managers, managers as men: Critical perspectives on men, masculinities and managements* (pp. 210–226). Thousand Oaks, CA: Sage.

Rorty, R. (Ed.). (1967). *The linguistic turn: Recent essays in philosophical method.* Chicago: University of Chicago Press.

Rosaldo, M. Z. (1987). Moral/analytic dilemmas posed by the intersection of feminism and social science. In P. Rabinow & W. M. Sullivan (Eds.), *Interpretive social science: A second look* (pp. 280–310). Berkeley: University of California Press.

Rosen, M. (1985). "Breakfast at Spiro's": Dramaturgy and dominance. *Journal of Management, 11*(2), 31–48.

Rosen, M. (1988). You asked for it: Christmas at the bosses' expense. *Journal of Management Studies, 25,* 463–480.

Rosenau, P. M. (1992). *Postmodernism and the social sciences.* Princeton, NJ: Princeton University Press.

Rosener, J. B. (1990). Ways women lead. *Harvard Business Review, 68,* 119–125.

Rothschild-Whitt, J. (1976). Conditions for facilitating participatory-democratic organizations. *Sociological Inquiry, 46,* 75–86.

Rothschild-Whitt, J. (1979). The collectivist organization: An alternative to rational bureaucratic models. *American Sociological Review, 44,* 509–527.

Rotundo, E. A. (1993). *American manhood: Transformation in masculinity from the revolution to the modern era.* New York: Basic Books.

Sachs, R., Chrisler, J. C., & Devlin, A. S. (1992). Biographic and personal characteristics of women in management. *Journal of Vocational Behavior, 41,* 89–100.

Said, E. W. (1994). *Representations of the intellectual.* New York: Pantheon.

Saussure, F. de (1960). *Course in general linguistics.* London: Peter Owen.

Savage, M., & Witz, A. (Eds.). (1992). *Gender and bureaucracy.* Oxford, UK: Basil Blackwell/The Sociological Review.

Sawicki, J. (1991). *Disciplining Foucault: Feminism, power, and the body.* New York: Routledge.

Scarr, S., Phillips, D., & McCartney, K. (1989). Working mothers and their families. *American Psychologist, 44,* 1402–1409.

Scheibel, D. (1992). Faking identity in clubland: The communicative performance of "fake ID." *Text and Performance Quarterly, 12,* 160–175.

Scheibel, D. (1996). Appropriating bodies: Organ(izing) ideology and cultural practice in medical school. *Journal of Applied Communication Research, 24,* 310–331.

Schein, E. H. (1992). *Organizational culture and leadership* (2nd ed.). San Francisco: Jossey-Bass.

Schein, V. E. (1973). Relationships between sex role stereotypes and requisite management characteristics. *Journal of Applied Psychology, 57,* 95–100.

Schein, V. E. (1975). Relationships between sex role stereotypes and requisite management characteristics among female managers. *Journal of Applied Psychology, 60,* 340–344.

Schein, V. E., & Mueller, R. (1992). Sex role stereotyping and requisite management characteristics: A cross cultural look. *Journal of Organizational Behavior, 13,* 439–447.

Schrag, C. O. (1986). *Communicative praxis and the space of subjectivity.* Bloomington: Indiana University Press.

Schrag, C. O. (1997). *The self after postmodernity.* New Haven, CT: Yale University Press.

Scott, E. K. (1998). Creating partnerships for change: Alliances and betrayals in the racial politics of two feminist organizations. *Gender & Society, 12,* 400–423.

Scott, J. C. (1990). *Domination and the arts of resistance: Hidden transcripts.* New Haven, CT: Yale University Press.

Scott, J. W. (1988). Deconstructing equality-versus-difference: Or, the uses of poststructuralist theory for feminism. *Feminist Studies, 14,* 33–50.

Sealander, J., & Smith, D. (1986). The rise and fall of feminist organizations in the 1970s: Dayton as a case study. *Feminist Studies, 12,* 321–341.

Seccombe-Eastland, L. (1988). Ideology, contradiction, and change in a feminist bookstore. In B. Bate & A. Taylor (Eds.), *Women communicating: Studies of women's talk* (pp. 251–276). Norwood, NJ: Ablex.

Segal, L. (1990). *Slow motion: Changing masculinities, changing men.* New Brunswick, NJ: Rutgers University Press.

Seidler, V. J. (1989). *Rediscovering masculinity: Reason, language and sexuality.* New York: Routledge.

Seidler, V. J. (1994). *Unreasonable men: Masculinity and social theory.* New York: Routledge.

Seidman, S. (Ed.). (1994). *The postmodern turn: New perspectives on social theory.* Cambridge, UK: Cambridge University Press.

Sewell, G. (1998). The discipline of teams: The control of team-based industrial work through electronic and peer surveillance. *Administrative Science Quarterly, 43,* 397–428.

Sewell, G., & Wilkinson, B. (1992). "Someone to watch over me": Surveillance, discipline, and the just-in-time labor process. *Sociology, 26,* 271–289.

Sex held reason for pilot's loss. (1935, November 7). *The Evening Star,* p. A2.

Shepherd, G. (1993). Building a discipline of communication. *Journal of Communication, 43,* 83–91.

Sheppard, D. (1989). Organizations, power and sexuality: Image and self image of women managers. In J. Hearn, D. Sheppard, P. Tancred-Sheriff, & G. Burrell (Eds.), *The sexuality of organization* (pp. 139–157). London: Sage.

Shuler, S. (2000, November). *Breaking through the glass ceiling without breaking a nail: Portrayal of women executives in the popular business press*. Paper presented at the annual conference of the National Communication Association, Seattle, WA.

Silverman, D. (1970). *The theory of organizations*. London: Heinemann.

Simon, H. (1976). *Administrative behavior* (3rd. ed.). Glencoe, IL: Free Press.

Smircich, L. (1983). Concepts of culture and organizational analysis. *Administrative Science Quarterly, 28*, 339–358.

Smircich, L., & Calás, M. (1987). Organizational culture: A critical assessment. In F. Jablin, L. L. Putnam, L. Porter, & K. Roberts (Eds.), *The handbook of organizational communication* (pp. 228–263). Newbury Park, CA: Sage.

Smith, D. (1997). Comment on Hekman's "Truth and method: Feminist standpoint theory revisited." *Signs: Journal of Women in Culture and Society, 22*, 392–398.

Smith, F. L., & Keyton, J. (2001). Organizational storytelling: Metaphors for relational power and identity struggles. *Management Communication Quarterly, 15*, 149–182.

Smith, H. L. (1942). *Airways: The history of commercial aviation in the United States*. New York: Alfred A. Knopf.

Smith, P. L., & Smits, S. J. (1994). The feminization of leadership? *Training and Development, 48*, 43–46.

Smith, R., & Eisenberg, E. (1987). Conflict at Disneyland: A root metaphor analysis. *Communication Monographs, 54*, 367–380.

Sotirin, P., & Gottfried, H. (1999). The ambivalent dynamics of secretarial "bitching": Control, resistance, and the construction of identity. *Organization, 6*, 57–80.

Spitzack, C. (1998a). The production of masculinity in interpersonal communication. *Communication Theory, 8*, 143–164.

Spitzack, C. (1998b). Theorizing masculinity across the field: An intradisciplinary conversation. *Communication Theory, 8*, 141–143.

Spitzack, C., & Carter, K. (1987). Women in communication studies: A typology for revision. *The Quarterly Journal of Speech, 73*, 401–423.

Spitzack, C., & Carter, K. (1988). Feminist communication: Rethinking the politics of exclusion. *Women's Studies in Communication, 11*, 28–31.

Spradlin, A. L. (1998). The price of "passing": A lesbian perspective on authenticity in organizations. *Management Communication Quarterly, 11*, 598–605.

Stabile, C. A. (1995). Postmodernism, feminism, and Marx: Notes from the abyss. *Monthly Review, 47*(3), 89–107.

Staley, C. C. (1988). The communicative power of women managers: Doubts, dilemmas, and management development programs. In C. A. Valentine & N. Hoar (Eds.), *Women and communicative power: Theory, research, and practice* (pp. 36–48). Annandale, VA: Speech Communication Association.

Stecopoulos, H., & Uebel, M. (Eds.). (1997). *Race and the subject of masculinities.* Durham, NC: Duke University Press.

Steeves, H. L. (1987). Feminist theories and media studies. *Critical Studies in Mass Communication, 4,* 95–135.

Steeves, H. L. (1988). What distinguishes feminist scholarship in communication studies? *Women's Studies in Communication, 11,* 12–17.

Sternberg, R. J., & Soriano, L. J. (1984). Styles of conflict resolution. *Journal of Personality and Social Psychology, 47,* 115–126.

Stewart, J. (1991). A postmodern look at traditional communication postulates. *Western Journal of Speech Communication, 55,* 354–379.

Stewart, J. (1992). Philosophical dimensions of social approaches to interpersonal communication. *Communication Theory, 2,* 337–346.

Stewart, L. P., & Clarke-Kudless, D. (1993). Communication in corporate settings. In L. P. Arless & D. J. Borisoff (Eds.), *Women and men communicating.* Fort Worth, TX: Harcourt Brace Jovanovich.

Strine, M. (1992). Understanding "how things work": Sexual harassment and academic culture. *Journal of Applied Communication Research, 20,* 391–400.

Tannen, D. (1990). *You just don't understand: Men and women in conversation.* New York: Ballantine.

Tannen, D. (1994). *Talking from 9 to 5: Women and men in the workplace: Language, sex and power.* New York: Avon Books.

Tasker, Y. (1993a). Dumb movies for dumb people: Masculinity, the body, and the voice in contemporary action cinema. In S. Cohan & I. R. Hark (Eds.), *Screening the male: Exploring masculinities in Hollywood cinema* (pp. 230–244). New York: Routledge.

Tasker, Y. (1993b). *Spectacular bodies: Gender, genre, and the action cinema.* New York: Routledge.

Taylor, B. C. (1993a). Fat Man and Little Boy: Cinematic representation of interests in the nuclear weapons organization. *Critical Studies in Mass Communication, 10,* 367–394.

Taylor, B. C. (1993b). Register of the repressed: Women's voice and body in the nuclear weapons organization. *Quarterly Journal of Speech, 79,* 267–285.

Taylor, B. C. (2002). Organizing the unknown subject: Los Alamos, espionage, and the politics of biography. *Quarterly Journal of Speech, 88,* 33–49.

Taylor, B. C., & Conrad, C. (1992). Narratives of sexual harassment: Organizational dimensions. *Journal of Applied Communication Research, 20,* 401–418.

Taylor, B. C., & Trujillo, N. (2001). Qualitative research methods. In L. L. Putnam & M. Pacanowsky (Eds.), *The new handbook of organizational communication: Advances in theory, research, and methods* (pp. 161–196). Thousand Oaks, CA: Sage.

Taylor, J. R. (1993). *Rethinking the theory of organizational communication: How to read an organization.* Norwood, NJ: Ablex.

Taylor, J. R. (1995). Shifting from a heteronomous to an autonomous worldview of organizational communication: Communication theory on the cusp. *Communication Theory, 5*, 1–35.

Taylor, J. R., Cooren, F., Giroux, N., & Robichaud, D. (1996). The communicational basis of organization: Between the conversation and the text. *Communication Theory, 6*, 1–39.

Taylor, J. R., & Van Every, E. J. (2000). *The emergent organization: Communication as its site and surface.* Mahwah, NJ: Lawrence Erlbaum.

Taylor, V. (1995). Watching for vibes: Bringing emotions into the study of feminist organizations. In M. M. Ferree & P. Y. Martin (Eds.), *Feminist organizations: Harvest of the new women's movement* (pp. 223–233). Philadelphia: Temple University Press.

Thompson, P. (1993). Postmodernism: Fatal distraction. In J. Hassard & M. Parker (Eds.), *Postmodernism and organizations* (pp. 183–203). London: Sage.

Todd-Mancillas, W. R., & Rossi, A. N. A. (1985). Gender differences in the management of personnel disputes. *Women's Studies in Communication, 8*, 25–33.

Tompkins, P. K. (1984). The functions of human communication in organization. In C. Arnold & K. Frandsen (Eds.), *Handbook of rhetorical and communication theory* (pp. 659–719). Boston: Allyn & Bacon.

Tompkins, P. K., & Cheney, G. (1985). Communication and unobtrusive control in contemporary organizations. In R. D. McPhee, & P. K. Tompkins (Eds.), *Organizational communication: Traditional themes and new directions* (pp. 179–210). Beverly Hills, CA: Sage.

Tong, R. (1989). *Feminist thought.* Boulder, CO: Westview.

Townley, B. (1993). Performance appraisal and the emergence of management. *Journal of Management Studies, 30*, 221–238.

Townsley, N. C., & Geist, P. (2000). The discursive enactment of hegemony: Sexual harassment in academic organizing. *Western Journal of Communication, 64*, 190–217.

Trethewey, A. (1997). Resistance, identity, and empowerment: A postmodern feminist analysis of clients in a human service organization. *Communication Monographs, 64*, 281–301.

Trethewey, A. (1999a). Disciplined bodies. *Organization Studies, 20*, 423–450.

Trethewey, A. (1999b). Isn't it ironic: Using irony to explore the contradictions of organizational life. *Western Journal of Communication, 63*, 140–167.

Trethewey, A. (2000). Revisioning control: A feminist critique of disciplined bodies. In P. M. Buzzanell (Ed.), *Rethinking organizational and managerial communication from feminist perspectives* (pp. 107–127). Thousand Oaks, CA: Sage.

Trethewey, A. (2001). Reproducing and resisting the master narrative of decline: Midlife professional women's experiences of aging. *Management Communication Quarterly, 15*, 183–226.

Triece, M. E. (1999). The practical true woman: Reconciling women and work in popular mail-order magazines, 1900–1920. *Critical Studies in Mass Communication, 16,* 42–62.

Trujillo, N. (1992). Interpreting (the work and talk of) baseball: Perspectives on ballpark culture. *Western Journal of Communication, 56,* 350–371.

Trujillo, N., & Dionisopoulos, G. (1987). Cop talk, police stories, and the social construction of organizational drama. *Central States Speech Journal, 38,* 196–209.

Tsoukas, H. (2000). False dilemmas in organization theory: Realism or social constructivism? *Organization, 7,* 531–535.

Van Maanen, J. (1988). *Tales of the field: On writing ethnography.* Chicago: University of Chicago Press.

Van Maanen, J. (1995a). Fear and loathing in organization studies. *Organization Science, 6,* 687–692.

Van Maanen, J. (1995b). Style as theory. *Organization Science, 6,* 133–143.

Vogel, L. (1993). *Mothers on the job: Maternal policy in the U.S. workplace.* New Brunswick, NJ: Rutgers University Press.

Walker, H. A., Ilardi, B. C., McMahon, A. M., & Fennell, M. L. (1996). Gender, interaction, and leadership. *Social Psychology Quarterly, 59,* 255–272.

Wants equal rights in the air. (1929, August 14). *Wichita, Kansas Beacon.* 99s Museum of Women Pilots, Oklahoma City, OK, Helen Richey file.

Weber, M. (1978). *Economy and society* (G. W. Roth, C., Trans.). Berkeley: University of California Press.

Wecter, D. (1941). *The hero in America: A chronicle of hero-worship.* New York: Charles Scribner's Sons.

Weedon, C. (1987). *Feminist practice and poststructuralist theory.* Oxford, UK: Basil Blackwell.

Weick, K. (1979). *The social psychology of organizing* (2nd ed.). Reading, MA: Addison-Wesley.

Weick, K. E. (1995). What theory is not, theorizing is. *Administrative Science Quarterly, 40,* 385–390.

Welshimer, H. (1937, July 18). The women who mark the air lanes. *San Francisco Chronicle.* 99s Museum of Women Pilots, Oklahoma City, OK, Helen Richey file.

Wendt, R. F. (1995). Women in positions of service: The politicized body. *Communication Studies, 46,* 276–296.

Wertin, L., Medlecker, S., & Pearson, T. (1995, February). *An investigation of sexual harassment in restaurants: Employees' experiences, responses, feelings, definitions, and training.* Paper presented at the annual conference of the Western States Communication Association, Portland, OR.

West, C., & Fenstermaker, S. (1995). Doing difference. *Gender & Society, 9,* 8–37.

West, C., & Zimmerman, D. (1987). Doing gender. *Gender & Society, 1,* 125–151.

West, G. (1990). Cooperation and conflict among women in the welfare rights movement. In L. Albrecht & R. M. Brewer (Eds.), *Bridges of power: Women's multicultural alliances* (pp. 149–171). Philadelphia: New Society.

Wiegman, R. (1993). Feminism, "The Boyz," and other matters regarding the male. In S. Cohan & I. R. Hark (Eds.), *Screening the male: Exploring masculinities in Hollywood cinema* (pp. 173–193). New York: Routledge.

Wiley, M. G., & Eskilson, A. (1985). Speech style, gender stereotypes, and corporate success: What if women talk more like men? *Sex Roles, 12,* 993–1007.

Wilkins, B. M., & Anderson, P. A. (1991). Gender differences and similarities in management communication. *Management Communication Quarterly, 5,* 6–35.

Will woman drive man out of the sky? (1911). *American Examiner.* 99s Museum of Women Pilots exhibit, Oklahoma City, OK.

Willis, P. (1977). *Learning to labor: How working class kids get working class jobs.* New York: Columbia University Press.

Willmott, H. (1990). Subjectivity and the dialectics of praxis: Opening up the core of labor process analysis. In D. Knights & H. Willmott (Eds.), *Labour process theory* (pp. 336–378). London: MacMillan.

Willmott, H. (1994). Bringing agency (back) into organizational analysis: Responding to the crisis of (post)modernity. In J. Hassard & M. Parker (Eds.), *Towards a new theory of organizations* (pp. 87–130). London: Routledge.

Willmott, H. (1998). Towards a new ethics? The contributions of poststructuralism and posthumanism. In M. Parker (Ed.), *Ethics and organizations* (pp. 76–121). London: Sage.

Wilson, F. (1996). Organizational theory: Blind and deaf to gender? *Organization Studies, 17,* 825–842.

Witten, M. (1993). Narrative and the culture of obedience at the workplace. In D. K. Mumby (Ed.), *Narrative and social control: Critical perspectives* (pp. 97–118). Newbury Park, CA: Sage.

Witz, A., & Savage, M. (1992). The gender of organizations. In M. Savage & A. Witz (Eds.), *Gender and bureaucracy* (pp. 3–64). Oxford, UK: Basil Blackwell/The Sociological Review.

Wolf, M. (1992). *A thrice-told tale: Feminism, postmodernism and ethnographic responsibility.* Stanford, CA: Stanford University Press.

Woman pilot teaching men art of flying. (circa 1947). 99s Museum of Women Pilots, Oklahoma City, OK, Helen Richey file.

Women fliers prepared to split on regulations. (1931, September 1). *New York Herald.* 99s Museum of Women Pilots, Oklahoma City, OK, Helen Richey file.

Wood, E. M. (1995). What is the "postmodern" agenda? An introduction. *Monthly Review, 47*(3), 1–12.

Wood, J. T. (1995). Feminist scholarship and the study of relationships. *Journal of Social and Personal Relationships, 12,* 103–120.

Wood, J. T. (1997). *Gendered lives: Communication, gender, and culture.* Belmont, CA: Wadsworth.

Wray-Bliss, E. (2002). Abstract ethics, embodied ethics: The strange marriage of Foucault and positivism in labor process theory. *Organization, 9,* 5–40.

Wray-Bliss, E., & Parker, M. (1998). Marxism, capitalism, and ethics. In M. Parker (Ed.), *Ethics and organizations* (pp. 30–52). London: Sage.

Wright, R. (1996). The occupational masculinity of computing. In C. Cheng (Ed.), *Masculinities in organizations* (pp. 77–96). Thousand Oaks, CA: Sage.

Young, E. (1989). On the naming of the rose: Interests and multiple meanings as elements of organizational culture. *Organization Studies, 10,* 187–206.

Author Index

Subject Index

About the Authors

Karen Lee Ashcraft (Ph.D., University of Colorado at Boulder) is an Assistant Professor of Organizational Communication in the Department of Communication at the University of Utah. Her research examines gender, power, professional identity, and alternative organizational forms and has appeared in such forums as *Communication Monographs, Administrative Science Quarterly,* and *the Academy of Management Journal.*

Dennis K. Mumby (Ph.D., Southern Illinois University-Carbondale) is a Professor in the Department of Communication Studies at the University of North Carolina at Chapel Hill. His research focuses on the relationships among discourse, power, gender, and organization. He has published in journals such as *Academy Management Review, Communication Monographs,* and *Management Communication Quarterly.*